INSIDE AL-QAEDA AND THE TALIBAN

Inside Al-Qaeda and the Taliban

Beyond Bin Laden and 9/11

Syed Saleem Shahzad

PlutoPress
www.plutobooks.com

palgrave
macmillan

First published 2011 by Pluto Press
345 Archway Road, London N6 5AA
www.plutobooks.com

and

PALGRAVE MACMILLAN
15–19 Claremont Street, South Yarra 3141
Visit our website at www.palgravemacmillan.com.au
Associated companies and representatives throughout the world.

Distributed in the United States of America exclusively by
Palgrave Macmillan, a division of St. Martin's Press LL C,
175 Fifth Avenue, New York, NY 10010

British Library Cataloguing in Publication Data
A catalogue record for this book is available from the British Library

Please contact the National Library of Australia for Australian cataloguing in
publication data

US Library of Congress Cataloging in Publication Data applied for

ISBN 978 0 7453 3102 7 Hardback
ISBN 978 0 7453 3101 0 Paperback (Pluto Press)
ISBN 978 1 4202 5671 0 Paperback (Palgrave Macmillan Australia)

This book is printed on paper suitable for recycling and made from fully managed
and sustained forest sources. Logging, pulping and manufacturing processes are
expected to conform to the environmental standards of the country of origin.

10 9 8 7 6 5 4 3 2

Designed and produced for Pluto Press by Curran Publishing Services, Norwich.
Simultaneously printed digitally by CPI Antony Rowe, Chippenham, UK,
Edwards Bros in the United States of America and Griffin Press in Australia

CONTENTS

MAPS

PREFACE

I have never worked for any well-funded international news organizations. Nor have I worked for the mainstream national media. My affiliations have always remained with alternative media outlets. This has left me with narrow options and very little space to move around in. Those who loom large on the political horizon by and large target mainstream information outlets and well-financed news organizations for the launch of their media campaigns, interviews and/or disclosures. Alternative media persons need to work twice as hard as others to draw their attention. However, independent reporting for the alternative media best suits my temperament as it encourages me to seek the truth beyond "conventional wisdom." As a result, I study people and situations from a relatively uncompromised position, in isolation and seclusion. For instance, I have avoided repetitive reflection on well-known figures in the Al-Qaeda ambit and instead chosen to focus on those close to the bottom of the ladder, looking to share their understanding of the world, their lives, and their behind-the-scenes contributions, which are what actually what determine the fate of movements. (Some little known figures I explored and interviewed included Commander Muhammad Ilyas Kashmiri,[1] Sirajuddin Haqqani,[2] and Qari Ziaur Rahman.[3] They all later emerged as the real leaders of the movement.)

The world of today primarily pictures Osama bin Laden, who launched a resistance movement against Western imperialism, as the embodiment of Al-Qaeda, but there is more to Al-Qaeda than just bin Laden. There are as many characters, personalities, and twists in the tale of Al-Qaeda as were narrated by Queen Scheherazade to her husband King Shaharyar of the legendary *Alf Laila Wa Laila* (or *A Thousand and One Nights*). In these fables, there surface thousands of lesser-known characters who shaped the world of their time through the type of love and loyalty that even today constitutes the essence of humanity.

Alf Laila Wa Laila is a collection of Middle Eastern and South Asian stories and folk tales compiled in Arabic during the Islamic Golden Age. They are of uncertain date and authorship. The framing device of the collection, however, hinges on the vengeful King Shaharyar, having been cuckolded by his promiscuous first wife, determining to marry and execute a new wife each day as a lesson to womanhood. The resourceful Scheherazade, understood to be of Indian extraction, brought an end to this. She captivated King Shaharyar with stories spread over a period of a thousand and one nights both to avert an early execution and to restore the king's faith in the virtues of womanhood.

Scheherazade's odyssey encompassed stories from India, Iran, Iraq, Egypt, Turkey, and possibly Greece. It is believed that the collection is a composite work originally transmitted orally and developed over a period of several centuries. The collection has a long and convoluted history which mirrors complex narrative structures and draws the reader into a whirlpool of celebrated sagas from which there is no easy escape.

I have tried to unravel some of Al-Qaeda's *Alf Laila* legendary figures to present them in parallel fashion. These are the stories of characters who performed behind the scenes, but at the same time, played a decisive part in creating an environment through which Al-Qaeda, an organization believed to be buried under the rubble of the Tora Bora mountains[4] as a result of US bombing in 2001, was able to spread its wings from North Africa to Central Asia and emerge as a real global resistance movement against Western hegemony.

I visited Iraq, Lebanon, North Waziristan, and Afghanistan to meet with Al-Qaeda personalities, but to my surprise found the source of my real inspiration in a little-known person, retired Captain Khurram Askhiq (since killed fighting UK troops in the Helmand province of Afghanistan), who had once been a member of the Pakistan Army's Special Services Group (SSG), Pakistan's elite commandos. When I met him, Captain Khurram had resigned from the army and joined forces with the Taliban in Afghanistan. Kurram's imprint on Al-Qaeda was unmistakable. On his death, his friend, retired Major Abdul Rahman and Khurram's brother, retired Major Haroon, who later became the two main strategists of the attacks in Mumbai on 26 November 2008 (often referred to as 26/11) and turned around Al-Qaeda's war against the Western coalition, met me and broadened my views and perception on Al-Qaeda's strategy.

After meeting them I began to see the world of Al-Qaeda from an entirely new perspective – that of unmeasured energy emerging purely on the strength of conviction and human ingenuity against the sophisticated might of advanced technology to provoke the United States (the world's sole surviving superpower) with 9/11. The aim was to draw the United States to fight in a region where people lived in the stone age – an age where hi-tech meant nothing and untutored wisdom for survival was all that was to be had. It was not surprising, then, that Al-Qaeda lost hundreds of adherents in the initial battle, while the survivors retreated rapidly into caves to watch the US victory celebrations.

Al-Qaeda continued to watch closely, but abstained from fighting, as the Ibnul Balad, or the sons of the soil (also known as the Taliban), went to war against the foreign intruders. But they remained engaged in something else all the time, and this was to commandeer these sons of the soil into "blood brothers" and bring them under Al-Qaeda's direct command.

Al-Qaeda's first objective was to win the war against the West in Afghanistan. Its next objective was to move on to have the fighting extend all the way from Central Asia to Bangladesh to exhaust the superpower's resources, before bringing it on to the field in the Middle East for the final battles to revive the Muslim political order under the Caliphate, which would then to lead to the liberation of all Muslim territories.

This book is written at the critical juncture when the defeat of the Western coalition appears imminent. Some commentators have painted the dreaded picture of a nuclear-armed Al-Qaeda supported by Muslim states threatening the world, but after many years of fighting, what stands out above all else is that Al-Qaeda's arsenal is not its weaponry, but its uncanny ability to exploit unfolding events to engineer the collapse of its hi-tech enemies.

The Western coalition is now looking for a way out of the Afghan theater of war. However, if and when it finally does achieve this, it will not end Al-Qaeda's war against the West. It will merely signal the end of one round and mark the beginning of another. This is the perspective I have tried to explore throughout the book.

Syed Saleem Shahzad

PROLOGUE

The 9/11 attacks in 2001 aimed to provoke a war in South Asia. The 26/11 Mumbai assaults in 2008 warned that Al-Qaeda was expanding its war to the east, from Central Asian republics to India and Bangladesh, and that many more such actions would follow. In the ideological perspective of Al-Qaeda, this was to be a preparation for the "End of Time" battles which were referred to by the Prophet Muhammad (in what is now known as the *Hadith*). These pointed to parts of modern-day Iran, Afghanistan, Pakistan, and Central Asia as ancient Khurasan. Khurasan was to be the first battleground for the End of Time battles, before a decisive confrontation against the West, with the last battle being fought in the Middle East for the liberation of Palestine and all occupied Muslim lands.

In the meantime, Al-Qaeda aimed to trap the world's most powerful states in the impossible terrain of Afghanistan. The aim was to lead them to exhaust their energies there, before the expansion of the theater of war against the West from Central Asia to Bangladesh.

On October 9, 2009, some years after the attack on the United States on 9/11, Al-Qaeda's Military Committee chairman, Commander Muhammad Ilyas Kashmiri, who was confirmed as the mastermind of the 26/11 (2008) Mumbai assaults after revelations from the arrested US citizen David Headley,[1] sketched his future strategies during an interview with me. He said:

> We planned this battle to bring the Great Satan [that is, the United States] and its allies into this swamp [Afghanistan]. Afghanistan is one of the most unique places in the world where a hunter has all sorts of traps to choose from. The traps might be set in deserts, rivers, mountains, or even in urban centers. This is our thinking. We are sick and tired of the Great Satan's global intrigues and aim for its demise to make this world a place of peace and justice. The Great Satan is full of the arrogance of its superiority and thinks of Afghans as helpless statues who can be

easily hit from all four sides by America's war machine without the power or capacity to retaliate.

(*Asia Times Online*, October 15, 2009)

The seeds of Al-Qaeda's thinking on the war against the West, which began in 2001, were planted during the decade-long Jihad (or holy war) against the Soviet occupation of Afghanistan in the 1980s. The Arabs who poured into the country to join hands with the Afghan resistance fell broadly into two camps, the Yemeni and the Egyptian. Religious zealots from elsewhere, who had come to Afghanistan after being inspired by clerics in their home countries, mostly joined the Yemeni camp. Once they had joined together, they exercised hard, undertaking military drills all day long when they were not engaged in fighting. They cooked their own food and then slept straight after the *Isha* (the last prayers of the day). As the Afghan Jihad tailed off toward the end of the late 1980s, most of these Jihadis returned to their home countries. Others merged with the Afghan population, or went to Pakistan, where many married. In Al-Qaeda circles, these last were called *dravesh* (easy-going).

The Egyptian camp had many men who were extremely political, as well as ideologically motivated. Though they had largely been members of the Muslim Brotherhood, they were unhappy with that organization for its insistence on attempting to bring about change in their societies through democracy and elections rather than revolution. The Afghan Jihad served as powerful glue for these like-minded individuals, many of whom had trained as doctors and engineers. Others were former military personnel from the Egyptian Army who were associated with the underground Egyptian Islamic Jihad movement of Dr Ayman al-Zawahiri, who is now bin Laden's deputy. This group had been responsible for the assassination of President Anwar Sadat in 1981 after he had signed a peace deal with Israel at Camp David, and were united in the core belief that the reason for the Arab "doom and gloom" was the United States and its puppet governments in the Middle East. The Egyptian camp was in the hands of al-Zawahiri, and after *Isha* prayers its men would sit and discuss contemporary issues in the Arab world. One of the stronger messages its leaders gave out was that they should invest in efforts to ideologically motivate the armies of Muslim countries.

In the mid-1990s, when then Afghan president Professor Burhanuddin Rabbani and his powerful defense minister, Ahmed Shah Masoud, allowed bin Laden to move from Sudan to Afghanistan, the Egyptian camp drew many people into its fold, and ran *maaskars* (training camps) to teach strategy for the future fight. By the time the Taliban had emerged as a force to be reckoned with in Afghanistan in the mid-1990s, the Egyptian camp had settled on its strategies. The most important were:

- to speak out against corrupt and despotic Muslim governments and make them targets, with the aim of destroying their image in the eyes of the common people who interrelated with the state, rulers, and the nation
- to focus on the role of the United States, which was to support Israel and the tyrannical governments of Middle Eastern countries, and make everyone understand this role.

Those were the years of the Afghan Jihad against the Soviets, and during this period the Egyptian camp molded the minds of many Muslim youths drawn from all over the world.

Al-Qaeda itself emerged from another organization. This was the Maktab al-Khidamat, the services bureau that Abdullah Yusuf Azzam[2] set up in the early 1980s to facilitate young Arabs coming from the Middle East to fight the Soviets in Afghanistan. Azzam was assassinated in 1989 and was succeeded by bin Laden, one of his leading disciples. Osama bin Laden transformed the organization into Al-Qaeda. However, his was no more than a structural change. Al-Qaeda would not have had the same impact if it had not been preceded by al-Zawahiri and the Egyptian camp's ideology and pattern of struggle. In fact, al-Zawahiri was the one who actually made Al-Qaeda into the organization the world knows today.

Al-Qaeda set up the dialectic of the struggle, which initially redefined the Islamic faith to meet the needs of contemporary world politics. Al-Qaeda emphasized monotheism as the basis of the Muslim faith, which stipulates, "There is no god but Allah and Muhammad is His final messenger." For Al-Qaeda this monotheistic concept defines Islamic traditions at both the individual and collective levels.

The concept of "No god but Allah" does not only have ritualistic connotations. Al-Qaeda also drew on the perspective that the concept of god is synonymous with authority, and monotheism demands that Islam should therefore be the sole authority. Any political system or other authority that refuses to be subservient to God's will effectively creates a form of polytheism. The word NO (No God but Allah) symbolizes a rebellion against any human-made system. Muslims who take this stance automatically reject

XVI   PROLOGUE

governance systems based on democracy, socialism, or any ideology that is dependent on human-made laws as polytheistic, and argue that Muslims are required to struggle against any such system.

This automatically casts any Muslim majority state that has adopted a secular form of government as heretic, and gives rise to the concept of *takfeer* (the act of declaring a non-practicing Muslim an apostate). Strategic alliances between Muslim majority states and non-Muslim states which might operate against Muslims are also denounced under *takfeer*. This precept is the basis of the whole Al-Qaeda strategy, and sometimes seems close to the Marxist dialectic. Marx defined his dialectic in terms of an economic class war, whereas the neo-Islamist dialectic polarizes society on the basis of faith and practices, before categorizing two levels of struggle – Islamists versus polytheists in the Muslim world, and Islam versus the West. However, this is a theoretical divide, designed to clarify the essence of the struggle to win over the allegiance of majority Muslim populations. In practice, Al-Qaeda deals with the polytheism of both the Muslim world and the West through its battle strategy.

Al-Qaeda is primarily an Arab organization, but it did not choose Egypt or any other Middle Eastern country for the launch of its struggle. Its choice fell on South Asia, which has traditions, religious ideologies, and customs that are diametrically opposite to those of Al-Qaeda's ethnically Arab members. The main reason for this choice, which might appear odd to some, is rooted in faith. The Prophet Muhammad prophesied that ancient Khurasan would be the initial theater of war for the "End of Times" battles, so Al-Qaeda set out to fulfil this prediction.

It bears repeating that the geographically defined Khurasan theater of war includes parts of modern Iran, the Central Asian republics, Afghanistan, and parts of Pakistan. The initial battle-ground also incorporates Ghazwa-e-Hind (a term used in the Prophet Muhammad's sayings), or the battle for India, and this serves to locate Al-Qaeda's initial theater of war between Central Asia and Bangladesh. (Bangladesh is not the battlefield but comes into the loop for logistical reasons in the war against India.)

It is a part of the Islamic faith that the Prophet's predictions will come to pass, and that once the Muslim armies have won the battle of Khurasan and India, they will march to the Middle East to join forces with the promised Mahdi (the ultimate reformer), and do battle against the Antichrist and its Western allies for the liberation of Palestine.

Al-Qaeda effectively arrived in its "Khurasan" in the mid-1990s, during the Taliban rule in Afghanistan, and its objective then was to create circumstances that would turn the regions from Central Asia to Bangladesh into a battlefield. Its main focus became the Taliban-ruled Islamic Emirates of Afghanistan, where all the regional liberation movements from Uzbekistan, Tajikistan, Chechnya, and the Chinese Xingjian province were based. These latter organizations were the flag bearers of Islam, but very much like the Taliban militia, they had local agendas. Their strategy did not extend beyond localized boundaries. Al-Qaeda has an agenda that stretches beyond borders.

This book discusses in detail the period from 1996 to 2010, and explains that throughout this period Al-Qaeda and Taliban appeared the same to most observers. However, they were never identical in either personnel or objectives. Only a few people, including the top leadership of the Taliban, recognize this reality. Al-Qaeda supported the Taliban and has contributed considerably to the Taliban's military successes, first against the Northern Alliance[3] during the Afghan civil war in the late 1990s, and then against the United States after the US attack on Afghanistan in October 2001. However, this does not make the two a single entity. Theirs is a unique relationship, in which Al-Qaeda aims to bring the Taliban and all Muslim liberation movements into its fold and to use them to forward its global agenda.

As a consequence, the Taliban and all the liberation movements in countries and regions such as Uzbekistan, Chechnya, the Chinese province of Xingjian, and Kashmir are wary of Al-Qaeda's design, but Al-Qaeda has laid its trap meticulously. It aims to ensure that all resources are funneled through Al-Qaeda channels, so that these movements are left with no choice but to follow Al-Qaeda directives. Yet Al-Qaeda is not self-centered. It is geared towards the broader Islamic cause. In fact, if we look at events from the mid-1990s through to 2010, we can see that Al-Qaeda has repeatedly placed itself on the altar of sacrifice.

The Taliban's initial successes against the Northern Alliance were not sustainable in northern Afghanistan during the mid-1990s. Al-Qaeda provided the Taliban with support from its Arab fighters. Among the Islamists, Arab fighters were the real heroes of the Afghan Jihad against Soviet Russia. Therefore when Al-Qaeda joined forces with the Taliban against the Northern Alliance it gave lot of credibility to the Taliban. Arabs tend to be more resilient fighters than Afghans. The inclusion of Arabs changed the dynamics of the conflict between the Northern Alliance and the Taliban. The

Northern Alliance force, then led by Ahmad Shah Masoud (who has since been killed), lost territory until it controlled only a few areas in northern Afghanistan. At times Masoud faced such a difficult situation that he planned an escape to Tajikistan. This was the case when the Taliban forced its way around the Northern Alliance command center, the Pansher Valley.

Al-Qaeda's support of the Taliban against the Northern Alliance went a long way in influencing the Taliban. Mullah Muhammad Omar (the spiritual leader of the Taliban) was personally indebted. This was the time for Al-Qaeda to capitalize on the situation. Al-Qaeda took over effective charge of the entire defense policies of the Taliban, which included running their training camps and formulating strategies to fight against the Northern Alliance. As a result, Al-Qaeda gained immediate access to the camps of the Chechen, Pakistani, Uzbek, and even Chinese liberation movements. In the process of doing this, Al-Qaeda changed the nature of the Taliban rule in Afghanistan, and turned it into a "national security state," creating war hysteria throughout the country. This involved actions like blowing up the Bamiyan Buddhas[4] and other activity that isolated the Taliban from the world community.

Three countries in the world recognized the Taliban government of Afghanistan: Pakistan, Saudi Arabia, and the United Arab Emirates. They made intensive efforts to have the Taliban move into territory near the Chinese border. However, the Taliban assured China that nobody would be permitted to use the territory under Taliban control for offensive purposes against it. The Islamic Movement of Eastern Turkestan would be allowed to live peacefully in Afghanistan, but it would not be permitted to instigate insurgency in Xingjian as the Chinese feared.

China was about to recognize the Taliban government in Afghanistan and establish diplomatic ties when the Bamiyan Buddhas incident occurred. This was followed by 9/11, which saw China backing away. Had China recognized the Taliban government, it would have gone to a long way towards making Taliban-controlled Afghanistan a member of the international community, but this was not Al-Qaeda's aim, since it was against its broader interests. Al-Qaeda needed to turn the region into a theater of war and trap the United States in an Afghan quagmire, and when 9/11 ignited the region, this was in keeping with Al-Qaeda's plans. Al-Qaeda saw the invasion of Afghanistan by the United States as just as inevitable as the Taliban's defeat and retreat into Pakistan's border regions.

There are seven tribal agencies (that is, locally administered areas) situated between Pakistan and Afghanistan:

- the Khyber Agency
- the Orakzai Agency
- the Kurram Agency
- the Mohmand Agency
- the Bajaur Agency
- the South Waziristan Agency
- the North Waziristan agency.

There are routes from these territories through the Pakistani city of Dera Ismail Khan into Pakistan's south-western Balochistan province, which borders the Afghan provinces of Helmand and Kandahar. This loop provided bases for Afghan national resistance against the Soviet Union. The residents of this area are for the larger part ethnic Pashtuns but there are some Baluch as well. All are natural warriors. During the Taliban rule in Afghanistan many of these Pashtuns and Baluch fought or worked with the Taliban. They therefore had no hesitation in providing sanctuary in this belt (which stretches over 1,500 km) to the retreating Taliban and Al-Qaeda forces after their defeat in Afghanistan.

Al-Qaeda needed a resting place – a safe haven – but it did not intend simply to hole up in its sanctuary. What it wanted was a natural fortress from which it could incite the whole region to evolve into a theater of war. It could then trap the United States and its Western allies in the natural guerilla terrain of Afghanistan, and expand the sphere of its operations into Central Asia in the north and India to the east.

Al-Qaeda never aimed to launch a Jihad in Pakistan, but it was left with a dilemma when Pakistan sided with the United States in Afghanistan. (It did so half-heartedly and under duress, but it sided with the United States nevertheless.) This left Al-Qaeda with no option but to consider Pakistan as no less an enemy than the Western allies of the United States. Al-Qaeda felt it had been left with no alternative other than to expand its operations into Pakistan.

From 2002 onwards, therefore, Al-Qaeda geared its strategy to focus on Pakistan's tribal region – the natural fortress in which it was based – and inundate the region with its ideology. It carried out a few small operations in Pakistan, hoping to neutralize Pakistan's support for the US actions in Afghanistan, but it still did not open a major front in Pakistan. Then once it had regrouped its forces in the tribal areas, Al-Qaeda went to Afghanistan in 2006, to support the Taliban's spring offensive that year. This in fact marked both the comeback of the Taliban and a watershed for Al-Qaeda.

In 2007 Al-Qaeda briefly returned to its caves in the tribal areas, once more to regroup, but this time in order to open a war front in Pakistan, whose allegiance to the US actions in Afghanistan was now unequivocal. It carried out some major operations there, including the assassination of the prime minister, Benazir Bhutto, then again retreated into the tribal areas and began a procedure to turn its ideologically inspired tribal comrades into its "blood brothers."

From these developments the Tehrik-e-Taliban Pakistan (TTP) came into being in the late 2007 and early 2008, and Al-Qaeda developed a new generation of leaders and commanders woven into a "shadow army" (Laskhar Al-Zil). Its aim was to coordinate Muslim resistance movements across the world, including in Indian Kashmir and on the Indian mainland, while bringing Palestine, Somalia, and Iraq into the picture, with the *Ibnul Balad* (sons of the soil) fighters. For Al-Qaeda strategy and ideology were now combined, and the 26/11 Mumbai attacks and Chechnya's Muslim resistance movement jointly set the stage for renewed Al-Qaeda attacks in India.

The whole world is currently obsessed with the Afghan war, and 26/11 is seen as an independent incident. This book looks to go beyond that perception. It provides an overview of all that has transpired since 9/11, which present a very different picture, and argues that beginning with bringing India into its theater of war, Al-Qaeda aims to extend its war against the West all the way to the Middle East for the final "End of Time" battles to liberate Palestine.

1

A NEW WORLD: DESTRUCTION, MIGRATION, FRIENDS, AND FOES

Soon after 9/11, Osama bin Laden broadcast messages on television channels while moving from one secret location to another to evade capture. This phase of Al-Qaeda tactics began well before the US invasion of Afghanistan on October 7, 2001. Bin Laden's emissaries in the meantime made new connections in Pakistan through contacts already established there. They hired houses in Pakistan to which they planned to relocate the family members of Al-Qaeda fighters. Abu Zubaida, a Palestinian, was sent to Lahore (in Pakistan) with US$100,000 to meet with the chief of Laskhar-e-Taiba[1] (LeT), Hafiz Muhammad Saeed,[2] make formal arrangements for the women's and children's passports and tickets, and arrange for their interim accommodation. Saeed was selected for this sensitive mission because he was an old confidant of both Osama bin Laden and the Al-Qaeda leadership.

In 1988 Abu Abdur Rahman Sareehi, a Saudi and one of bin Laden's deputies, had founded an organization in the Afghan Kunar Valley to recruit Pakistanis from the Bajaur Agency (a Federally Administered Tribal Area – FATA) to fight the Soviets. Sareehi was the brother-in-law of Zakiur Rahman Lakhvi, who is now the commander in chief of LeT and the main suspect for the Mumbai attack on November 26, 2008. (He has been named by the US Treasury and the Security Council as head of operations for LeT.)

Seed money for the training camps was provided by bin Laden, and the organization flourished in the Kunar Valley and Bajaur. Hundreds of young men from Pakistan belonging to the Salafi[3] school of thought joined the organization to fight alongside their Afghan brethren. In short, by 1989 bin Laden had set the tone and tenor of a global resistance movement.

In 1990 Iraq invaded Kuwait. Bin Laden offered Saudi Arabia his volunteers to defend the country, so that it had an alternative to looking for help from the United States, and sent the details of the resources he could control. They included Sareehi's set-up in the Kunar Valley. Laskhar-e-Taiba was born in Kunar Valley in those days, as a branch of Sareehi's set-up whose foundation was laid by Osama Bin Laden. Soon after, the communist regime in Afghanistan fell, and before the Taliban took up the reins of government, an Islamic Emirate, based on Salafi tenets supported by Kuwait and Saudi Arabia, was founded in the valley.

On October 7, 2001, the United States and its allies attacked Afghanistan. A one-sided war (with the United States dominant) continued for about two months, after which the entire leadership of Al-Qaeda and the Taliban retreated to Pakistan. This was not the end of the war as the United States had optimistically supposed, but the beginning of a new global conflict.

The 9/11 attacks had become the focal point of a global war against Western hegemony and interests. The origins of this lay with the dissident Muslim groups who had met up in the militant camps of Afghanistan two decades earlier. The first arrivals were Egyptian youths from the Muslim Brotherhood, and they were later joined by others from a number of underground organizations opposed to various Arab governments. This was the nucleus of the movement that, by defeating communism in Afghanistan, played a major part in bringing the great Soviet empire to an end.

But taking on the mighty US war machine, along with the hostility of the Western world, was another matter. The combined onslaught of the US and allied forces was lethal, and it saw most of the militants annihilated. The US casualties numbered just twelve in the two-month-long war, whereas thousands of Al-Qaeda militants (and civilian bystanders) were killed by aerial bombing. When this two-month phase of the long Afghan war ended in December 2001, it was estimated that at least 3,000 Al-Qaeda fighters had been killed. Dozens more had been arrested, and by the time the remaining trickle reached Pakistan's tribal areas of Bajaur, Mohmand, South and North Waziristan (near the Hindu Kush mountain range, these territories have among the world's most inhospitable terrain, and provide natural mountain strongholds), their numbers had been reduced to a few thousand. There is no credible information on the exact numbers of foreign fighters who escaped from Afghanistan after the US invasion, but a rough estimate is that 10,000 Uzbek, Chechen, Uighur, Chinese, and Arab fighters in total arrived in

Pakistan. Of these, no more than 2,000 could be considered bona fide Al-Qaeda members.

Al-Qaeda was in no shape to challenge US hegemony when these remnants of the Afghan resistance were in such a pathetic condition, but in reality its losses were less heavy than might have been imagined, because core Al-Qaeda members had not really fought in Afghanistan during the invasion. The only exceptions were special circumstances like the Tora Bora siege, where its men were trapped, and left with no option but to fight. Al-Qaeda's strategy had always been to conserve its energies and resources for the next phase of the war, after US forces had been completely routed in Afghanistan. It launched its war of attrition to this end from the Pakistani tribal areas.

PLAYING WITH FIRE

Shortly after the Taliban's defeat in Afghanistan, Al-Qaeda's network in Pakistan – its main strategic backyard to fight the Afghan war – had seemingly collapsed. In March 2002 a top Al-Qaeda commander, Abu Zubaida, was arrested. A few months later, on September 11, 2002, Ramzi bin Al-Shib was captured. The arrest of Abu Zubaida in particular reflected the weakness of Al-Qaeda's planning in Pakistan. He had been assigned to contact the LeT chief Hafiz Saeed and arrange the onward travel of Al-Qaeda family members to safe destinations. I documented this fact in *Asia Times Online* on January 27, 2006:

> According to sources in the LeT, the amount of money was US$100,000, which was to be used to take care of Arab Jihadis and their families displaced from Afghanistan by the US-led invasion of 2001. The LeT was the only organization in Pakistan the Arabs from Afghanistan would deal with. There were a number of reasons for this, apart from both having Salafi backgrounds. The most important of these being the ties established during the Afghan resistance against the Soviets in the 1980s. So the LeT organized temporary housing for many Arab families after the fall of Kabul and Kandahar. The next step was to arrange forged travel documents and air tickets. But Hafiz and the money were not forthcoming. Abu Zubaida, who was living in a safe house of the LeT in Faisalabad, traveled to Lahore to speak to Hafiz, who complained he did not have enough money to help the Arabs. Abu Zubaida was

incensed, and returned to his safe house. A few days later the house was raided and he was arrested. These events are part of Jihadi folklore. However, what's new is added by a source that left the Pakistani army to join the LeT, with which he soon became disillusioned and parted for Africa to become a businessman. Abu Jabran was the chief bodyguard of Abu Zubaida. He was also arrested along with Abu Zubaida. "The logical conclusion is that he should be in Camp X-Ray, the US military base at Guantanamo Bay, Cuba," my source had said. "But he is serving as the personal adviser to the No 1 man in the Laskhar-e-Taiba, Zakiur Rehman, commander-in-chief of the LeT in Indian-administered Kashmir." *Asia Times Online* inquiries indicate that Abu Jabran was freed by the US Federal Bureau of Investigation eight days after being arrested with Abu Zubaida. As soon as he was released, he was elevated as adviser to Zakiur Rehman. Abu Jabran is known in the internal circles of the LeT as Janab Jabran Chaca.

In her book *The Dark Side: The Inside Story of How the War on Terror Turned into a War on American Ideals* (2008), Jane Mayer wrote that a CIA official had said the United States had paid US$10 million to the Pakistani government, which in turn bribed an informant to learn of Abu Zubaida's whereabouts. Abu Zubaida's capture led to dozens of other arrests. Within months Al-Qaeda's network was in a shambles – so much so that its very survival became questionable.

Pakistan had been under pressure from Washington since the fall of the Taliban in Afghanistan in late 2001, and launched a major operation against the Taliban on June 22, 2002, at Azam Warsak, in South Waziristan, which is located near the Afghan border. The Azam Warsak operation by Pakistan's armed forces was their first-ever attack on Al-Qaeda. The assault included paramilitary forces from the Frontier Corps and the Waziristan Scouts. The total number killed was 17: 11 members of the security forces and 6 Chechen and Uzbek militants. More than 50 foreigners are said to have fled the attack. But the operation failed because of the sympathy of Pakistan's tribes for the defeated Taliban regime and its allied foreign fighters. Their anger heightened at the US-led invasion of Afghanistan, and when Pakistan's armed forces tried to catch fleeing members of Al-Qaeda, the tribesmen turned on the Pakistanis. Their fury manifested itself when the Mehsud tribe, long known for its pro-establishment view, resisted Pakistan's military and provided safe passage to foreign fighters. The Wazir chiefs and elders of other tribes warned Pakistan of retaliation. They denounced the operation as US-sponsored, and announced that if more operations were carried out in the tribal areas it would be tantamount to declaring open war on all of the Pashtun tribes.

On June 27, 2002, several Pakistani army officers, including Brigadier Shaukat Hayat and Colonel Saeed Khan, met with the tribal *jirga* (council). The two military officers pledged that before any future action was taken against Al-Qaeda, the tribes would be given an opportunity to handle the issue themselves. They promised the army would only enter the fray if the tribes failed to deliver. Despite this agreement, however, Pakistan's security forces and the local administration continued to conduct small operations in which foreigners were arrested. The tribes took serious exception to this, but did not make as much of an issue of it as might have been expected. Then on October 2, 2003, Pakistan armed forces blatantly violated his understanding when, without warning, 2,500 commandos were airlifted into the village of Baghar, near Angor Ada, with aerial support from 12 helicopter gunships.

According to local residents, some of the helicopters had flown from the Machdad Kot US airbase across the border in Afghanistan. Witnesses reported that 31 Pakistani soldiers and 13 foreign fighters and local tribesmen died in the attack. However, a large number of militants escaped. Major-General Faisal Alvi commanded the operation, and several high-profile Al-Qaeda commanders, including Abdul Rahman Kennedy, were killed. Al-Qaeda took its revenge for the attack when Major-General Alvi was shot dead in 2008 by retired Major Haroon Ashik. (There is a detailed account of that event and the life of Major Haroon on pages 85–6.) But the situation demanded that Al-Qaeda move to a new battle strategy, and with that, one of the main characters of this real-life *A Thousand and One Nights* tales emerges.

The October 2003 military operation forced the Al-Qaeda leaders to act quickly. Al-Qaeda now understood that the only useful function of the old Taliban cadre was to play host to its members. Commanders like Jalaluddin Haqqani had only survived because of their Pakistani connections. They did not have the backbone to stand up to the Pakistani establishment. Al-Qaeda had been on the lookout for new young blood with no connections to Pakistan's security establishment. It had been interacting with dozens of such young tribesmen, and its trained eyes spotted Nek Muhammad as the man for the hour. This was the beginning of the Neo-Taliban

– the new generation of South Asian youths born of Al-Qaeda's ideology and strategic vision.

AL-QAEDA'S NEW APPROACH

Nek Muhammad was a half-literate and poor man in his mid-twenties hailing from the Wazir tribe of South Waziristan. The Al-Qaeda leaders found in him a natural warrior. He was provided with guns and money. Nek and his tribal friends, who used to run around the mountains on public transport when they wanted to visit the tribal headquarters in Wana, now had several smart SUVs to move about in. Armed guards accompanied him. In Pashtun tribal societies, guns, money, and men signify a leader. With all this at his disposal, Nek Muhammad was acknowledged as the real leader of South Waziristan.

The old fiefdoms of the tribal elders started to collapse. Young men in their teens and twenties were organized by Nek Muhammad to challenge the old order. Within months, the centuries-old tribal structure had melted. The younger generation was calling the shots. Their insubordination knew no bounds. Tribal elders and senior Muslim clerics lost their grip. The traditional tribal dynamic had literally changed overnight. The younger militants were not ready to tolerate the presence of anybody who might rival them. The tribal chiefs were either killed or fled to the cities. Their fiefdoms fell into the hands of this new generation, who were totally committed to Al-Qaeda.

Pakistan's military establishment evaluated these setbacks as temporary, and was confident that a proper military operation would wipe out all signs of Al-Qaeda's ideology. The establishment became certain of this when Nek Muhammad was killed by a CIA predator drone strike in South Waziristan in 2004. However, both the United States and Pakistan had underestimated Al-Qaeda. Al-Qaeda did not rely on individuals. It had devised a dynamic strategy. Behind the force of Nek Muhammad's personality, it had raised a motivated cadre that could both perpetuate the war against the US–NATO forces in Afghanistan, and fend off pressure from Pakistan.

Under the command of Al-Qaeda were the twin forces of Jundullah and Jaishul al-Qiba al-Jihadi al-Siri al-Alami in South Waziristan, which had been formulated in 2003–04 by Al-Qaeda's high command. Jaishul al-Qiba was assigned the work of conducting international operations, including those in Afghanistan, while Jundullah was to target US and other Western interests in Pakistan, and conduct operations to neutralize Pakistan's support to the United States. (Jundullah in Pakistan was different from the Iranian organization that was also called Jundullah.)

These organizations were raised not for military operations alone, but also to promote Al-Qaeda's mission among the masses and add to its strength. In fact, this was investment for Al-Qaeda's future plans. The organizations also produced propaganda literature, including documentary films, and had a studio named Ummat, which undertook similar work for Al-Qaeda's media wing, as did the Al-Sahab Foundation.

By the end of 2004 Al-Qaeda had released a state-of-the-art CD containing Osama bin Laden's selected speeches from 2002 to December 2004. This was circulated in Afghanistan, Pakistan, and the Middle East. It was the first step towards the broader Al-Qaeda goal of shedding its former "shadowy" image, and openly announcing mass Jihad against the United States and other foreign occupation forces in the Middle East and Afghanistan. The speeches on the CD addressed several specific audiences. The one from 2002 addressed the Pakistani nation, the 2003 speech was aimed at the United States, the 2004 one at Europe, and the December 2004 speech addressed the people of the Arabian Peninsula (Saudi Arabia).

The lengthiest and most impressive of these speeches was Osama bin Laden's December 2004 video address to the people of the Arabian Peninsula. In this he explained why the rulers of Saudi Arabia were being targeted by Al-Qaeda. The reasons given included their corruption, tyranny, human rights abuses, and finally deviation from the true Islamic faith. The CD included horrifying images of war and destruction in Iraq, and paid tribute to the Iraqi resistance. In contrast to some earlier Al-Qaeda productions, this CD appeared to have been made by professionals in a modern and well-equipped studio. The audio and visual effects are clear, with English subtitles for non-Arabic speakers. Additionally, separate files included transcripts in languages such as Urdu, Persian, English, Pashtu, and Arabic.

The package clearly showed that Al-Qaeda had regrouped and, in an organized manner, was ready to spread its message to the whole of the Muslim world. But unlike in the past when Al-Qaeda's propaganda only urged people to join the Afghan resistance, from 2005 onward its aim was to connect with Muslim masses for worldwide resistance. The speeches selected for the CD were therefore not pure and simple propaganda designed to stir people to make war, but an in-depth analysis of Al-Qaeda's approach and clarification of its various actions – with justifications. Generally, underground groups do not engage in debate to justify their actions. They resort to rhetoric to attract fresh blood. However, when they do try to connect with the masses through the media to cultivate collective thinking, it shows their interest in linking with mainstream activities, which include mass mobilization and mass participation programs for a larger purpose.

In 2004–05, Al-Qaeda was looking to do precisely that – especially in Pakistan. The idea of launching Jundullah was to open Al-Qaeda doors to Pakistani youths through these media outlets and charge their sentiments through films. This was the basic tool used to create a new generation of Jihadis. But Al-Qaeda did not organize Jundullah for this purpose alone. It also aimed to raise a Pakistani Jihadi cadre which could work towards limited objectives in Pakistan followed by Afghanistan, then move forward to the field of international operations, working against Western interests through Jaishul al-Qiba al-Jihadi al-Siri al-Alami. Jundullah's most sought-after audience was members of the Pakistani Jihadi organizations fighting in Indian-occupied Kashmir. They were to be convinced that the liberation of the Muslim lands would only be possible if struggles were waged under the Al-Qaeda banner. Prospective recruits were then invited to work for the cause of a global Jihad. In a few months the stage was set for this new game.

Al-Qaeda understood that Pakistan was fertile soil for ideological cultivation. There were at least 600,000 youths there who had been trained and had fought in Afghanistan and Kashmir since 1979. At least 100,000 Pakistanis were active members of different Jihadi cadres. Over 1 million students were enrolled in various Islamic seminaries, and there were several hundred thousand supporters of Pakistan's Islamic religious parties. The main handler of the Afghan Jihad against the Soviets had been Pakistan's army, which itself was not immune to the influence of radicalism. Several army officers had pledged their allegiance (*bait*) to different Jihadi spiritual leaders, including Maulana Akram Awan of Chakwal. These groups were known in the Pakistan army as *pir bhai* groups (*pir bhai* are those who pledged their allegiance to a person, in a way that means the whole circle of disciples act as brothers to each other). Although General Pervez Musharraf had purged some of these elements from the Pakistan Army after 9/11, including his very close friend, the then deputy chief of army staff, Lt.-Gen. Muzaffar Usmani, he was unable to completely eradicate the radical tendency, which had become deep-rooted in Pakistan's security services during the period from 1979 to 2001. Al-Qaeda aimed, through organizations like Jundullah, to divert the allegiances of this impressive pool of Islamists into its own fold, along with others.

The vitriolic Laskhar-e-Jhangvi (LJ), an underground banned anti-Shiite militant organization, was the first to join the ranks of Al-Qaeda's affiliated structures. LJ is a breakaway faction of the later banned political party Sepah-e-Sahaba Pakistan (SSP). LJ adherents had killed dozens of Shiite clerics and Shiite professionals, and the state had put all its members on the wanted list. After the fall of the Taliban they did not have any place to go, and most of them had been hiding in Afghanistan during the Taliban regime. To take advantage of the situation Al-Qaeda provided these LJ members with a precise role in the global Jihad. On Al-Qaeda's regrouping in Pakistan's tribal areas, LJ members were welcomed in South Waziristan and encouraged to support Al-Qaeda's multifaceted operations in Pakistan. LJ was permitted to continue with its targeted anti-Shiite killings, but some members, like Qari Zafar (who was killed in 2010 in North Waziristan), were also used in Al-Qaeda operations such as the attack on the Federal Investigation Agency (FIA) offices in Lahore. At the same time, other leaders like Qari Hussain were tellingly deputed to raise suicide brigades for Al Qaeda's anti-US operations. Slowly and gradually this strategy began to work, and brought thousands of new recruits into the Al-Qaeda fold. Among them were two well-known brothers, Dr Akmal Waheed and Dr Arshad Waheed, who had earlier been affiliated with Jamaat-e-Islam.[4] These two top physicians from the southern port city of Karachi were now linked to Al-Qaeda through Jundullah. Dr Arshad Waheed was later killed in Wana in South Waziristan in a CIA drone strike, and soon afterwards Al-Qaeda's media wing Al-Sahab released a documentary on his life and exploits to inspire the younger generation. Subsequently several army officers joined the Al-Qaeda cadre (see later in the book).

In July 2010 a spokesperson of Punjabi Taliban (the non-Pashtu speaking section of the Taliban) confirmed that the influence of Arshad and Akmal Waheed had split Pakistan's largest student organization, Islami Jamiat-e-Taliba (IJT), and other organizations, especially those whose members who came from Karachi. Many joined forces with Al-Qaeda in North Waziristan. IJT had been formed in the 1948 as the offshoot of Jamaat-e-Islami, and by the 1970s it dominated all the country's major educational institutions, including the University of Karachi, University of Punjab, and University of Peshawar. Most of the middle-class members of Pakistan's leadership had belonged to the IJT as students, including Pakistan's ambassador to the United States, Husain Haqqani, Pakistan Muslim League leaders Javed Hashmi and Ehsan Iqbal, Pakistani law minister Dr Babar Awan, and almost 80 percent of Urdu-language newspaper and electronic media opinion writers and television talk show anchors in Pakistan.

While Jundullah and the other organizations that took shape in South Waziristan from 2003–04 under the influence of Al-Qaeda provided broad guidelines to local insurgent groups, Al-Qaeda was not behind each and every attack inside Pakistan. The existing ideological fault lines created problems for Al-Qaeda, as when sectarian Jihadis carried out the killings of innocent Muslim civilians in Pakistani cities, just as they had done in Iraq. But the worldview of Jihadis such as the members of LJ did eventually change from narrow sectarianism to the perspective of an international Muslim resistance movement.

Al-Qaeda initially struggled to broaden its struggle by acquiring new members and allies, after its migration into the Pakistani tribal areas. However, this was a comparatively easy task because much of the ground had already been laid out. In addition, Al-Qaida benefited as the alliance between United States and Pakistan grew closer, and the Pakistan military establishment gradually pushed Islamists out of the loop. As a consequence, a large number of pro-Pakistan Islamic militants who had been engaged in fighting against the Indian forces in Kashmir were put on the suspect list, and badly roughed up. This caused thousands of others to withdraw their first loyalty from Pakistan and join hands with Al-Qaeda. Al-Qaeda then picked a select group to reshape its strategy, while thousands of others helped it change from a purely militant group into a real Islamic resistance movement.

2

THE POLITICS OF WAR AND PEACE

Afghanistan is central to Al-Qaeda's policy. Terror operations in Pakistan were not. In fact, after 9/11 there was a tacit agreement between the then director general of Pakistan's premier intelligence agency, Inter-Services Intelligence (ISI), Lt.-General Mehmood, and Al-Qaeda members (made when Mehmood visited Kandahar to convince Mullah Omar to hand over Osama bin Laden) that Pakistan would not be hostile to Al-Qaeda if Al-Qaeda did not harm Pakistan's interests. Under US pressure Pakistan mounted a few military operations against Al-Qaeda in 2002 and 2003, but Al-Qaeda abided by its commitment to avoid enmity with Pakistan until late 2003, when militants carried out an attack on General Pervez Musharraf. This led to a long and continuing period of hostilities between Pakistan and Al-Qaeda.

The two attacks on Musharraf's motorcade, one following shortly after the other in late 2003, were masterminded by Amjad Farooqui, a former LJ leader killed in an encounter in September 2004. He was working in close collaboration with Al-Qaeda at the time, but the plan he devised was of his own making. The attack on Musharraf prompted a massive crackdown on Jihadi structures. In a matter of few months several thousand Jihadis were rounded up by the intelligence agencies and detained without trial. Soon after this Al-Qaeda planned a Pakistan terror operations strategy, although it did so half-heartedly.

Up to that time, Al-Qaeda had viewed Pakistan as an essential component of its strategic base and a recruiting ground for personnel, not as a theater in which terror was to be spread. However, when the tide of US pressure forced Pakistan to wage war against Al-Qaeda, the Taliban, and other militant groups, it was inevitable that Al-Qaeda would resort to counter-strategies such as its terror campaign in Pakistan. This strategy conveyed the message that if the United States was capable of pressurizing Pakistan through military means, the militants were equally capable of changing the course of Pakistan's future direction with attacks of this nature. The strategy certainly succeeded in slowing down Pakistan's support for the US-led "War on Terror." As the war progressed, the militants flexed more muscle, forcing Pakistan to recognize them as serious players. Pakistan was then forced to sit down with them to negotiate the terms for a truce.

Later on, this initially half-hearted strategy morphed into a well-planned dialectic under which Al-Qaeda planed the course of its war, based on three prominent features:

* Regrouping of its cadre and a battle strategy in the Pakistani tribal areas against the Pakistan Army.
* Buffering this arrangement through ceasefire agreements before venturing back to its main battlefield, Afghanistan, to launch the spring offensive of 2006 (Al-Qaeda's watershed to enable it to strengthen its strategic base in Pakistan's tribal areas).
* Expanding the war into Pakistan (which by 2007 had become a vital ally of the United States against Al-Qaeda), and from there strategizing the expansion of the theater of war from the Central Asian Republics to India, for the express purpose of defeating NATO forces in Afghanistan.

In order to pursue this strategy, Al-Qaeda regrouped its forces and erected new militant structures in Pakistan's tribal belt (issues covered in Chapter 1), then expanded the formation of the structures from Central Asia to Bangladesh. (Subsequent chapters discuss the detail of this.)

In March 2004, under intense US pressure, thousands of Pakistan Army troops launched the Kalusha Operation in the Wana subdivision of South Waziristan. They were under the misguided belief that a short, sharp, surgical operation would eliminate the militants. But unlike in the 2002 and 2003 operations, this time the Al-Qaeda structures were active. The Pakistan Army had not anticipated such a fierce reaction, and the operation failed, with the militants ambushing the troops and inflicting heavy losses. Pakistan's officers and soldiers were lured into traps and captured, while the pride and honor of the armed forces suffered public humiliation when young tribal boys slapped around both the officers and the men they held in captivity. Finally the Pakistan Army surrendered, and a ceasefire (the Shakai Agreement) was signed on April 24, 2004.

This was the first success for Al-Qaeda's strategy in South

Waziristan. The militants used this breathing space to shore up their struggle against the United States and its Pakistani allies. In the coming months more such ceasefires fitted in perfectly with Al-Qaeda's broader war strategy, allowing the militants to maneuver battles from one region to another, and eventually enhance their capabilities to draw the boundaries of battlefields to their own liking. (Later chapters discuss this further.)

Nek Muhammad, the Yargulkhel Wazir, emerged as the hero of Wana. He successfully rescued Al-Qaeda operatives from Pakistan's military onslaught and saved the life of the chief of Uzbekistan's Islamic Movement, Qari Tahir Yaldochiv, during the Kalusha Operation. This was the first operation in which foreign militants were publicly acknowledged as real players.

NEW AL-QAEDA PLAYERS AND ACTIONS

The Shakai Agreement witnessed the emergence of many more characters in Al-Qaeda's version of *A Thousand and One Nights*. Tahir Yaldochiv was prominent among them. He later played a key role in the recruiting such tribal militants as Abdullah Mehsud, alias Muhammad Alam, and Baitullah Mehsud, together with an Uzbek force of 2,500 men. The Uzbeks were to give the Pakistani militants lessons in brutality to establish a reign of terror: their tactics included routinely slitting the throats of their foes.

The following are details of the main signatories to the treaty. Each one of them was important. In the official document Nek Muhammad was noted as a *mujahid* (holy warrior). According to documents the signatories to the Shakai Agreement were:

- Muhammad Miraj Uddin
- Maulana Abdul Malik
- Maulana Akhtar Gul
- Muhammad Abbas
- Nek Muhammad (*mujahid*)
- Haji Sharif
- Baitullah Mehsud
- Noor Islam
- Muhammad Javed
- Muhammad Alam alias Abdullah.

Muhammad Miraj Uddin and Maulana Abdul Malik were two Pakistani parliamentarians from the pro-Taliban six-party religious alliance, MMA (Muttehida Majls-e-Amal). Maulana Akhtar Gul was a local pro-Taliban cleric. Muhammad Abbas, Nek Muhammad, Haji Sharif, Noor Islam, and Mohammad Javed were pure militants. Muhammad Alam, alias Abdullah, was the famously defiant Abdullah Mehsud who became the top leader of the Pakistani Taliban. (He was killed in Pakistan's south-western province of Balochistan, in the district of Zhoab, in July 2007.) This quick glance at the list shows how in 2004 the political alliance of the Taliban and Al-Qaeda had replaced the pro-establishment tribal leaders.

The main clauses of the agreement were:

* The government would release all prisoners.
* The government would pay compensation for the *suhada* (martyred)/injured during the operation.
* The government would pay compensation for collateral damage to material during the military operation.
* The government would not take action against Nek Muhammad and other wanted individuals.
* The government would allow foreign *mujahideen* to live peacefully in Waziristan.

Against this:

* The *mujahideen* (local militants) would not resort to any action against the land and government of Pakistan.
* The *mujahideen* from Waziristan would not undertake any action against Afghanistan.

The agreement failed because of conflicting interpretations regarding the clause of "foreigners' registration." The government claimed that the militants would register "foreign fighters" in the area and surrender them. The militants claimed that no such clause had been present in the agreement. This began a new period of confrontation, with Pakistan's military starting another operation in South Waziristan. But Al-Qaeda was ready to retaliate. The first reaction to the operation came in Pakistan's largest city, the southern port of Karachi, where the then Corps commander, General Ahsan Saleem Hayat (later promoted to Pakistani vice chief of army staff) was attacked. He survived the attack, but several of the military men around him were killed. The attack was credited to Jundullah's Karachi cell. The attackers were arrested, and Pakistan resolved to take more serious action against the militancy after a hellfire missile launched from a US Predator drone on 19 June 2004 had killed Nek. The duration of the agreement was less than 50 days, but its effects were pervasive:

- The tribal dissidents grew into a powerful militant group which became a permanent feature of the tribal landscape and reinforced the polarization.
- The government of Pakistan strongly supported the stance of the United States on the "War on Terror" and militarized the situation.
- Militants were given "equal party status" which was superior to the tribes.

Nek Muhammad's demise was the end of a legend, but new characters of equal stature had already been reared by Al-Qaeda, and in the coming months, they emerged one after the other. Al-Qaeda visionaries helped them expand their horizons.

Haji Omar was in his fifties, and marked out to be Nek Muhammad's successor. He was from the same tribe, but Al-Qaeda did not believe in hereditary leadership, especially in the case of Haji Omar, who was too old to be molded into Al-Qaeda's strategy. They were looking for someone in his twenties – like Nek Muhammad. Two youths, Abdullah Mehsud and Baitullah Mehsud, were chosen by the Al-Qaeda leadership. The Uzbek warlord Tahir Yaldochiv was close to both of them. Like Nek Muhammad, both youths came from ordinary backgrounds. However, their Mehsud tribe was the difference. Unlike the Wazirs, the Mehsud tribe had always been close to the Pakistani establishment. They were better educated and better off than most tribespeople. Money had little to do with their recruitment. Tahir supported them with over 2,500 Uzbek militia, and with that they resorted to a culture of vandalism.

Born in 1974 in the village of Nano in South Waziristan, Abdullah Mehsud's real name was Muhammad Alam Mahsud. He was a member of the Mehsud clan, Saleemi Khel, in South Waziristan. He had a diploma in commerce (D.Com.) from Peshawar. Abdullah Mehsud had fought against the United States and the Northern Alliance forces in Afghanistan, and had lost a leg to a landmine in 1996 during the opening days of "Operation Enduring Freedom." In December 2001, he surrendered to the Uzbek warlord Abdul Rashid Dostum in the "Battle of Kunduz." He was then handed over to the United States and spent 25 months in the Guantanamo

Bay detention camp, where he was fitted with a prosthetic limb. Mehsud was later released by the United States and returned to South Waziristan. Imprisonment had not eroded his faith in the Taliban and Al-Qaeda, and when he returned to South Waziristan, he became close to Tahir Yaldochiv, who then pitched him against Pakistan's security forces. He next went to the Afghan province of Helmand to fight alongside the Taliban against NATO troops, but while passing through the district of Zhob, in Pakistan's Balochistan province, on his way back from Afghanistan to South Waziristan, he was surrounded by Pakistan's security forces. He refused to surrender and committed suicide by blowing himself up with a hand grenade.

Baitullah Mehsud was born in early 1974 in the village of Landi Dhok in the Bannu district of Pakistan's former North West Frontier Province (NWFP), which is now called Khyber Paktoonkhwa. He hailed from the Broomi Khel side of the Shabi Khel subtribe of the Mehsud, and was one of five brothers. He avoided media attention and refused to be photographed in conformity with his religious beliefs. He never finished formal school but received instruction in a *madrassa* (Islamic seminary). As a young *madrassa* student, Baitullah would often travel into Afghanistan to assist the Taliban in their implementation of *sharia* (the sacred law of Islam), and their fight against the Northern Alliance. He emerged as another major tribal leader after the 2004 death of Nek Muhammad.

In a ceremony attended by five leading Taliban commanders, including Mullah Dadullah, Baitullah was appointed Mullah Omar's governor for the Mehsud area. He then became close to the Uzbek leader Tahir Yaldochiv, and Tahir's ideological commitment left a deep impression on him. Al-Qaeda had differences over Baitullah Mehsud's modus operandi, but it did not have much choice as he was the guardian of the movement in the two Waziristans. (Mehsud was killed in a CIA drone strike in August 2009.)

Abdullah Mehsud and Baitullah Mehsud developed differences, and Abdullah was forced to abdicate command in favor of Baitullah. This notwithstanding, both Pakistani militants played a crucial role in the demolition of the tribal structure by forcing the tribal elders to flee from their respective areas. They then became the biggest warlords of the region.

The Pakistan government was once again forced to surrender – this time to the now militant Mehsud tribe. The terms of surrender surfaced in the shape of the Srarogha peace deal in February 2005. This deal was agreed between the pro-Taliban militant Baitullah

Mehsud and the government of Pakistan through local *jirga* mediation on February 7, 2005 at Srarogha, South Waziristan. It was a six-clause, written agreement which included:

- Baitullah and his group would neither harbor nor support any foreign fighter in his area.
- Baitullah and his supporters would not attack any government functionary or damage government property. Also, they would not cause any hindrance to development activities.
- The government would not take action against Baitullah and his supporters for their past acts. However, if found to be involved in any kind of terrorist or criminal activities in the future, they would be dealt with according to the prevailing laws in the Federally Administered Tribal Areas (FATA). If any culprit were found present in the Mehsud area, he would be handed over to the government.

The agreement read:

- We pledge that if any culprit (not from the Baitullah group) is found in this area, the Mehsud tribe will hand him over to the government and the government is empowered to take action under FCR (Frontier Crimes Regulations).[1]
- All those issues not covered under this agreement will be resolved through mutual consultation between the political administration and the Mahsud tribe.
- In case of violation of any of the above clauses, the political administration is empowered to take a legal course of action.

The agreement was signed by Baitullah Mehsud and members of the *jirga* (Malik Inayatullah Khan, Malik Qayum Sher, and Malik Sher Bahadar Shamankhel).

A few comments on this agreement:

- No clause was inserted in the agreement regarding cross-border infiltration or attacks in Afghanistan.
- There was no clause that foreign fighters would be surrendered.
- There was no clause requiring the militants to lay down arms.
- Controversies arose over reports of money payments to the militants during peace negotiations.
- Abdullah Mehsud, the second most important commander, opted out of the agreement.

Technically, the Shakai Agreement in 2004 granted a new lease of life to Al-Qaeda by allowing Al-Qaeda's local tribal allies to strengthen their control and provide the space Al-Qaeda required to spread the tentacles of its war game. Having gained complete control of South Waziristan (held by the Mehsud and Wazir tribes), Al-Qaeda now had huge bases to operate from. But that was not enough. The network of Al-Qaeda's influence in the tribal region and in Pakistani cities required it to broaden its bases to include a steady supply of new recruits and form cells which could effectively smooth the sharp edges of Pakistan's alliance with the United States over the war in Afghanistan. Then Al-Qaeda could emerge strong enough to fight the war in Afghanistan with focused minds. From here we can see how Al-Qaeda's moves eventually shaped the course of future battles.

With Al-Qaeda having planted its feet firmly in South Waziristan, some of the top Arab ideologues moved to the town of Razmak, situated at the crossroads between North Waziristan and South Waziristan. Close by is the town of Mir Ali in North Waziristan. The opportunities to launch operations from North Waziristan were better than those in South Waziristan. South Waziristan was more a Taliban outpost of Helmand province, directly under the influence of the Afghan Taliban. North Waziristan was different. Most of the militants there were stand-alone operators. Therefore North Waziristan provided much more space for Al-Qaeda to use as its international headquarters.

Jalaluddin Haqqani had been a legendary fighter against the Soviets. He pledged his allegiance to the Taliban, but was not part of the Taliban movement when it emerged, in 1994, as a student militia against the warlords of Afghanistan. Even after the US attack, Haqqani remained attached to the Taliban, but he still personally micro-managed his strategies in his fight against NATO troops. His sons Naseeruddin Haqqani and Sirajuddin Haqqani, however, were very close to the Arab fighters.

Unlike South Waziristan, where despite ideological unanimity the Mehsud and Wazir tribes often had differences with each other, North Waziristan was a united Wazir domain. The Dawar tribe also lives in North Waziristan, but is subservient to the Wazirs, and thus has never taken a stand against them.

Al-Qaeda understood that US pressure would obligate Pakistan to launch more operations, and ultimately the theater of war would expand to other Pakistani tribal areas where the United States would engage directly with Al-Qaeda followers. Al-Qaeda therefore sought to establish a series of strong ideological "forts," so that the conquest of one fort by the United States and/or its allies would not end the struggle. The aim of the Al-Qaeda exercise was to convince the tribesmen to forge a united front against the Pakistani government.

Jalaluddin Haqqani was the leading Taliban warlord in North Waziristan. Pakistan's ISI intelligence service had contacted him and assured him that the military operations in North Waziristan were superficial, and that once the situation changed, Pakistan would support the Taliban again. Haqqani believed this and so he was not ready to take up arms against Pakistan. However, Al-Qaeda knew on the basis of its previous experiences in 2002 and 2003, that given the rising influence of the United States in Pakistan, one day Pakistan would have to fight a real war against the Taliban. That understanding took Sheikh Essa Al-Misri (Al-Qaeda's ideologue: for more about him see page 27), then in his seventies, to North Waziristan.

Essa did not speak to any of the major *mujahideen* leaders. Instead he picked up two clerics from the Dawar tribe, Moulvi Sadiq Noor and Abdul Khaliq Haqqani, and convinced them that there was no difference between Pakistan's establishment and that of the United States. Rather, the Pakistan armed forces were worse, because although they had been born Muslims, they were supportive of the US and Israeli agenda.

Moulvi Sadiq Noor and Abdul Khaliq Haqqani's Friday sermons against Pakistan's armed forces turned the towns of Mir Ali and Darpa Khail in North Waziristan into Al-Qaeda fortresses. These were just microcosms of the wider situation. There were hidden hands macro-managing higher developments. At one level some Al-Qaeda ideologues were winning the hearts and the minds of the local clerics and warlords, but at another level Al-Qaeda strategists covertly advised local warlords to gather collective strength from the Mujahideen Council and cement relationships on the basis of ideology, rather than tribal customs.

In December 2005, the Pakistani Taliban stunned the world with the execution of several robbers in North Waziristan. This was an indication that they had taken over the security of the area. Previously, the Pakistani Taliban had distanced itself from local affairs. As a consequence, the two Waziristans had become a paradise for drug smugglers, car thieves, bandits, and child abductors. These criminals had mostly committed their crimes in Pakistani cities and then retreated to their villages in the two Waziristans. However, they now also began to run rampant in the tribal areas. They raided other villages to loot and plunder, and they set up checkpoints and collected money from all travelers. The Pakistani Taliban had turned a blind eye to these activities, since they were obsessed with their Jihad against the United States and NATO in Afghanistan. However, Al-Qaeda now wanted the Pakistani Taliban to engage in local politics, in conformance with its strategy of turning the tribal areas into its strategic base. Thus, for the first time the Pakistani Taliban openly announced that they would run affairs in the territory, and not the Pakistani armed forces, or the local bandits, or the tribal elders. They executed almost 30 bandits in public. They hanged them before dragging their bodies through the streets. They took film footage of all these events, and released it initially to *Asia Times Online*. When the images were released in February 2006, a month before President Bush's visit to Pakistan, they created a storm around the world. Media outlets acquired the films from this author, and the footage was released on major international TV channels. Not long after their retreat from Afghanistan, the Taliban and Al-Qaeda announced the establishment of the Islamic State of North Waziristan, with a Taliban police to combat vice and crime.

The outside world saw the development simply as the formation of the Islamic State of North Waziristan, but Al-Qaeda had already restructured this part of the tribal areas to establish an Islamic state. Al-Qaeda's larger plan was to lay the ground for the restructuring all of the tribal areas in this fashion – to have them fully functional as Al-Qaeda forts, before expanding into the whole of the former NWFP as well as Balochistan. In this way it could cut all of NATO's supply lines through Pakistan and thus force the Western allies to engage in a long, draining war.

However, the real battlefield was always Afghanistan, and Al-Qaeda gains in the two Waziristans in 2005 were intended above all to advantage the Afghan Taliban in fighting the United States and its NATO allies there. The story, which started after 9/11 with Al-Qaeda migrating to the Pakistan tribal areas for a large-scale indoctrination campaign, targeted victory in Afghanistan's Helmand province and then the whole of south-west Afghanistan.

Al-Qaeda ensured that the Taliban would return to Afghanistan with finance, a strategy, recruits, and a restructured command system. The Taliban's resurgence in Afghanistan in summer 2006 alarmed the Western coalition. The summer 2006 battle literally floored them, for they had had no idea of the developments that had taken place in the shadows of Pakistan's tribal areas. They were convinced the Taliban and Al-Qaeda's back had been broken once and for all. The Taliban's comeback in 2006, with the help of Al-Qaeda, established the militants as the major regional player. Time proved that the Taliban's successful 2006 spring offensive was Al-Qaeda's watershed. After this time, Al-Qaeda clearly dominated Pakistan in 2007 and 2008, expanded its operations into India in late 2008, and opened up a theater of war in Chechnya in 2010. Thus during and before the spring of 2006, we see Al-Qaeda providing space for the Afghan Taliban to operate freely and go back into a kind of withdrawal mode. But in reality it was planning the 2006 offensive to put pressure on the United States, and it had well prepared the stage for this.

THE SPRING OFFENSIVE 2006: AL-QAEDA'S WATERSHED

The developments in the two Waziristans had been extraordinary. Al-Qaeda had quietly reinvented itself there and was aiming to pass on the benefit to the Afghan Taliban, to enable them tighten the noose around the NATO troops who had been so sure of an easy victory in Afghanistan. This was the first milestone Al-Qaeda had passed in its pursuit of its targets.

Al-Qaeda created this situation from 2002 to 2005, so that in 2006 the Taliban in Afghanistan were able to make an impressive comeback. This comeback tells the stunning story of the 2006 Taliban spring offensive and the emergence of a new cast of characters. They have shocked a world that thought the Taliban had become a relic of the past.

In 2006, Al-Qaeda had all but departed the scene. Its structures were woven into the tapestry of the Taliban, and its immediate aim was to have the Taliban emerge buoyant in Afghanistan. Further strategy had to wait until that was achieved. Meanwhile, with the Taliban regrouping in the Pakistani tribal areas and in contact with the Iraqi resistance, the Taliban leadership in south-west Afghanistan spent the better part of 2005 preparing for the coming offensive. Their preparations included a high-frequency exchange of training workshops with a group of emboldened veterans from the Iraqi resistance. Collectively the Iraqis and Pakistanis compiled a modified primer on the tactics of terror which should be deployed henceforth by the pro-Taliban forces in Waziristan. These tactics were widely disseminated among the scattered groups of heavily armed tribal Pashtuns and the mosaic of ideological mercenaries. Fighters of Arab, Uzbek, Chechen, and Afghan origin had regrouped after the fall of Kandahar at makeshift mini-bases south of the border. These bases were located deep in the heart of the secluded Pakistan-administered tribal areas of North Waziristan and South Waziristan, in the porous underbelly of the Durand Line.[2]

Revitalizing the pro-Taliban groupings in the southwest, rather than attempting to provoke an immediate all-Afghan uprising against the Karzai government and its Western allies, was the intended rationale of the now-celebrated spring offensive of 2006. First, though, the unholy mess of internecine strife that had periodically plagued pro-Taliban groups in the area needed to be sorted out.

Reuniting and mobilizing seemingly disparate groups in these two tribal areas became the immediate objective of Al-Qaeda, Mullah Omar, and Taliban central command. The intended result was to strike a life-threatening blow to the morale of the mighty US war machine in south-west Afghanistan, and to proclaim mastery over southern Afghanistan and Pakistan's adjoining tribal areas to a spellbound international audience. This would pave the way for the comeback of the Taliban and Al-Qaeda as a major regional force.

Despite the orchestrated hype, early spring 2006 witnessed no more than the usual limited sporadic encounters in south-west Afghanistan. In the tribal capital of South Waziristan, Wana, it was widely held that the trumpeted Taliban spring offensive of 2006 would soon be extinguished, and that the continuing resistance would peter out well before summer, leaving the Jihadis' picture of a resurrected Taliban "Kingdom of Heaven" in south-west Afghanistan as a distant memory.

At the end of May 2006, an apparently insignificant low-profile visit by an emissary from the Taliban central command to the bases in Waziristan radically altered the existing balance of power in the south-west. The emissary was a one-legged military commander renowned for his diplomatic skills. His presence in the area in early summer radically affected the perceived course of Taliban fortunes. He was none other than Mullah Dadullah, a name that still arouses a quiet reverence when it is whispered by military commanders on either side of the divide in the south-western area of conflict.

Preparations for the Taliban's spring offensive of 2006 had begun a year earlier. The Taliban leadership concentrated on restoring relations once again with various elements of the political leadership in Kabul, irrespective of whether these were US collaborators or dissidents. Fresh emissaries were also dispatched to the semi-autonomous warlords whose changing domains spanned most of

Afghanistan's 34 provinces. Above all, strategic contacts were initiated with the two important groups from amongst the militant *mujahideen* factions that had earlier shared the honors in expelling the Soviets from Afghanistan – the Hizb-i-Islami Afghanistan (HIA) faction led by former prime minister and strongman Gulbaddin Hikmatyar,[3] and the Hizb faction led by the hardline orthodox cleric Moulvi Younus Khalis.[4]

Because of the hostility between the Hikmatyar and Khalis factions, managing to attract both of these powerful groups of mujahideen to join a common anti-Karzai platform would be a notable triumph for the new-vision Taliban diplomacy. An additional measure of success would be virtually assured for a grand anti-Karzai popular front by drawing in formerly hostile Pashtun commanders, as well as their Tajik and Uzbek counterparts, to synchronize actions with the resurgent Taliban force in south-west Afghanistan through emissaries. The problem with this grand strategy was the continued existence of infighting amongst the pro-Taliban forces in North Waziristan and South Waziristan. These potential recruiting grounds had failed to merge into a single fighting arm, or to provide the requisite manpower and public sympathy that was essential to the intended Taliban resurgence.

It is against this background that the significance of Mullah Dadullah's visit to the two Waziristans in the heart of Pakistan's FATA must be viewed. A failed offensive in the south-west could lead cynical commanders and warlords across Afghanistan to write off any prospect of a successful Taliban comeback in the future. Mullah Dadullah was therefore keen to expend all of his energies on ensuring that the spring offensive would not fail.

Mullah Dadullah was then 40 years old. With a long bushy beard and sharply chiseled Kandahari features, he was one of the most feared Taliban commanders in the region. With the spring offensive expected to produce a visible change in Taliban fortunes, his unique ability to mediate successfully between the warring factions would add another feather to his military and diplomatic cap. He hailed from the Helmand province of Afghanistan, in the area adjoining Kandahar. In 1994 he had been undergoing a rigorous education in a religious seminary in Quetta (the capital of Pakistan's large western province of Balochistan), but in response to the Taliban call to arms, he left his religious texts behind and joined the Taliban movement at its very inception in Afghanistan. He was wounded at the Maidan Shehr front near Kabul, leading to the amputation of his left leg. In recognition of the services he had rendered, Mullah

Dadullah was then appointed as one of the key commanders on the Northern Front, with a 12,000 strong force under his control.

In the late 1990s, to the surprise of many observers, Dadullah inflicted a stunning and decisive defeat on the battle-hardened veterans of the Hizb-i-Islami led by Hikmatyar, at Kunduz. In the heady days before the fall of Kabul to the Taliban, observers had believed Dadullah to be a covert supporter of the Panjsheri warlord, Ahmed Shah Masoud, but they were forced to a reassessment after Dadullah successfully fought against Masoud's forces during the last year of the Taliban government. December 2001 brought the invasion of the Northern Alliance and their Western allies, and witnessed Dadullah entrenched in a Kunduz under siege.

A plethora of senior Taliban commanders negotiated with the Uzbek warlord General Rashid Dostum for the safe passage of their forces trapped in the north. Rashid Dostum betrayed many such Taliban commanders by handing them over to the United States after they had surrendered to him. Some of them are still languishing in the confines of Guantanamo Bay. Dadullah made good his escape in a way that was to define his distinctive brand of battle valor and shrewd native intelligence. In a daring maneuver outside the walls of Kunduz, he kidnapped one of Dostum's key commanders, using him as a human shield and releasing him only upon reaching the relative safety of Kandahar. For the next three years Dadullah would organize a series of wildcat operations in the ceaseless war of attrition that was being waged by Taliban elements in the south-western theater. With the assumption of his role as Mullah Omar's special envoy to the two Waziristans on the eve of the late spring offensive of 2006, Mullah Dadullah swiftly rose to the top echelons of the Taliban hierarchy (He was killed in 2007 in Helmand.) As his popularity spread, it became clear that he was a man to be reckoned with.

What caused the reclusive Mullah Omar to select this one-legged veteran for this critically important mission? Was his choice of Mullah Omar governed by the trust factor, or was there sufficient evidence available before the Taliban leadership that the energetic Dadullah was uniquely suited to deliver results on a high-risk mission, given his former relationships with many of the northern commanders now seeking refuge south of the Durand Line? Or was it simply his availability that proved to be the critical factor in the choice? Whatever the reason, results would soon justify the confidence the tenacious Mullah Omar had placed in the wide-ranging skills of his trusted protégé.

The period between 2002 and the commencement of the spring offensive in April 2006 witnessed the gradual resurgence of Taliban power in south-west Afghanistan. The same period also witnessed setbacks in the Karzai government's attempt to bring about national reconciliation and create an ethnically diverse coalition. At the same time, there was a heightened apprehension within the military establishment in Islamabad that the Taliban's bases in Pakistan's tribal areas had begun to radically transform the ideological topography of the two Waziristans, leading to a strategic imbalance on the Durand Line that the resurgent Taliban were certain to utilize to their advantage.

Although the Taliban Central Command in adjoining south-west Afghanistan loudly proclaimed that over 300,000 Taliban ideologues (read militants) would rise at a suitable signal from the reclusive Mullah Omar, in reality the missing 300,000 ideologically inclined militants had already been safely reabsorbed into the urban and rural tribal demography of post-Taliban Afghanistan during the period of the Karzai government. More critical to the future success of the Taliban's military fortunes would be the vanguard role played by the few thousand pro-Taliban militants, in addition to the rapidly dwindling group of approximately 4,000 foreign fighters – Arabs, Chechens, Uighurs, Uzbeks, and Chinese – ensconced in the mountainous Waziristan. It was they who would play a central role in leading the Taliban comeback, and mobilize the large and sympathetic tribal populations in pursuit of their political and military aims.

The tribe that formed the core of the Taliban support was the Waziris. These were described as the "wolves" by military observers of the "Great Game" (the strategic rivalry and conflict between the British Empire and the Russian Empire for supremacy in Central Asia) 100 years ago. Their traditional rivals, the Mehsud tribesmen (the "panthers" of the "Great Game") had kept their sympathies with the Pakistan Army, providing a check to any strategic imbalance. After the army made a bloody incursion into South Waziristan in 2004 which left scores of Mehsud tribesmen dead, the tribe changed its allegiance from the Pakistan Army to the Taliban.

A couple of seasons of hard occupation had also driven the commercially minded Dawar tribe (comprising occupational castes including tradesmen and shopkeepers) to a stage of hostility towards the Pakistan Army. Thus, as 2005 dawned, there were virtually no major tribal groupings in the two Waziristans that had not hitched their wagons to the Taliban cause.

Meanwhile, many Arab families had returned to their countries of origin, while a large number of other foreign Al-Qaeda fighters decided to embed themselves in the teeming cities of what tribesmen refer to as the "settled areas" of Pakistan. From here they could continue to wage their war against the United States and its Pakistani allies. Some of these operatives are even today being held behind the walls of Guantanamo Bay.

As mentioned earlier, the intervening years before the spring offensive were characterized by the rise of the two organizations that were to prove central to the successful deployment, mobilization, and training techniques used by the pro-Taliban forces in the offensive. The first was the Jaishul al-Qiba al-Jihadi al-Siri al-Alami (Secret Army of International Jihad), which concentrated on training and ideological indoctrination of the new generation of Jihadis in the region. The Jaishul al-Qiba was empowered to train Afghans and foreign militants already present in the territory, in addition to the tribesmen resident in Waziristan.

The second revolutionary organization that was established in South Waziristan was Jundullah (Army of God: see page 6), which was given the task of training militants who had originated from and who would in future operate not just in the two Waziristans, but also in the settled areas of Pakistan. The fortunes of Jundullah, however, considerably diminished when it masterminded the attempted assassination of a senior general in Pakistan's coastal metropolis, Karachi. The daring plan for a morning shootout was aborted, and Jundullah's high command was rapidly unmasked and arrested en masse, signaling an end to its brief moment in the history of revolutionary adventurism.

Although both organizations collapsed with relative speed in Waziristan, they succeeded in training and disseminating the requisite dose of militant ideology and military discipline to a generation of new Jihadis. Trainees from these two organizations would, over the next twelve months, effectively direct the middle-level cadre of the pro-Taliban resurgence in the area.

Meanwhile in August 2003, a massive military operation with gunship helicopters and ground troops started under the surveillance of CIA operatives. During the operations, all lines of communications between Al-Qaeda and the Taliban members in various areas were disrupted, and dozens of Al-Qaeda members who were confidently sitting in their South Waziristan headquarters, Wana, were forced to flee to the cities of Pakistan, where they were later arrested. The military operation played havoc with Taliban interests.

Commanders like Nek Muhammad were killed and Al-Qaeda training facilities destroyed. The Taliban and Al-Qaeda were forced to hide in the mountains for over a year and a half. During that period, the Taliban in Afghanistan, and the Al-Qaeda and Taliban members in South and North Waziristan, lost contact with each other. It was during this period that the Taliban and Al-Qaeda subdivided into groups, which later caused complications. The core division was between the Al-Qaeda group led by Osama bin Laden and the group led by Dr Ayman al-Zawahiri. Both groups took refuge in the far-flung area of Shawal, situated at the crossroads of Afghanistan, South Waziristan, and North Waziristan, but technically part of North Waziristan. Osama and al-Zawahiri were there along with few hundred diehard fighters, holed up in the various valleys. Both leaders were on the defensive. They were out of contact with their men in other places and with the central Taliban leadership.

Sheikh Essa was an ultra-radical Egyptian ideologue. He had stayed on in North Waziristan with a few dozen men, and exercised great influence over some local clerics. Abdul Khaliq and Sadiq Noor were two such prominent clerics in North Waziristan who became his followers. Sheikh Essa preached the need for a war against Pakistan, as he believed it was only because of the Pakistan Army that the United States had been successful against the Afghan Taliban. He also blamed the suffering of North and South Waziristan on Pakistan. He even went to the extent of saying that those who crossed the border to fight against the United States in Afghanistan were deviants – that the real battle had to be fought against Pakistan's ruling military establishment.

As Sheikh Essa and his Pakistani followers gained momentum, their guns turned on Pakistan's military. In fact, that meant only a small deviation from the Al-Qaeda cause, which was not surprising given there were so many veteran commanders, ideologues, and groups operating side by side. Al-Qaeda's principal aim was to fight the NATO troops in Afghanistan. It bears repetition that its terror tactics in Pakistan had the sole objective of neutralizing Pakistan's support for the US-led "War on Terror".

This is also a point at which to draw attention again to the powerful group of militants led by Tahir Yaldochiv from Uzbekistan. Yaldochiv was really an extremist, even by Al-Qaeda and Taliban standards. Several hundred Uzbeks fought under him, but many of them were taken aback by his ruthlessness. Yaldochiv himself was based in South Waziristan, but several of his men had found homes in the North Waziristan town of Mir Ali. Those who were in North Waziristan decided to sever their ties with Yaldochiv, who in any case appeared focused on issues pertaining to Uzbekistan rather than Afghanistan. In the meantime, however, Yaldochiv had found a great supporter in South Waziristan's Abdullah Mehsud, the dominant local commander.

As mentioned earlier, Mehsud had been captured in Afghanistan during the US invasion and sent to a Cuban prison, from where he was released in 2004. Another one-legged fighter who had lost his leg fighting for the Taliban in late 1990s, Mehsud succeeded to the command of Taliban forces against the Pakistan Army in South Waziristan on the demise of Nek Muhammad. At the time of Nek Muhammad's final battle, Mehsud narrowly escaped arrest, was badly wounded, and reported dead. But he resurfaced again in South Waziristan with Tahir Jan (Tahir Yaldochiv). (Mehsud later committed suicide to avoid arrest.)

Sirajuddin, the son of legendary Afghan commander Jalaluddin Haqqani, was in North Waziristan, and Baitullah Mehsud and Haji Omar in South Waziristan were the representatives of Mullah Omar there. The men they commanded were committed to the Afghan resistance movement only. Scattered in various nooks and crannies of the two Waziristans, these pro-Taliban factions sheltered in Birmal, in Afghanistan's Paktia province, Shawal, in North Waziristan, and Shakai and Angor Ada, in South Waziristan, in the belt that runs along the Durand Line. The mountains here were filled with global Jihadis. The terrain facilitated their efforts as these men fought ferociously against the Pakistan security forces, aiming to leave the Pakistani troops exhausted in impossible-to-follow "hide and seek" games.

Remote-controlled bombs and improved explosive devices (IEDs) were the only weapons imported from the Iraqi resistance and used in the two Waziristans against the Pakistani troops. But they were enough to force the Pakistani troops to withdraw to their barracks in the tribal headquarters there.

For the Jihadis, the retreat of Pakistan's forces was their first victory, and it presented an opportunity for the ambitious ideological mercenaries to boot out all of the Pakistan government's connections in these tribal territories. They took it. As a result by late 2005, downtrodden youngsters in their teens and twenties were ruling the streets of North and South Waziristan.

A single incident at the end of 2005 turned the tables. A group of local thugs led by an Afghan, Hakim Khan Zadran, a bandit, confronted a Taliban faction in North Waziristan in a tussle for control. In the bloody gun battle that followed the Taliban prevailed and the surviving thugs were executed. Headless bodies and severed heads hung all around Dand-i-Darpa Khail in North Waziristan in a show of terror by the pro-Taliban forces, who now called themselves the Pakistani Taliban. The centuries-old structure of the tribal Jirga, comprising clerics and tribal elders, fell before these Pakistani Taliban as they announced the Islamic State of North Waziristan.

Calls were then made to the settled areas of Pakistan for men to join forces with the Pakistani Taliban in North Waziristan, and in a matter of days former Jihadis who had been sitting idle after Pakistan had closed its camps in Kashmir rushed to join the Pakistani Taliban in their hundreds. Soon afterwards the Pakistani Taliban flooded the tribal capital of North Waziristan, Miranshah, and the Pakistani security forces fled the area without firing a shot. They informed the Peshawar Corps that without air cover they could not fight the militants. The Pakistan Army came back in full force to crush the Pakistani Taliban, only to find they had vanished like smoke in the mountains.

But before that, the Pakistani Taliban had established courts, a police system, and a tax collection arrangement in South Waziristan, while Pakistan's security forces remained passive in their military headquarters. Astutely, however, the Pakistani Taliban decided not to play rough around these headquarters.

Meanwhile, the news of the Islamic State of North Waziristan and Islamic State of South Waziristan had spread like wildfire. Over 10,000 Jihadis from Pakistan's cities: Karachi, the central city of Lahore, the western city of Quetta, and the smaller former NWFP cities of Peshawar, Bannu, Mardan, and Dir, reached North Waziristan. Along with these there were approximately 12,000 local tribal activists, of which over 3,000 were of Afghan origin and about 2,000 were foreign fighters, including Uzbeks, Chechens, and Uighurs, with a sprinkling of Arabs.

In South Waziristan, most of the pro-Taliban factions were local, but there were in addition a few hundred Uzbek and a few dozen Arabs, to make for a total strength of 13,000. So 27,000 in North Waziristan and 13,000 in South Waziristan, or 40,000 fighters, was the combined strength of the pro-Taliban factions Mullah Omar had to launch his spring offensive. As this was not considered enough, Mullah Dadullah was asked to convey Mullah Omar's message to all factions in the two Waziristans that they were to abandon all other activities and join forces with the Taliban in Afghanistan. A message was then sent across the two Waziristans about the arrival of Mullah Omar's emissary, also asking Tahir Jan (that is, the Uzbek leader, Qari Tahir Yaldochiv), the Egyptian Sheikh Essa, Abdullah Mehsud, and local clerics like Abdul Khaliq Haqqani to congregate in South Waziristan. Dadullah distributed copies of Mullah Omar's letter and in some places read out Omar's message personally. This was:

> Immediately stop attacks on Pakistani security forces. This will lead to chaos and cannot be termed as Islamic Jihad .... Jihad is being waged in Afghanistan so leave your places and come to Afghanistan to join the Jihad against the Americans and its infidel allies.

The reclusive one-eyed leader of the Taliban, Mullah Omar, had always been a charismatic binding force for all of the Taliban commanders, irrespective of their personal differences, and the message he sent through his emissary had a magical effect. The coming days saw his efforts to effect reconciliation between the militant groups in the two Waziristans and Pakistan's armed forces bear fruit. There were 27,000 men in North Waziristan and over 13,000 in South Waziristan. Most of them had usually held their guns back against Pakistan's security forces. The pro-Taliban groups in Waziristan regrouped and geared up ready to go back to Afghanistan. But before that, they all gathered in Shakai in South Waziristan, and in Shawal and Birmal near the Ghulam Khan Mountains in North Waziristan. When Dadullah arrived, these activities gained momentum from his visit.

Dadullah aired video and audio CD presentations acquired from the Iraqi resistance. A three-member delegation from the Iraqi resistance representing Abu Musab Al-Zarqawi had come to Afghanistan and Waziristan in March 2006, where they met with Osama, Zawahiri, and Mullah Omar. They pledged their allegiance to Mullah Omar on behalf of al-Zarqawi. The same delegation brought along with them dozens of other motivational videos and CDs, as well as training video CDs for suicide missions.

Mullah Dadullah had the same sort of material with him when he came to Waziristan, but he also had messages and speeches from leading Arab scholars and the speeches of Mullah Omar to shed light on how and why suicide attacks were allowed in Islam. There was no precedent for suicide attacks in the history of Afghanistan (although it is seen as a successful weapon of Muslim resistance these days all over the world), as suicide had hitherto been strictly prohibited in Islam. It was therefore difficult to persuade the rigid Afghan society to use suicide as a strategy. There had been a few suicide missions in Afghanistan in the more recent past, but they were largely isolated incidents. Dadullah highlighted suicide as a legitimate form of attack, and spread audio and video messages to show how the Iraqi resistance had used suicides as its most effective weapon.

In 2005 there were exchanges between many Taliban and Iraqi delegations who examined and compared their know-how on the battlefield. There were, in addition, many Taliban commanders including Mullah Mehmood Allah Haq Yar who had trained with the Iraqi resistance and knew how suicide could be used as a form of attack. Prior to this, although the Taliban were aware that others had used suicide attacks, they had a dearth of men ready to volunteer for such an act. Dadullah's mission bore fruit on this front as well. He succeeded in impressing on groups coming from Uzbekistan, Tajikistan, Waziristan, and various cities of Pakistan, the importance of suicide attacks. The first squad of prospective bombers was taken into the Kunar Valley for training shortly thereafter. Dadullah motivated an astonishing 450 suicide attackers, notably including 70 women, to rewrite history. While Afghanistan has a centuries-old tradition of fighting invaders, it had never seen a role for women in war. The suicide squad female bombers were mainly the widows of fighters from Arab and Central Asian states who had been killed either in Afghanistan or in Waziristan, but there were some from Waziristan too who had been persuaded by their husbands or fathers to join suicide squads. The first batch of suicide bombers was just the tip of the iceberg. In the coming days, the success of the Taliban emissary in Waziristan would be apparent in a long supply chain of suicide bombers.

These developments came about when spring had started and the Taliban had initiated a sporadic armed struggle, with a scattered strength of a few thousand and with the help of local warlords in various Afghan districts. They would be able to mount a much more significant campaign if they could call on the 40,000 men in the two Waziristans. The Taliban had appointed the veteran Jalaluddin Haqqani as its commander-at-large for the spring offensive.

The decision to install Haqqani as commander-at-large was in line with the unfolding Taliban strategy, which was to destabilize the government in Kabul in the north, even before they managed to seize control of south-west Afghanistan. They intended to first mobilize their strength in the south-eastern provinces, then move on to Kabul.

Meanwhile, a command council comprising ten commanders responsible for specific regions was put in place. Mullah Omar's former minister of defense, Mullah Obaidullah Akhund, was appointed as the emissary to take directions directly from Mullah Omar and pass them on to the commanders for feedback before a final decision was taken. Again, while all the commanders, especially Dadullah, had the primary task of eradicating the writ of the government in the south-west and south-east of Afghanistan, Jalaluddin Haqqani was assigned to exploit the situation and drive the enemy, north, south, east, and west by employing so much terror that the Karzai administration would fall before the arrival of the Taliban troops.

An aging, thin, and short man, commander Jalaluddin Haqqani had kept a record of every victory against the Soviet army, including the first, the *mujahideen* victory in 1991 when they defeated the communist government and seized control of Khost, the home town of the then president of Afghanistan, Dr Najeeb. The Khost submission had been a major milestone in the fall of Kabul to the *mujahideen.*

When the Taliban emerged, unlike all the other leaders and commanders of Afghanistan, Jalaluddin Haqqani was the first and only example in Afghanistan who unconditionally surrendered (in this case Khost) to them. Haqqani was not a Talib or student, and nor had ever previously been part of the movement, so the Taliban never accorded him much importance. He was minister for border areas, but never consulted on any policy matters. Despite this, when the Taliban decided to retreat in December 2001, the veteran commander advised them to retain their control over Khost, Paktia, and Paktika provinces, and make Gardez their front line against the US forces. The Taliban leadership, however, paid no heed to his advice and evacuated all of the provinces. Yet Jalaluddin Haqqani remained loyal to Omar, even when Pakistan and the United States called him to Islamabad before the US invasion and asked him to carve out a structure for a "moderate" Taliban, become its head, and rebel against Omar.

All the foreign fighters who fled Tora Bora, Kabul, and the other places where they had been fighting, looked to Haqqani for sanctuary. And Haqqani provided it to all of them in his adopted home in North Waziristan. For those who wanted to stay with him, he arranged accommodation, and for those who wanted to go back their native lands, he arranged safe passage. Haqqani once again came into the limelight in 2006 when Mullah Omar recognized his worth. He was provided with money, men, and all the material resources he needed, and was also delegated the power to carry out actions in any region of Afghanistan. Today, after Mullah Omar, he is the most respected person in Taliban circles.

Jalaluddin Haqqani dyes his hair and beard to help him look younger; he has connections with all the Taliban commanders in Afghanistan, whether Uzbek, Tajik, or Pashtun; and he controls the main suicide squads, as he hammers out a two-pronged strategy to destabilize the political heartlands of Afghanistan: Herat, Kabul, Kandahar, Kunduz, and Jalalabad. His strategy was to employ suicide attacks and reconnect with veteran commanders from the Soviet era to help in manpower mobilization when the Taliban-led resistance started from south-west Afghanistan.

Under the new restructuring of the Taliban commanders for the spring offensive 2006, the following individuals emerged on the Afghan landscape.

- Mullah Dadullah: Even before he secured his success in the two Waziristans, Dadullah was Mullah Omar's choice for supreme commander in south-west Afghanistan, where he was ordered to seize control of cities and towns. Though one-legged, he was media-friendly and, unlike others, happy to have his photograph published. He successfully defeated the Afghan forces whenever he wanted, and pitched sustained battles against the Coalition forces. Dadullah was killed in a military raid in the Afghan province of Helmand in May 2007.
- Maulvi Abdul Kabeer: the governor of Nanagarhar province during the Taliban era, Kabeer has been keeping himself in hiding. Unlike Dadullah or Haqqani he does not have a power base. He was not a major player either in the Taliban era or before it, but as a trusted cohort of Mullah Omar he commands a wing of the Taliban in Afghanistan's Paktia province with the help of a strong pro-Taliban arm from North Waziristan, which supplements his supplies and manpower.
- Commander Mohammed Ismael is the chief commander of the Kunar province. Kunar has never been a comfortable place for the Taliban as most of its population, and that of adjoining Nuristan, are Salafi, and have differences with the Hanafi Muslims. Ismael therefore had a very narrow base to operate from, and that is why he has made Pechdara his center of gravity in Kunar. He

fights alongside Arab and Chechen militants, and employs suicide attacks and IEDs as his main strategic weapons.

- Kashmir Khan: of the other Afghan Taliban commanders, many are attached to slain commander Ahmed Shah Masoud's Jamaat-e-Islami in Afghanistan, while some important commanders are loyal to Gulbaddin Hikmatyar. Prominent among the latter is Kashmir Khan, who fought against the Taliban until Hikmatyar joined forces with them after 9/11. Khan fights against the United States as an independent commander from the mountaintops of Shegal.

- Mullah Gul Mohammed Jangvi, whom the author interviewed on the Pakistan–Afghanistan border in June 2006, is in his late thirties. He was the commander of Pul-i-Khumri during the Taliban rule and now commands Taliban forces in Argun, Qalat, and Kandahar. In 2003 he was betrayed to the US forces, arrested, and taken to Bagram base near Kabul, where he was tortured and then coerced into joining the Jaishul Muslim, a proxy US outfit established among the Taliban in an attempt to dislodge Mullah Omar as Taliban leader. By the time Gul Mohammed was released, Jaishul Muslim had evaporated and he rejoined the Taliban, along with 1,600 men. He is now one of the main commanders in the Qalat and one of the most prominent figures in the Taliban movement.

THE NEW TALIBAN STRATEGY

The new strategy of the Taliban has made a difference, especially with the placement of the right men in the right place. Taliban-led guerrilla operations today are many times more effective than the past. NATO forces have launched multiple operations against them in southern and eastern Afghanistan, but the Taliban remain defiant and gain more ground by the day.

The game plan for the reconstruction of Al-Qaeda and Taliban after 9/11 was completed by late 2005, when Al-Qaeda succeeded in establishing the Islamic State of North Waziristan and the Islamic State of South Waziristan to gather together thousands of tribal youths, Afghans, Pakistani Jihadis, and foreign fighters. The Pakistani tribal areas were made strategic bases for Al-Qaeda to wage war in the southern Afghan provinces, while the Taliban registered major successes in Kunar, Nanagarhar, Khost, Paktia, Paktika, Gardez, Urzgan, Zabul, and Kandahar, with seven important districts of Kandahar falling under their direct control by the end of 2006. However, their most successful action was in taking South Waziristan. This enabled them to launch operations from there into Afghanistan's adjoining Helmand province, which continues to see some of the bitterest fighting in the West's war against Al-Qaeda and its Taliban allies.

With the spring offensive of 2006, the majority districts of the Afghan province of Helmand fell to the Taliban. I visited Helmand in November 2006, by which time the most strategic southern regions of Helmand, like the Gramsir district that borders Pakistan, were under the control of the Taliban. From there a long stream of militants from South Waziristan had entered Helmand to fight NATO. Except for the towns of Greskh and Laskhar Gah (the provincial capital of Helmand), the whole of northern Helmand was under the control of the Taliban, facilitating their safe passage into the north-west Afghan provinces of Badghis, Farah, Herat, and Nimroz. The strategy, which began in South Waziristan and expanded to Helmand province in 2006, spread the Taliban-led insurgency all across Afghanistan.

BACK TO BASE

As dozens of body bags containing the remains of NATO soldiers were ferried back to their home countries in the West, news of the Taliban and Al-Qaeda's revival pointed directly at the two Waziristans as the primary conduit for the Taliban having re-emerged in Afghanistan to play havoc with the US–NATO-led war machine. The United States now had to come up with a plan to counter the Taliban advance on the Pakistani side of the border. When the news came that renewed pressure was being piled on Pakistan to carry out a military operation in the Pakistani tribal areas, a grand tribal council was called in Miranshah, the tribal headquarters of North Waziristan. It was conceded that the militants could not fight on all fronts. They needed to call a truce with Pakistan until the emergence of their next plan.

"I can see slit throats beneath these turbans and beards," were the words of Hajaj bin Yusuf, an eighth-century tyrant in what is now Iraq, as he witnessed a gathering of leading religious and political figures. A similar thought occurred to this writer in August 2006 when he attended the largest-ever gathering of the Pakistani Taliban, tribal elders, and politicians in Miranshah, the tribal capital of North Waziristan. Fire and blood were in the air as momentous events loomed over the tribal areas of North and South Waziristan, where the Taliban were in complete control. The militants' decision to reach a peace agreement with the Pakistani government was not meant to promote peace in any real sense, but was another strategic mode of engagement until the next war plan was finalized.

To confront the immediate threat, the militants were asked to stay in the background under a strategy that called upon local political leaders belonging to the pro-Taliban Jamiat-e-Ulema-e-Islam[5] to come to the fore. In the tribal council meeting the militants were not allowed to speak and were instead relegated to the backbenches. The militants agreed to stop all hostilities against Pakistan's armed forces, and the peace agreement was signed in September 2006. However, much like previous moves, this too was a lull before a storm.

This time, a pact was signed between the Pakistan government, represented by the political agent, the Uthmanzai tribe and tribal leaders, and the religious leaders of North Waziristan. It had 16 clauses and 4 sub-clauses.

The major points included:

A. The Uthmanzai Wazirs, including the local Taliban, religious leaders, elders, and tribesmen undertook that:

1. There would be no attacks on law-enforcement agencies and government property. There would be no targeted killings.
2. There would be no parallel administration established and the government's writ would stand. In case of any problem, the political administration would resolve the issue in consultation with the Uthmanzai tribes, according to traditions and customs and the FCR ordinance.
3. There would be no cross-border military activities inside Afghanistan. However, there would be no restriction on border crossings for the purposes of trade/business and meeting relatives according to the local *riwaj* (traditions).
4. There would not be any kind of terrorist activities in the adjacent districts of North Waziristan.
5. All foreigners residing in North Waziristan would either leave Pakistan or remain peacefully according to the prevailing laws and current agreement. The aforementioned clauses would apply stringently to all foreigners.
6. All captured government property during the operation in the shape of vehicles, weapons, wireless, etc. would be returned.

B. The government undertaking included:

1. All those apprehended during the operation would be released and not be arrested again on previous charges.
2. The government would release all political benefits.
3. The government would remove all newly established checkpoints on roads and post Levies and Khasadars on the old checkpoints, as in the past.
4. The government would return all vehicles and other items such as weapons captured during the operation.
5. After the agreement had been signed the government would stop all land/air operations and issues would be resolved according to custom and traditions.
6. The government would pay compensation for all collateral damage to those affected.
7. According to tribal traditions there would be no restrictions on carrying weapons. However, restrictions would continue to be imposed on heavy weapons.
8. The implementation of the agreement would start with withdrawal of the army from the checkposts to the barracks.

C. Miscellaneous:

1. According to the agreement, a ten-member committee would be established, comprising *ulema* (scholars)/elders and representatives of the political administration. The committee would be responsible for:
   a. establishing links between the government and the Utmanzai tribes
   b. reviewing and ensuring the implementation of the agreement.
2. If anyone or any group (foreigners or local) did not abide by the agreement and disrupted peace in Waziristan, action would be taken against him or them.

Unlike the previous agreements, this agreement was devoid of any mention of words like *mujahideen* or Taliban, and although the agreement was signed by the leading Pakistani military commanders, Hafiz Gul Bahadar, Maulana Sadiq Noor, and Maulana Abdul Khaliq, it was basically an accord between the government and the Utmanzai Wazir. This was done because the militants wanted to show the United States that any new military operations on their territory were unnecessary as the tribal leaders had taken responsibility for peace.

As a result of this peace agreement an unknown amount of money was transferred from Pakistani government coffers to the militants;

the clinical term "foreigners" was used to indicate Al-Qaeda and other foreign militants; and some 100 Taliban and Al-Qaeda men, ranging from commanders to footsoldiers, were released from Pakistani custody. During the signing ceremony of the agreement in the soccer stadium of Miranshah, the militants provided security cover, while Al-Qaeda's black flag (*al Rayah*) was fluttering over the stadium scoreboard.

The peace deal broke down on May 20, 2007 as the United States was pressurizing Pakistan to conduct operations against the militants and the militants were finalizing their new war plan. The strategy that had started after 9/11 and extended to South Waziristan, then on to Helmand, now saw a move up to the next level of war. As both the US and Pakistani security apparatus looked to wage a military operation in Pakistan's tribal areas, the militants turned their eyes towards Pakistan's cities. And by the end of 2007, the theater of war had expanded from Peshawar to Karachi.

THE WRATH OF THE UNITED STATES

A visibly upset Dick Cheney (the US vice president) arrived in Islamabad on February 26, 2007 to vent Washington's fury over the Taliban's spring offensive, for which the United States had been unprepared. The United States had realized in late 2006 that Al-Qaeda had been reinventing itself in Pakistan's tribal areas along with the Taliban, but its personnel were completely in the dark on more recent developments. South-west Afghanistan had slipped from their hands; the Taliban ruled Afghanistan's Helmand province and several important districts in Kandahar province; and the situation had seriously deteriorated in Urzgan and Zabul. For the first time the coalition troops felt the Taliban had become a major threat, and Cheney warned General Musharraf of serious consequences if Pakistan did not wage all-out war on the militants in its tribal areas.

During the visit Dick Cheney went over all the previous agreements between the government of Pakistan and the Taliban, in which Pakistan had given money to the Taliban warlords (as compensation for their losses during military operations). He accused Pakistan of having ties with some of the Taliban factions such as the Haqqani network. The situation became even more complex when Cheney visited Kabul the next day. While he was at the Bagram air base, a suicide attack killed 23 people and injured 20. The CIA later reported that the attack had been planned in North Waziristan by

Abu Laith al-Libi, who at the time was only loosely associated with Al-Qaeda. (He later joined Al-Qaeda as a regular member, and led its operations in Pakistan and Afghanistan.)

Cheney's visit was critical to the next course of events in South Asia. He understood that Pakistan's tribal areas were completely in the hands of Al-Qaeda and the source of the Taliban's strength. This new thesis changed the dynamics of thinking in Western capitals. Previously the West had believed Pakistan to be no more than a safe sanctuary for Taliban and Al-Qaeda fugitives, but now realization dawned on them that Pakistan was at the core of the problem. If the problem was to be resolved, it had to begin in Pakistan.

This new understanding gave impetus to US efforts to pressurize Musharraf's regime to democratize Pakistan. The United States wanted to continue with its support to Pakistan, but at the same time wanted to see a mechanism in place that would protect its strategic interests. This thinking process actually evolved after the Taliban's spring offensive of 2006. It eventually turned into Washington's Af–Pak policy in 2008, which assessed the entire Pakistan and Afghanistan region as a single theater of war, and Pakistan's tribal areas as the root cause of the problems.

Broadly speaking, from January 2006 onwards the United States remained behind the scenes, working on a strategy to give popular impetus to the "War on Terror." The United States thought that democratic reforms would create the needed space. Cheney's visit to Pakistan and Afghanistan had proved a milestone in changing minds. The forward strategy of the United States after identifying Pakistan and Afghanistan as one conflict zone was to promote democracy.

By the end of 2006 Musharraf agreed to the US formula of holding national elections, and at the beginning of 2008, power shifted to an alliance of a secular and liberal political parties led by the Pakistan People's Party (PPP).[6] The other members of the future coalition were the secular Pashtun subnationalist Awami National Party (ANP),[7] Muttehida Quami Movement (United National Movement, MQM), Jamiat-e-Ulema-e-Islam Fazlur Rahman group (JUI), and the Pakistan Muslim League (PML-Q).[8]

Under the new dispensation Musharraf agreed to shed his uniform, appoint a US-approved chief of army staff, then stay on as the civilian president of the country to oversee the whole system and the "War on Terror." Benazir Bhutto's role was considered crucial. A parliament led by her government could easily pass laws against Islamic seminaries and launch a powerful campaign against militancy in the country. The ANP and the MQM were to be her supporting arms, while the JUI was to endorse the format from the religious angle.

Washington and London next brokered a deal between Musharraf and Benazir Bhutto, as a result of which the notorious National Reconciliation Ordinance (NRO) was promulgated in October 2007. It negated all the charges of corruption against Ms Bhutto and her spouse Asif Ali Zardari, and allowed them to come back to Pakistan as free citizens to take part in national politics. This plot was hatched in February 2006 and came to fruition in April 2007 – the same month as the United States put pressure on Islamabad to launch an all-out war against the militants. As a consequence, the agreement signed by Hafiz Gul Bahadar, Maulana Sadiq Noor, and Maulana Abdul Khaliq in Miranshah in September 2006 broke down on May 20, 2007. What followed was the bloodiest chapter in Pakistan's history.

An overview of events after the US invasion of Afghanistan reveals a massive intelligence failure concerning Al-Qaeda's regrouping and its strategic vision, which successfully countered US moves in the region and prevented Pakistan from taking any winning measures against the pro-Taliban militants. The result was the spring offensive of 2006, which spurred the Taliban-led insurgency in Afghanistan to new heights. Meantime Al-Qaeda was looking minutely into developments in the South Asian theater of war, and assessing how Washington was planning political and military counter-moves against its structures in both Pakistan and Afghanistan.

This starts another real-life story in Al-Qaeda's *A Thousand and One Nights* adventures, with a new theme and a new cast of characters. Al-Qaeda's strategy was to take root in Pakistan's tribal areas in order to achieve a spillover effect in south-west Afghanistan, then establish Afghanistan's Helmand province as the main conduit to export insurgency all around the country. But it faced the challenge of the US reaction in 2007. The United States had by then correctly identified the Al-Qaeda sanctuaries and was in the process of devising the means to destroy them. Al-Qaeda had to protect them at all costs. Thus begins a game of strategic manipulation between the United States and Al-Qaeda.

The next phase of Al-Qaeda operations was to launch attacks in Pakistan's cities to cause disruption and thereby prevent any joint US–Pakistan attack on Al-Qaeda strongholds. In 2007 the United States started building a forward base in the Afghan province of Kunar, a few hundred meters away from Pakistan's Bajaur Agency.

The construction of similar bases and US military posts began simultaneously in Afghanistan, near the Pakistani tribal areas of Mohmand, North Waziristan, and South Waziristan. At the same time, the United States secretly contracted with Pakistan to use its airbases for drone strikes on militant hideouts in the tribal areas.

But while the United States was busy funneling billions of dollars to strengthen its forces in Pakistan and Afghanistan, Al-Qaeda played its wildcard of taking the war to Pakistan's cities. (Al-Qaeda was always a step ahead of Washington in the context of making political connections in Pakistan.) In fact, Al-Qaeda had planned to take the war to Pakistan's cities earlier, but the plan could only be implemented in 2007, after the Taliban's 2006 summer offensive against the United States had been blunted.

Dick Cheney was to oversee the US mission statement for the region. Under the guidelines set by Dr Ayman al-Zawahiri, Sheikh Essa Al-Misri was the director of Al-Qaeda's master plan for Pakistan. Sheikh Essa, an Egyptian ideologue whose record is discussed later in the book, was the Al-Qaeda emissary sent to meet various Islamic politicians and political organizations in Pakistan from 2003 onwards. He was intended to forge an Islamic political front in the country's urban areas to strengthen support for Al-Qaeda. The people whom Sheikh Essa met included:

- Qazi Hussain Ahmed, the then chief of the Jamaat-e-Islami (JI), a leading Islamic party of Pakistan which was considered a South Asian version of the Muslim Brotherhood.
- Hafiz Muhammad Saeed, the chief of Jamaatut Dawa (JD), formerly known as Laskhar-e-Taiba, a banned militant outfit of a Salafi and Wahhabi religious inclination.
- Maulana Fazlur Rahman, the chief of JUI, a society of Muslim scholars and an influential political party subscribing to the Deobandi school, which already supported the Taliban.
- Dr Israr Ahmed, an academic who called for the revival of the Islamic caliphate.

However, the people who responded most significantly to Al-Qaeda's call in both letter and spirit were two brothers, Maulana Abdul Aziz and Abdul Rasheed Ghazi, the prayer leaders of Islamabad's Lal Masjid. The Lal Masjid (Red Mosque) hosted two religious schools in Pakistan's federal capital, Islamabad. Jamia Hafsa, adjacent to the mosque, was the school for girls, and Jamia Faridia, situated in the upmarket E-7 district of the capital, was for boys. Over 7,000 students were studying in both schools. The mosque had been founded by Maulana Abdullah, a veteran Jihadi who had fought against the Soviets in Afghanistan, so the organization had strong ties with such radicals as Mullah Omar, Dr Ayman Al-Zawahiri, Tahir Yaldochiv, and Osama bin Laden. After Abdullah's assassination in the late 1990s, two of his sons, Maualana Abdul Aziz and Abdul Rasheed Ghazi, became Lal Masjid's prayer leader and deputy prayer leader respectively. Both brothers, like their father, were committed to the cause of Jihad.

The Pakistan Army had intensified military operations against the militants by mid-2003. The operations were unpopular from the very beginning, and even the secular political parties were not prepared to voice their support for them. The general public understood the Taliban as an anti-imperialist resistance movement. Thus the military operations against them were taken by the masses as Pakistan's support for neo-imperialism. Politicians such as Qazi Hussain Ahmed, Imran Khan, and Nawaz Sharif blamed the then president, Musharraf, for shedding the blood of innocent Pakistani tribal Muslims in order to prolong his incumbency as Pakistan's president by gaining support for his military dictatorship from Western governments. There were two attacks on Musharraf in late 2003 in Rawalpindi, and these upped the pace. Thousands of Jihadis were arrested as suspects. The United States then pressurized Pakistan to close down the Pakistani militant camps in Kashmir, and anti-Americanism in Pakistan soared to new heights. Only a small spin was required for Al-Qaeda to take advantage of the situation.

On the advice of Al-Qaeda, Maulana Abdul Aziz issued a religious decree in 2004 which declared the South Waziristan operation un-Islamic. The decree prohibited the burial of the soldiers in Muslim graveyards. Funeral prayers for those who had died in the action against the Muslim militants in South Waziristan were forbidden. The decree was circulated throughout the country and 500 clerics signed it. That was all the spin needed to further ignite anti-American feelings in Pakistan. All the combined guns of the militants could not have been as useful in belittling the Pakistan Army as that religious decree.

Matters did not end there. As a result of the religious decree, several cases were reported by the media of parents refusing to receive the dead bodies of their sons who had been killed fighting on the side of the armed forces. Religious clerics refused to say prayers over their bodies. The result was the demoralization of the rank and file of the Pakistan's armed forces. Dozens of lower-ranking non-commissioned officers defied the commands of their officers to fight and were court-martialed. Almost an equal number of officers resigned from service on receiving orders of their postings to South Waziristan. The Pakistan Army had been well placed to defeat the militants in 2004, but Al-Qaeda's timely spin by using Lal Masjid had clipped its wings.

The two brothers from Lal Masjid were in regular contact with major Al-Qaeda leaders including Tahir Yaldochiv and Sheikh Essa, which enabled them to receive directives on strategy. By 2007, Lal Masjid had become an Al-Qaeda powerhouse in the federal capital of Islamabad, directly in the face of Pakistan's powerful ISI in Islamabad, and the military's General Headquarters (GHQ) in the capital's twin-city, Rawalpindi. Meantime, the militants' strength kept increasing around the country. They expanded their influence from South Waziristan to North Waziristan, then moved on to Bajaur and the Mohmand and Orakzai agencies. The total strength of the militants in North and South Waziristan soared to around 50,000, and the security crackdown on militants associated with the Kashmir Liberation Movement (KLM) enhanced this number by causing a massive migration of other militants to the two Waziristans. This migration included such stalwart commanders of the KLM as Ilyas Kashmiri and Abdul Jabbar. (The next chapters discuss the situation in detail.)

The US CIA and Pakistan's ISI submitted report after report on the increasing strength of the militants, and advised Pakistan's government to take timely steps to prevent more damage. Pakistan tried to mount a bigger operation than the earlier ones, but Al-Qaeda held the Lal Masjid trump card. They did not have to resort to battle: Pakistan was forced to sign a ceasefire agreement.

Musharraf and his aides had planned to take serious action against the Lal Masjid lobby many times, but military intelligence always opposed the move. The reason was that in the already charged anti-American atmosphere, taking any such action against Lal Masjid and its adherents would have brought matters to a head. Dozens of the daughters of Pakistan's armed forces personnel, influential businessmen, and bureaucrats were day students in the Lal Masjid schools. Already wary after the soldiers' near-mutiny over the tribal area operations, Musharraf's government was unwilling to confront a political upheaval in the middle of the federal capital. This delay in dealing with Lal Masjid proved catastrophic.

It was hardly a shock to learn that Washington and London were pressing Pakistan to draw up a strategy that would lead to a conclusive defeat of the militants. It was at this time that Washington pressured Musharraf to strike a deal with Benazir Bhutto for a broad-based alliance of secular and liberal political parties, to counter the rising public support for the militants. At the same time, Western intelligence agencies drew a full map of the Al-Qaeda assets in Pakistan. These assets started with Islamabad's Lal Masjid, and moved into the Swat Valley through Malakand division in the shape of Mullah Fazlullah. Added to these was the Tehrik-e-Nifaz-e-Shariat-e-Mohammadi, which was connected to the militants in Bajaur, North Waziristan, and South Waziristan. In the face of this, US and British officials visited Pakistan, one after the other, to persuade Pakistan to urgently set up a coherent strategy for the defeat of the militancy.

This whole game plan was already on Al-Qaeda's radar, and it struck while the plan was only half-completed. In January 2007, the Pakistani Taliban in South Waziristan broke its ceasefire accord with the Pakistani security forces and unleashed a series of sudden attacks on their positions. Pakistan's GHQ in Rawalpindi was taken aback by this move and was still trying to comprehend it, when the Lal Masjid students took to the streets. To create an issue, they took up the demolition of a few mosques that had been built on illegally occupied land. To prevent the matter from spinning out of control the government quickly agreed to the students' demands and stopped further demolitions of mosques. The administration also agreed to provide alternative land for the congregations whose mosques had been demolished. However, the Lal Masjid radicals stuck to their guns and insisted that the new mosques should be rebuilt on the same land they had originally been erected on.

Baffled by the attitude of Maulana Abdul Aziz and Abdul Rasheed Ghazi, Pakistan's government had no idea that the brothers were in fact playing games under a broader Al-Qaeda strategy to sabotage US interests. The occupation by Lal Masjid female students of Islamabad's Children's Library, adjacent to the mosque, captured the world's attention. The students announced they would not evacuate the library until Islamic law (*sharia*) was enforced throughout the country.

Muslim academia, in both Pakistan and abroad, was stunned by the Lal Masjid affair. Mufti Taqi Usmani, the spiritual guide of the Lal Masjid brothers and a respected Islamic economist, flew up from Karachi to Islamabad for a detailed discussion with the brothers on their violent reformist agenda. Abdul Aziz could not answer Taqi Usmani's questions because in the light of the Quran, according to *Sunnah* (traditions set by the prophet Muhammad) and *Salaf* (the unanimously agreed traditions according to which Islam has been practiced over the last 1,400 years) he could only mumble that the steps taken were essential for the Islamization of Pakistan. Taqi Usmani was so disappointed and annoyed with the Lal Masjid cleric's attitude that he expelled Maulana Abdul Aziz from his spiritual guide circle. Usmani then publicly announced that all spiritual ties between them were severed from that point. Abdul Aziz could not have suffered greater public humiliation than this, but it did not deter him from continuing on the path he had embarked on.

As the news of Musharraf and Benazir Bhutto's secret meetings to plan a new alliance hit the media, Lal Masjid jacked up its protests to a higher level of violence. The female brigade of the seminary, Jamia Hafsa, abducted an alleged female pimp to trigger Lal Masjid's "Crisis Action" plan.

On March 9, 2007, the then President Musharraf dismissed the chief justice of Pakistan, Iftikhar Mohammad Chaudhary. This began the lawyers' movement. Within a few weeks, the media, civil society, and several political parties came out in support of the lawyers' movement. With this new sea of trouble compounding the Lal Masjid issue, it became impossible for the Musharraf government to undertake any effective military operations in the two Waziristans. As the lawyers' movement picked up pace, Lal Masjid activities also increased. In the center of Islamabad, Lal Masjid vigilantes forcibly closed down video and music shops. When their people were arrested by law enforcement agencies, they abducted civil law enforcement personnel so that they could exchange them with their own people in custody.

The Ministry of Interior put both Abdul Aziz and Abdul Rasheed Ghazi on the wanted list, and the police force was instructed to bring the mosque under blockade. But the Lal Masjid vigilantes inspired so much fear that the police kept their distance. At the same time, Abdul Aziz's firebrand Friday sermons continued to rouse the masses, including some of the police deployed around the mosque.

Al-Qaeda's leadership in North Waziristan was aware that sooner, rather than later, Lal Masjid's role would be over – that the government's tolerance level would reach its limit and a strong reaction to the Lal Masjid clerics was imminent. The Al-Qaeda *shura* (council) met in North Waziristan and, after prolonged discussion and debate, agreed that the high point of their struggle in Pakistan would come when the foreseeable military operation against Lal Masjid began. Open war against the US–Pakistan designs was now unavoidable.

In July 2007, the military conducted a military operation against Lal Masjid, and after several days of siege, troops entered the mosque. Maulana Abdul Aziz tried to sneak out in a burqa (a woman's covering veil) but was arrested. Abdul Rasheed Ghazi, his mother, and Abdul Aziz's son were all thoughtlessly killed by the security forces. A number of male and female students died with them. The first US objective had been achieved: an important Al-Qaeda asset in the federal capital of Islamabad had been eliminated. The US–Pakistan alliance would now prepare for an all-out war against Al-Qaeda.

On the political front, the deal between Benazir Bhutto and Musharraf had matured, with Ms Bhutto scheduled to return to Pakistan in October. On the military front, operations against the militants in Swat, as well as in the two Waziristans, were primed. But matters did not move on smoothly for the Musharraf regime. There was a massive reaction to the Lal Masjid massacre. Musharraf's ruling party, PML-Q, was not ready to own the operation; civil society movement picked up pace; Pakistan's Supreme Court restored a hostile Iftikhar Mohammad Chaudhary to his earlier position as chief justice of Pakistan; and the opposition leader Nawaz Sharif (who had been exiled by Musharraf under an agreement with Saudi Arabia) sought to return to Pakistan.

But the Lal Masjid saga was over. Abdul Rasheed Ghazi had been killed and his brother Abdul Aziz captured. The story had reached its climax. Al-Qaeda then released a video declaring Abdul Rasheed Ghazi a "righteous" leader (*Imam-e-Barhaq*) and vowed to avenge the Lal Masjid massacre. This marked the beginning of another chapter in the continuing Al-Qaeda *A Thousand and One Nights* drama.

After the Lal Masjid operation, the United States and its allies moved quickly to push Pakistan towards destroying Al-Qaeda once and for all in Pakistan. But Al-Qaeda restructured just as quickly to boldly confront each new challenge. With that, although Al-Qaeda was not able to destroy the whole US plan for South Asia, it did manage to put a serious dent in it. When next the Al-Qaeda *shura* met in North Waziristan to discuss future strategy, it was agreed that the time had arrived when Pakistan's alliance with the United States was so cogent that sporadic, stand-alone tactics against it would not work. The *shura* was of one voice on the issue of the Pakistan regime's *takfeer* (heresy) – the following chapters will spell this out in detail – and agreed on *khuruj* (revolt) against the state of Pakistan. The Lal Masjid clerics had set the scene for the next battle, and after the unpopular Lal Masjid operation, Al-Qaeda would capitalize on it.

In Islamic jurisprudence a revolt is only allowed against a Muslim state when the ruler and establishment transgress all limits. The first *khuruj* was attempted on the Prophet Muhammad's grandson, Hussain Ibn-e-Ali, when Ummayad ruler Yazid bin Mauvi was installed as the Caliph under a hereditary arrangement, in violation of established Islamic norms which only allow the selection of a Muslim ruler with the consent of the Muslim populace. Al-Qaeda decided on the kind of a strategy Ibn Taymiyyah (1263–1328) had adopted in identical circumstances when he was fighting a Jihad against the Mongols, a foreign occupation force who had converted to Islam, but had terminated Islamic law as the single source of law and instead introduced laws in which Islam and Mongol traditions were mixed to introduce two parallel legal systems in their empire. The Mongols had already occupied Baghdad at the time and were eyeing other Muslim cities. The Muslim ruler of Syria and Egypt, Nasir Al-Din, had doubts on the capacity of his forces to defend his realm against a Mongol attack, so he had assured the Mongols of his neutrality – that he would not fight against the Mongols if they were to retake control of Baghdad. For Tamiyyah it was a major deviation on part of any Muslim ruler to refuse Jihad in defense of a Muslim state. Tamiyyah felt this was sufficient reason to launch a revolt against the ruler. Tamiyyah then warned Nasir Al-Din if he did not break his agreement with the Mongols on the occupation of Baghdad, he would stop the Jihad against the Tartars and launch *khuruj* against him. He threatened Nasir Al-Din that he would first dethrone him and then fight the Mongols independently. Tamiyyah's threats compelled Nasir Al-Din to join forces with the resistance, and he fought against the Mongols.

Al-Qaeda decided to pursue the same principle in 2007 after the Lal Masjid operation. Osama bin Laden installed Abdul Hameed, aka Abu Obaida al-Misri, as the *imam-e-khuruj* (the leader of revolt) for Pakistan. And with his coming we see of a new strategy, with a new cast of characters in the continuing *A Thousand and One Nights* tales of Al-Qaeda.

SETTING UP THE AF–PAK THEATER OF WAR

The end of the Lal Masjid rebellion brought about a new and significant turn of events. The US blueprint for Pakistan was unveiled. This envisaged a new troika positioned to pursue the mission against Al-Qaeda. The troika included a military chief who was fully onboard with the United States in its "War against Terror," a US-supportive parliament comprising secular and liberal forces to drum up popular support for this, and a strong civilian president to oversee affairs and report to the US political administration on unfolding events. Both military and civilian US aid packages were to be routed through the president. While the preparations for this new dispensation were underway, the pro-Western General Ashfaq Parvez Kayani, who was very close to the US military command, was installed as the vice-chief of army staff in October and nominated as the future chief of army staff (COAS).

Kayani had not been Musharraf's preferred successor. Musharraf had wanted General Tariq Majeed (who was promoted to the ceremonial position of the chairman joint chiefs of the Staff Committee on October 7, 2007) as the army chief. But Kayani was the US choice. His appointment went against the traditions of the armed forces, as never before in the history of Pakistan's army had a director general (DG) of ISI been made COAS. The argument was that the DG ISI, whose concern was with intelligence needs, had to consort with politicians who might influence him to move away from the military's perspectives on both domestic and foreign policy issues. Intelligence chiefs also had to have close rapport with other countries' intelligence apparatus, and at times, even friendly relations with them. If, therefore, an intelligence chief was appointed as COAS, there was always the risk of national security interests being compromised.

Kayani's record showed he could be ruthless. As the vice-chief of army staff in October 2007, he had used Pakistan's air force to fire indiscriminately on alleged militants in Mir Ali and Swat. Scores of civilians were killed. Unlike Musharraf, Kayani was unconcerned about inflicting collateral damage. Similarly, in North Waziristan, South Waziristan, Bajaur, Mohmand, and Swat, Kayani had remained indifferent to the plight of millions of civilians forced to abandon their homes while military operations were being conducted in 2008 and 2009.

With Ms Bhutto's return affirmed on the political front, Pakistan was required on the military front to conduct operations to eliminate all of Al-Qaeda's strategic assets in Pakistan. The Swat Valley was where this was to start. Before the military could take up their positions in the valley, however, the militants scrapped the 2006 Miranshah Agreement, and by the time the Lal Masjid episode began, they were already attacking Pakistan's security forces' positions in both South and North Waziristan. Over the period from July 24 to August 24, 2007, 250 militants and 60 soldiers were killed.

On September 2, 2007, a few dozen militants led by Baitullah Mehsud ambushed a 17-vehicle army convoy and captured an estimated 247 soldiers – without a shot being fired. The event stunned the nation. Several officers were among those captured. To add insult to injury, the militants then invited the BBC to hear these officers (from the Baloch regiment) speak in favor of the insurgency. Following this the army returned to their Waziristan military headquarters and garrisoned the area, setting up a number of checkpoints. This did not deter the militants. In mid-September the Taliban attacked army outposts across North and South Waziristan. This led to some of the heaviest fighting in the Pakistani Taliban's war against the state security apparatus in these areas. The first Pakistani Army outpost was attacked and overrun by the Taliban on September 12, 2007. It resulted in the capture of 12 Pakistani soldiers. The next day, a suicide bomber in Ghazi Tarbela visited a Pakistani army base, destroying the main mess hall, killing 20 members of the elite Special Services Group (SSG) and wounding 29. A series of attacks followed, and by September 20, 2007 five of the Pakistani Army outposts had been overrun and an additional 25 soldiers captured. In all, more than 65 soldiers were killed or captured, and over 100 were wounded. Most of the attacks by the militants were knee-jerk reactions to the Lal Masjid massacre.

About two weeks later, the army counterattacked with helicopter gunships, jet fighters, and ground troops to hit militant positions near the town of Mir Ali. In heavy fighting over the next four days, between October 7 and October 10, 2007, 257 people were killed, including 175 militants, 47 soldiers, and 35 civilians.

Al-Qaeda then decided to revamp its plans to counter US designs in the region. While the theater of war was in the making in Pakistan's cities, Musharraf had instructed the ISI to work for a political solution in which the secular or liberal parties would dominate the politics of the country. An alliance was then forged between the Pashtun subnationalist ANP in NWFP, the JUI (Fazlur Rahman Group), a religious party ready to act as an intermediary between the religious forces and the establishment in NWFP and south-west Balochistan, the MQM, based in Sindh, which represented the Indian Muslims who had migrated to Pakistan after the partition of British India in 1947 (who were a real anti-Taliban secular force), and Musharraf's hand-picked PML-Q, mainly from the Punjab.

Musharraf ordered a National Reconciliation Ordinance to be proclaimed on October 5, 2007. This granted across-the-board amnesty to all politicians, political workers, and bureaucrats who had been accused of crimes including corruption, embezzlement, money laundering, murder, and terrorism between January 1, 1986 and October 12, 1999 (the time between the two periods of martial law). It was a discriminatory ruling whose prime intention was to cancel corruption cases against Benazir Bhutto and her spouse Asif Ali Zardari. As soon as the NRO came into legislation, Ms Bhutto announced her return to Pakistan.

This was the perfect opportunity for Al-Qaeda to take the bull by the horns. Ms Bhutto was a populist politician and as her image would inevitably compel her to move in wider and more open circles, she would be a soft target. Al-Qaeda got down to discussing the merits and demerits of assassinating her. They all agreed that killing her would change the political landscape. They realized that Al-Qaeda would not be the only beneficiary, but also knew that killing her would seriously dent US designs in the South Asian region.

The plan to kill Ms Bhutto was prepared a year ahead of the November 2008 US presidential elections. Al-Qaeda had foreseen the victory of the Democrat candidate, Barack Obama, and was sure that if Bhutto was hit during the transition phase of the Bush administration, it would come as a major blow to US designs on Pakistan. A number of Al-Qaeda-affiliated sleeper cells across the country were activated, including one in Karachi, where Ms Bhutto was supposed to arrive on October 18, 2007. On her landing at Karachi airport, thousands of people rallied to welcome and escort her back to her home in the city. The rally was hardly halfway through when suicide bombers struck. Ms Bhutto somehow escaped unharmed, but 136 people were killed and over 450 people seriously injured. The attack caused a serious rift between the Musharraf government and Ms Bhutto. The Musharraf government was roundly criticized for the security lapse, yet Ms Bhutto remained undeterred. She held rallies across the country, including in NWFP (now Khyber Pakhtoonkhwa), and spoke against the militants everywhere she went. She was the only politician in Pakistan who openly stood up for the operation against Lal Masjid.

For the first (and last) time in Ms Bhutto's political career, however, she was denied the opportunity to focus on national politics in her election campaign. All her addresses to the public were against the militants and Al-Qaeda. As a consequence militants followed her throughout her political gatherings, but they found no opening to strike until her arrival on December 27, 2007 in the garrison town of Rawalpindi. There she was assassinated. Within few hours, Pakistan found itself in total chaos. The entire country was in the hands of agitators, with law-enforcement agencies nowhere to be found. Dozens of trains were attacked in Ms Bhutto's home province of Sindh, while public and private property was destroyed all over the country. The post-December 27, 2007 situation exposed, for the first time, the weakness of Pakistan's internal security. Al-Qaeda had succeeded in creating a crisis situation in the urban centers of Pakistan, designed to deter Pakistan from collaborating with the United States in its designs against this revolutionary Islamic force. However, Al-Qaeda too went through its moment of crisis, which prevented it from taking full advantage of the situation. This came with the sickness of Amir-e-Khuruj, Abdul Hameed, alias Obaida al-Misri, who was suffering from hepatitis C. The deadly disease had made him so weak that he could not capitalize on this post-December 27 situation. Within a few days of Ms Bhutto's assassination, Abdul Hameed also died and Khalid Habib was installed as the new Al-Qaeda head for Pakistan's operations. He in turn was killed a few months later in a CIA predator drone strike.

Between January 2008 and February 2008, suicide attacks in Pakistan outnumbered the suicide attacks in Afghanistan and Iraq. But as there had been no coordination in the Al-Qaeda ranks because of the unexpected death of al-Misri, this could not be translated into multiple strategic advantages. However, there had been one important gain for Al-Qaeda: with Benazir Bhutto assassinated just before the scheduled January 8, 2008 elections, the US plan of reorganizing the secular and liberal political parties and Pakistan's security forces under one banner against Al-Qaeda had failed. This had driven the United States, Pakistan's army, and Musharraf into a corner. The entire US roadmap for the region had gone askew. The elections were postponed, and although Benazir Bhutto's assassination had gained her party (PPP) a huge sympathy vote, and it emerged as the majority party in the February 18, 2008 elections, in the eyes of the political pundits sitting in Western capitals, her shocking death had destroyed Pakistan's political equilibrium.

Musharraf shed his uniform on November 27, 2007. The reconciliation agreement between him and Ms Bhutto no longer existed (as one signatory, Ms Bhutto, was now dead). US Republican President George Bush's administration had been the chief guarantor, but

Bush was on his way out and the new administration was shortly to be ushered in. At that particular crossroads there was little room for effective political decisions.

Earlier, under Saudi Arabian pressure, Musharraf had been forced to allow the hostile Sharif brothers, Nawaz and Shahbaz, to return to Pakistan. The Lal Masjid massacre and the sacking of the judiciary on November 3, 2007 by Musharraf had left his staunchest ally, PML-Q, standing on very shaky ground. Inevitably Nawaz Sharif's party, the Pakistan Muslim League – Nawaz (PML-N), made more than expected inroads into parliament, and it now became impossible to form a government without PML-N's inclusion in a broad coalition government. This left Musharraf with problems. The new army chief, General Ashfaq Parvez Kayani, had as his first objective restoring the army's image among the masses. It had deteriorated because of the armed forces' repeated involvement in politics, and this had been aggravated by the judicial crisis and the unpopular Lal Masjid operation. In the prevailing circumstances the now retired General Musharraf was a liability. The military began to distance itself from politics, and issued a notification for the early withdrawal of armed forces personnel from civilian posts. Kayani moved away from Musharraf, who was still Pakistan's president, and instructed his military colleagues to do the same.

Musharraf, as president, was still the supreme commander of the armed forces, and he tried to remove the COAS twice, by offering the post to the chairman joint chiefs of the Staff Committee, General Tariq Majeed. But Majeed refused as he saw this as a breach of military discipline. He believed that a potential crisis would arise in army circles if there were any such move, and as a professional soldier, he was totally averse to this prospect. His failure to remove Kayani as COAS meant that Musharraf's position deteriorated further.

Pakistan's politicians watched these developments closely, and began to scramble for new positions. Musharraf's main allies, PML-Q and MQM, looked in other directions. Musharraf's supporters such as the JUI-F and the ANP switched their allegiance to the emerging political alliance. Musharraf's sworn enemies in the PML-N then launched a campaign to drive him out of power. The PPP, the party that had won the largest vote in the February 2008 elections, sought to win over Washington to Pakistan's changed military establishment. Pakistan's new ambassador in Washington, Professor Husain Haqqani, and the US ambassador in Islamabad, Anne W. Patterson, moved to convey to Washington why Musharraf's removal was imperative. In August 2008, Musharraf barely avoided an impeachment motion compelling him to step down from Pakistan's presidency. In the weeks that followed Asif Zardari was elected the new president of Pakistan, which was not an option Washington had thought of, as Zardari had always been disliked by Pakistan's military establishment. Nevertheless, Zardari became the head of state, and supreme commander of the Pakistani armed forces by virtue of this position. Worse still as far as the army (and others) were concerned was that despite the stigma of corruption attached to him, Zardari as Pakistan's president was entitled to manage all the US-sponsored economic development programs in the federally administered tribal areas.

After his wife Benazir Bhutto's death Zardari had become head of the PPP, the governing partner of a coalition government ready to fight against the terror war. In addition he had personal enmities with the major opposition political parties, especially PML-N which had earlier put him in jail and filed criminal charges against him. Noted newspapers such as the *New York Times* and *Washington Post* ran detailed stories of his alleged corruption during his wife's premierships. These raised alarm bells in most Western capitals. With Pakistan's political symmetry thus out of kilter, Al-Qaeda emerged as the sole beneficiary.

The whole year from Ms Bhutto's death to the resignation of Musharraf provided space for the militants to act more aggressively. After a brief backdown in 2007, the militants in Swat resurfaced at the beginning of 2008. Swat's theater of war was a perfect diversion for Al-Qaeda and the Neo-Taliban's regional ambitions. This was to have Pakistan's armed forces disengage from the Pakistan–Afghanistan border areas, to leave NATO exposed on that front. The Pakistan Army's continuing operation in the Swat Valley could not have served Al-Qaeda's purpose better, and they successfully regrouped in the Khyber Agency, Orakzai, and Dara Adam Khail to besiege the former NWFP's provincial capital, Peshawar. Meantime Al-Qaeda went on with its reorganization in the tribal areas, with a show of strength in Afghanistan, while penetrating Pakistan's cities. It then fashioned a parallel entity, the Tehrik-e-Taliban Pakistan (TTP), to reinforce its positions in the natural fortresses of seven of Pakistan's tribal agencies.

TEHRIK-E-TALIBAN PAKISTAN: AL-QAEDA'S BROOD

Al-Qaeda is fighting for complete ideological control over all Muslim resistance movements worldwide. It wants these resistance movements to fight their wars within the broader Al-Qaeda parameter, perceiving the United States as at the root of all the problems that affect the world. It believes the United States must fail on every front for peace to prevail. Al-Qaeda has fully indoctrinated the Taliban in Afghanistan, but the peril of defiance still exists. Al-Qaeda had a bad experience in Iraq, where it gave unconditional support to the Iraqi resistance. The US commander, General David Petraeus, held out the bait of dialogue to Iraq's Sunni tribal insurgents in 2007, and the leaders of the Iraqi resistance abandoned Al-Qaeda and held negotiations with their sworn enemies, the United States, to expel Al-Qaeda from its strongholds. This left Al-Qaeda with no choice except to migrate from Iraq to Yemen, to Somalia, and back into Pakistan's tribal areas. Al-Qaeda believes it has much deeper roots in Pakistan's tribal areas than in Iraq, where it surfaced only after the US invasion. It admits that its leadership at the time was naïve, but still fears the US strategy employed in Iraq. The spin-offs of this strategy almost sank the organization in Pakistan, as in early 2007 with the clash between the foreign Uzbek fighters and the loyalists of Mullah Nazir, the commander of the Taliban in Wana, in Pakistan's South Waziristan.

Born in 1975, Mullah Nazir was associated with the Hizb-i-Islami Afghanistan of Gulbaddin Hikmatyar during the Soviet invasion on Afghanistan, before he joined up with the Taliban. He was an Ahmadzai Wazir with dual Pakistani and Afghan nationality. Nazir was sympathetic to Al-Qaeda, but his real allegiance was to Mullah Omar. He was less into ideology and more into tribal traditions. For Nazir, Al-Qaeda members were no more than guests whose protection was the responsibility of the local tribes under tribal laws and the patronage of Mullah Omar. Mullah Nazir did not view them as his ideological guides. On the ideological and strategic fronts, he owned allegiance only to Mullah Omar.

Although the Taliban and Al-Qaeda, at least on the surface, enjoyed good relations with each other, the Taliban were uncomfortable with the recent developments in North and South Waziristan. Almost 40,000 fighters including Chechens, Uzbeks, Arabs, and Pakistanis had gathered in the two Waziristans in early 2006, but the leader of the Islamic Movement of Uzbekistan, Tahir Yaldochiv, had issued a *fatwa* (opinion) to prioritize fighting against the Pakistan army over waging the war against the Western coalition in Afghanistan. This took the Afghan Taliban aback. Although Al-Qaeda had raised the strength of the Pakistani Taliban to benefit the Afghan resistance, it also aimed to use this strength against Pakistan's army to neutralize Pakistan's support of the US "War on

Terror" by any means possible. Al-Qaeda saw Afghanistan as its real theater of war, and considered it imperative to deter Pakistan's support of the United States. The Afghan Taliban were not ready to adopt this approach. They did not want to fight Pakistan's army.

Al-Qaeda was strategizing events from future perspectives, but the Afghan Taliban wanted to keep the strategy limited to fighting the Western coalition forces in Afghanistan. There was a failure in communications. Mullah Omar's envoy, Mullah Dadullah, who was later assassinated, traveled to Pakistan's tribal areas in 2006 to keep the focus of the fight on Afghanistan, but a difference of opinion developed on this, leading to suspicion and animosity. Mullah Nazir expressed his concerns to Dadullah over the growing influence of the Uzbek militia in South Waziristan. They had taken little part in the Afghan campaign, but were actively fueling the insurgency against the Pakistani armed forces.

Pakistan's military establishment tried to exploit the developing differences, cognizant of the fact that Mullah Nazir was the only important Taliban commander in the two Waziristans who, despite providing them with protection, had kept his distance from Al-Qaeda's ideology. The Pakistan Army then actively supported Mullah Nazir with arms and money to eliminate the Uzbeks. In early 2007, this resulted in an internecine conflict between the Uzbeks and the Taliban loyal to Mullah Nazir. Hundreds of Uzbeks were massacred. The rest took refuge with Baitullah Mehsud.

But there was more to the story. Mullah Nazir comes from the Wazir tribe in South Waziristan, the traditional rivals of the Mehsud tribe. Despite their common ideological identity, Baitullah Mehsud and Nazir were rival militia commanders, and Nazir was jealous of the Uzbeks always putting their weight behind Baitullah Mehsud. Al-Qaeda had a limited interest in the event as the Uzbeks were not strictly tied to its organizational network. They were only associated with Al-Qaeda's broader aims. However, Al-Qaeda feared that the emerging contradictions and minor differences within the several factions operating under its ideological banner might be exploited by the enemy at some stage to spoil its hard-earned successes. This fear gave birth to the TTP in early 2008. Al-Qaeda gathered all the Pakistani pro-Taliban groups under the TTP flag. Baitullah Mehsud was then installed as its first chief, and Hafiz Gul Bahadar and Molvi Faqir appointed as his lieutenants. To allay suspicions, Mullah Omar was declared the chief patron, but the TTP served as the catalyst to draw the Afghan Taliban away from his influence, to carry forward the Al-Qaeda agenda in the region.

Commanders such as Gul Bahadar and Mullah Nazir had been against Mehsud's command from the very beginning, but Al-Qaeda helped Mehsud garner strength and broaden the TTP base all the way down from Pakistan's Khyber Agency to South Waziristan, and later from Peshawar to Karachi. Although the Afghan Taliban tried to distance themselves from the TTP, they could not condemn them outright as the TTP still sent a good number of fighters to support their war against the US–NATO coalition in Afghanistan. Baitullah Mehsud alone sent some 250 groups in 2008 to Helmand in support of the Afghan Taliban fighting there. By the end of 2008, the TTP had succeeded in establishing its presence in seven of Pakistan's tribal agencies and the bordering regions of Afghanistan, and its influence now ran all the way to the southern Pakistan province of Balochistan. TTP's formations were then able to erode Pakistan's connections in the tribal areas, and at the same time to minimize Mullah Omar's influence there. From 2008, onwards Mullah Omar had repeatedly urged the TTP to shun violence against Pakistan's security apparatus, but the TTP paid no attention to him.

The TTP now had a long natural bunker running along the Hindu Kush and some of the smaller mountain chains in the region, to stand as a formidable shield against the military designs of the mighty US war machine. With that Al-Qaeda decided to move forward and resume international operations, which had been obstructed by security crackdowns on their cells in Pakistan's cities, hitherto their only passage to the outside world. Iran's Jundullah presented a solution to their problem. Al-Qaeda established a connection with the Iranian Jundullah in 2009.

IRANIAN JUNDULLAH: AL-QAEDA'S NEW SYNDICATION

A passage through Iran was the simplest and most convenient way for Al-Qaeda to move from Pakistan to the Middle East after 9/11. Under an arrangement, the Iranian government turned a blind eye to its activists' travels through Iran. Abu Hafs Al-Mauritani was Al-Qaeda's coordination officer with Iran. However, the sudden emergence of Abu Musab al-Zarqawi in Iraq proved to be bad news for Al-Qaeda–Iranian relations.

Born in 1966 in Jordan, al-Zarqawi ran a militant training camp in Afghanistan. He became known after he went to Iraq, and was responsible for a series of bombings, beheadings, and attacks during the Iraq War. Dr Muhammad Bashar al-Faithi, a leading light in the Muslim Scholars' Association and a member of the Iraqi resistance to the United States, told me in Amman (Jordan) in 2007 that though the Iraqi resistance did not require foreign assistance after the US invasion of Iraq in 2003, they tolerated foreign fighters like al-Zarqawi who carried out operations which gave both himself and the Iraqi resistance a boost. But al-Zarqawi turned to killing Shiites, which was totally unacceptable to both the Iraqi Sunni resistance movement and Al-Qaeda. He thought this was strictly in line with the Al-Qaeda thinking, but it was not. Al-Qaeda sought to discard him as fast as they could, but were not able to do so before both Iraq and Iran had been alienated.

According to a document published by *USA Today* (on June 15, 2006), the purpose of al-Zarqawi launching anti-Shiite strife was to drag Iran into the war. The upshot was a bitterly antagonized Iran turning completely against the Al-Qaeda leaders and their grand designs of resistance to the Western presence in the Middle East. Iran then went on to guard all its entry and exit points to stop the flow of Al-Qaeda operatives through its territory. In fact Iran's security services arrested several Al-Qaeda members and handed them over to the Saudi Arabian and Egyptian authorities. So much damage was done by al-Zarqawi that even after his death, Al-Qaeda did not find it safe to travel through Iran. However, a solution to Al-Qaeda's problems on this count appeared in 2009 in the form of the Iranian Jundullah leader, Abdul Malik Rigi.

Rigi was a Baloch nationalist and drug smuggler. He moved around in off-road vehicles and kept a gang of 20 to 25 youths with him at all times. In 2008 he was in Mehmoodabad, a slum in Karachi close to the upscale Defense Housing Authority. Here, he had a quarrel with a rival gang and gunshots were exchanged, during the course of which he was injured. A former member of the Rigi gang said that he had initially been involved in the Baloch Liberation Organization (BLO) and moved freely from his Lyari base to Turkey, carrying heroin. Rigi was never apprehended because of his close connections with corrupt security personnel in both Pakistan and Iran, who turned a blind eye to drug smugglers in exchange for money. As a BLO stalwart Rigi had been hostile to Iran, and he used a wide range of disguises to evade capture. Rigi had links with a number of regional and international sensitive agencies, but was unsuccessful in stirring up a rebellion in Iranian Balochistan. A few years ago, Rigi changed colors after interactions with the banned Pakistani group, Sepah-e-Sahaba, in Lyari. His anti-Iranian stance as a Balochi shifted to one of being anti-Shi'ite. Not too long afterwards, he joined with Sepah's breakaway faction, the Laskhar-e-Jhangvi, the anti-Shiite Al-Qaeda-linked militant outfit. Through this connection, Rigi went to the Afghan province of Zabul, but the Taliban refused him entry into their ranks because of their suspicion that he had forged links with US intelligence. He was then driven out of Afghanistan. However, in 2009, his LJ connections arranged a meeting with Al-Qaeda in the Pakistani area of Turbat, and took responsibility for his loyalty. Al-Qaeda agreed to support Rigi's insurgency in Iranian Balochistan, and in return urged him to facilitate its members' movements back and forth to Turkey and Iraq from Pakistan's side of Balochistan through Iran on his smuggling routes. Rigi agreed. This rejuvenation of the Iranian Jundullah through Rigi in 2009 turned out to be the deadliest year for the Iranian government. Several high-profile attacks were carried out in Iranian Balochistan, and during one of them a top commander of the Iran Revolutionary Guard was killed.

Al-Qaeda operatives found safe passage on Rigi's smuggling routes. However, on February 2010, Rigi was arrested by the Iranian authorities after a tip-off provided by Pakistan. But Rigi's arrest did not prove to be the end of the world for Al-Qaeda. A few more events took place that normalized Al-Qaeda relations with Iran. Of these, the abduction of Iranian diplomat Heshmatollah Attarzadeh from Peshawar in November 2008 was perhaps the pivotal event. Tehran set about trying to get its emissary home, starting with official Pakistani channels. This included appeals to the Foreign Office and Pakistan's powerful ISI. Nothing happened. The Iranians then turned to their Afghan contacts in Zabul province, who in turn used their tribal connections to make contact with the top Taliban commander Sirajuddin Haqqani (the son of veteran *mujahid* Jalaluddin Haqqani). Through Sirajuddin, Tehran negotiated the release of its diplomat and swapped him with several high-profile figures who had been held in Iran, including Abu Hafs al-Mauritani and Sulaiman Abu Gaith, as well as two frontline figures: Iman bin Laden, the daughter of Osama bin Laden, and the Egyptian Al-Qaeda leader Saif al-Adil. The process of negotiation ran several months, and in the course of that time, Al-Qaeda and Iran grew to be on reasonable terms. Iran once again allowed Al-Qaeda members safe passage through the country into Turkey, Central Asia, and Iraq.

Meanwhile, Al-Qaeda zeroed in on the South Asian theater in its war against the US military machine. It had opened new travel routes through Iran to various destinations on the one side, and planned to cut NATO's supply line going through Pakistan into Afghanistan on the other.

PLANNING NATO'S WATERLOO

The years 2002 through 2009 highlighted Al-Qaeda *A Thousand and One Nights* tales in which the organization worked its way through sundry crises, throwing up various characters to make Afghanistan a US nightmare. But for the final victory, Al-Qaeda had a different game plan. Osama bin Laden and Dr Ayman al-Zawahiri were among the veteran Arab-Afghan fighters who had orchestrated the defeat of the former USSR. The militants kept foremost in mind one aspect of the *mujahideen* victory: their success in severing the Russian supply line from Northern Afghanistan. The spring offensive of 2006 was the watershed for the struggle. Al-Qaeda was looking for a strategy that could become the tipping point for NATO's defeat in Afghanistan. After discussion and debate, the Khyber Agency was chosen as the theater for that.

The Khyber Pass had been the main supply line for NATO troops since 2002. At least 80 percent of their supplies came through the Khyber Agency. The rest came through Kandahar, while small quantities of supplies were dropped by air. NATO was lucky that the Khyber Agency had very few Al-Qaeda sympathizers. The area has always been a trade route, and the majority of its inhabitants are followers of the Brelvi school of thought, which adheres to Sufi Islam. A member of Pakistan's parliament of this area is also an anti-Taliban Brelvi cleric. In the prevailing circumstances, making the Khyber Agency a war front was still a huge challenge for Al-Qaeda. This was surmounted when Al-Qaeda managed to convince the Afghan Taliban of the need to cut NATO supply lines to force the Western alliance out of Afghanistan. With the consent of Mullah Omar, Ustad Yasir, an old Afghan commander belonging to the Ittehad-e-Islami Afghanistan during the former USSR's invasion of Afghanistan, was appointed commander of the Khyber Agency. A small group of Taliban from the South Waziristan, including Hakimullah Mehsud, then aged 28, who became the chief of TTP after the death of Baitullah Mehsud, was sent to conduct hit and run operations there, with a local tribal group promising to facilitate them.

That was the beginning of the new war front. The organized attack on NATO supply convoys began in January 2008, and by April 2008, NATO could see the writing on the wall. The attacks intensified and the situation deteriorated for NATO to the point where some aircraft engines were seized by the Taliban, along with Humvees (military four-wheel-drive vehicles), which the Taliban were seen to be operating freely in the tribal areas before they were destroyed by Pakistan's security forces.

NATO commanders knew from past experience that new Taliban strategies were a constant factor, and so were concerned. The only alternative supply line was through the Iranian port of Chabahar, but to make use of that, a highway through Afghanistan was needed. The work began almost immediately and, though delayed by Taliban attacks to prevent its completion, it was finally completed in late 2008. But then there was the tricky business of persuading Iran to allow NATO shipments through its territory.

There is another route. This comes through Europe and Russia down to the Central Asian republics, then on to northern Afghanistan, crossing the length of Afghanistan, to the largest NATO base in Bagram at one end, and then across to the second largest NATO base in Kandahar. This route is long and impractical because of the huge cost entailed. In addition, shipments have to pass through two landlocked regions before reaching their final destinations. But the situation had become so desperate that NATO was forced to negotiate an agreement with Russia and the Central Asian republics to provide an alternative supply route. At the same time, in February 2009, on the sidelines of the 45th Munich Conference, Washington was compelled to initiate back-channel diplomacy with Iran, compromising all its previous positions for the single objective of Iran allowing the NATO troops a passage through to its Chabahar seaport from Afghanistan to oversee supplies.

Iran eventually approved non-military shipments, but only for a few European countries in their individual capacities, not as NATO member nations. This move was not a sustainable solution, however, and the United Kingdom and the United States had to fall back on Islamabad to guard their supply routes. But the monster of the militancy in Pakistan did not allow Pakistan to address the issue properly. With its troops engaged on several fronts, Pakistan had no choice but to regret its inability to provide security to NATO convoys. The success of the strategy employed to cut NATO's supply routes emboldened the Taliban, and they carried out relentless attacks on the Peshawar truck terminal where NATO convoys parked for the night before going through the Khyber Pass. They simultaneously moved into Karachi, where NATO cargo was unloaded. They abducted the contractors employed by NATO to deliver supplies northwards, and threatened the drivers of the vehicles with dire consequences if they continued to work for them. As a result, by December 2008 NATO supplies had come to a grinding halt, with sections of the UK press reporting that in the places like Helmand and Ghazni NATO stocks had dried up completely.

Al-Qaeda and Taliban's successes caused concern in Western capitals. They were beginning to realize that they had been trapped in a quagmire. They then turned to the strategy of fighting Al-Qaeda and its extremist Taliban allies by trying to strike a deal with the more malleable Taliban. It was a desperate "better late than never" type of approach.

Leading UK and US think tanks had been mulling over the Taliban's successes in Afghanistan and pointing out that after the spring offensive of 2006, southern Afghanistan had become virtually ungovernable. With that, Western capitals began to look in the direction of alternative end-game strategies. In August 2007, a Grand *Jirga* (tribal council) was held in Kabul, attended by delegates from Pakistan and Afghanistan. The then Pakistani president General Musharraf led the Pakistan side. The Grand *Jirga* decided on the need to hold regional *Jirgagai* (small *Jirgas*) from the November 2007 onwards to attract the regional commanders of the Taliban. The aim was to isolate the extremists within the Taliban aligned to Al-Qaeda.

After the Grand *Jirga*, the United Kingdom, the United States, and Pakistan worked jointly on this strategy. Maulana Fazlur Rahman, the then leader of the opposition in the Pakistani parliament, was chosen as the point-man, and he made several secret trips to Quetta, where he held negotiations with the middle cadre of the Taliban. The new US strategy appeared to be paying dividends with some Taliban commanders like Mullah Abdul Salam, who even struck a deal with UK troops in Helmand province and assumed charge as the administrator of the province's Musa Qala district.

Meanwhile British MI6 agents were active in the areas of Kunar, Paktia, and Paktika, with the new British ambassador to Afghanistan, Sir Sherard Cowper-Coles, working on the old Afghan traditions of *arbakai* (the raising of tribal militias to fight an enemy). The situation seemed to be improving in the southeastern Afghan provinces of Kunar, Paktia, and Paktika in favor of *Jirgagai* as well, and there were chances that if the regional *Jirgas* were held, it might split the Taliban. However these efforts could have borne fruit only if the Pakistani army had a breathing space. Al-Qaeda did not allow that to happen.

A SWAT WHIRLPOOL SET TO SINK THE AF–PAK STRATEGY

The dialogue process was the main component of the end-game, but not the only component. There was also the rapid construction of a US base on a mountaintop at the Kunar–Bajaur border crossing, and many other similar bases in south-east Afghanistan in 2007. Other agreements with Pakistan permitted the use of Pakistan bases for drone attacks and gave consent for US security contractors to operate in Pakistan. On one hand, Western governments were negotiating with the Taliban, and on the other they were setting up an agenda to eliminate Al-Qaeda from the Pakistani tribal areas. Pakistan was very much onboard for this new battle, which was to be fought in early 2008.

Inside informants had already alerted Al-Qaeda to the realities, and newspaper reports confirmed that a new game was about to begin not too long afterwards. Al-Qaeda had only one counter, and this was to raise the temperature of the war in Swat. The Taliban in Swat had risen against the Pakistani security forces soon after the Lal Masjid operations in mid-2007, but had been beaten back in the first phase of the military operation against them. Nevertheless the government of Pakistan was ready to strike a ceasefire deal, and agreed to their demand that Islamic courts be set up in the Malakand division. But Al-Qaeda had other ideas. It had already plotted the strategy of soliciting Pakistani tribal warlords to organize themselves into the TTP. Baitullah Mehsud was made the chief of the new set-up, with the Swat Taliban a tentacle of that camp. Then Al-Qaeda persuaded the TTP to send a team of suicide bombers into the Swat Valley, and one of its most astute commanders, Qari Hussain Mehsud, followed, as the war flared up there again. Mehsud was the ruthless Pakistani Taliban commander who had trained and raised squads of suicide bombers. His men played havoc with the local administration in Swat, and all the police stations were destroyed. Mehsud and his Uzbek allies upped the ante of viciousness by slitting of throats of their opponents, establishing a brutal reign of terror in the once peaceful valley.

To establish the TTP on the model of the Afghan Taliban to bring about an Islamic revolution in Pakistan through franchises was Al-Qaeda's long-term plan for gaining control. But now Al-Qaeda decided to move at an accelerated pace to realize its strategic objectives. On one hand it had to counter the dialogue strategy of the United States with the Taliban, and on the other it aimed to stir up open revolt in Pakistan's cities. In essence this strategy clashed with Mullah Omar's agenda because the Taliban were essentially fighting a war against the Western coalition troops in Afghanistan. The Pakistani militants were now required to fight another war, albeit under Omar's command. This meant a division of purpose. Mullah Omar and the Taliban in Afghanistan did not like the idea, but as long as the TTP pledged their allegiance to him and his resistance against the foreign troops in Afghanistan, he had no moral grounds to discourage the Pakistani militants from assembling on this Jihadi front as well. This was seen as a betrayal by Pakistan's military establishment which, while it had not actively discouraged the Taliban in Afghanistan, had not wanted it to spread its tentacles into Pakistan.

For Al-Qaeda, however, it was another story. There was now a new dimension to Islamic resistance in the region. It established the first-ever popular local and fully tribally supported Al-Qaeda franchise in the world. Thus, if in future the Afghan Taliban and the Pakistani military establishment were ever to plan reconciliation with the West, this body of the Neo-Taliban was there to oppose them and to remind their Afghan comrades that the Jihadi agenda did not end in Afghanistan, but was set to circle the world. In the meantime, Al-Qaeda could deploy the TTP to help break any obstructions erected by Pakistan's government.

Deploying the TTP in Swat worked well for Al-Qaeda, at least in the short term. As soon as it was established there, senior commanders from the Uzbek and Punjabi camps of North Waziristan and South Waziristan, together with several hundred fighters, were sent into the Swat Valley. This Jihadi brigade changed the dynamics of the Swat insurgency. Qari Hussain, a former leader of the anti-Shiite Laskhar-e-Jhangvi (LJ), brought about a new level of hostilities against the Pakistan army. Along with local commander Bin Yameen, he slit the throat of captured Pakistan Army soldiers and released photographs and video footage to the media. He launched a terror campaign which completely demoralized the Taliban's enemies. He abducted policemen and their relatives and beheaded them. Anti-Taliban leaders and workers from the secular Pashtun sub-nationalist ANP were executed in public. Their houses and even funerals were bombed. The campaign wiped out the civil administration and the police system in Swat. The Pakistan Army was helpless without the support of local administration and the police. As a result, it was incapable of carrying out an effective military campaign against the militants. By January

2008, the Taliban had succeeded in occupying 90 percent of Swat. The Pakistan Army was left with a few checkpoints and bases on mountaintops.

In February 2008, the chief of banned Pakistani militant group Tehrik-e-Nifaz-e-Shariat-e-Mohammadi (TSNM), Maulana Sufi Mohammad, who was also the father-in-law of Mullah Fazlullah, negotiated a peace deal with the former NWFP government. In the same month a peace deal was signed which agreed on the enforcement of Islamic laws and establishment of Islamic courts in Swat. This was the first surrender of the Pakistani establishment to the Neo-Taliban. But the agreement to enforce Islamic laws in the Malakand division was just a face-saving ploy for the Pakistan Army, which was desperate to withdraw its forces from there. It was also a face-saving exercise for the Pakistani Taliban, who were exhausted after their year-and-a-half-long battle.

Paradoxically, the enforcement of Islamic law had never been the aim of the Neo-Taliban. The Swat battle in 2007 was not fought because the government had refused to comply with the Taliban's demand that it introduce Islamic law. It was a bid to set up another smokescreen to eradicate the US presence in the region, and discourage any thoughts of dialogue with the Taliban. And, with that, Al-Qaeda expanded military operations across the border. Throughout the military operations no one heard the Pakistani Taliban make demands for the enforcement of Islamic law in Malakand to justify the attacks on the military convoys. The Swat war, in fact, was contrived by Al-Qaeda and the Neo-Taliban to disengage Pakistan's armed forces from the Pakistan–Afghanistan border areas, thus allowing Al-Qaeda more free rein to fight the war in Afghanistan. During the Pakistan Army's presence in the Swat Valley, the Taliban were successful in regrouping in the Khyber Agency, Orakzai Agency, and Dara Adam Khail.

Al-Qaeda's war in Swat had always been to phase out the US master plan of holding *Jirgagais* (small *Jirgas* on a regional basis) and talking to the Afghan Taliban's regional commanders. In holding these *Jirgagais*, the involvement of Pakistan was crucial, but if it were otherwise engaged in a war against the Taliban, it would be unable to help the United States and its NATO allies on the other side of the border.

Back in Afghanistan, the United States had the Saudis invite former Taliban and Hizb-i-Islami leaders to Saudi Arabia during Ramadan in 2008. This set up a communication channel between the Saudi intelligence chief Prince Muqrin and Mullah Omar through a Taliban official, Tayyab Agha. But talks broke down before the last Afghan presidential elections, when Mullah Omar categorically told Muqrin, through Agha, that he was not ready to talk to the Afghan government.

A new dialogue process was planned after the presidential elections in 2009, but it remained one-sided. The United States, through the Afghan government, offered astonishing new incentives to the Taliban. A former Taliban leader, at present a senator in Afghanistan, Moulvi Arsala Rahmani, told me during the Afghan presidential elections in 2009 that a few Afghans, including himself, were given an open mandate by the Afghan government (read Washington and London) to bargain with the Taliban as a first step in persuading them to stop attacks on the infrastructure, such as bridges, buildings, dams, and public places. Rahmani said to me:

> If the Taliban comply with this primary demand, then the next step of facilitating them would begin. For instance, the Taliban would be allowed to open offices in countries like Turkey, the UAE, and Saudi Arabia, from where regular rounds of talks could be held between the Taliban and the Afghan government. These talks would cover issues like the withdrawal of troops and the setting-up of a new political government with the participation of the Taliban and other insurgent groups.

The Taliban showed no interest. Why should they have? According to influential UK think tanks they were already ruling 73 percent of Afghanistan, and the US–NATO forces were in retreat from their border positions, even from the strategic Nuristan province.

OLD WINE IN NEW BOTTLES

Benazir Bhutto's murder had undone the US scheme for Pakistan. Washington was compelled to change its entire roadmap. Under the new arrangement General Musharraf was an irritant and he was bade farewell. The United States then welcomed Asif Zardari as the new president. However, the military establishments of the United States and Pakistan still had a role to play. As in the case of the earlier Bush and Musharraf association, it was now Admiral Mullen and General Ashfaq Parvez Kayani who were central to the Pakistan–US equation.

This is what was negotiated:

- The Pakistan Army was to be in sole charge of military operations in Pakistan. Its parliament and the civil administration were there simply to provide coordination and moral support.
- Central to the new theme was a US$1 billion plan to expand the US presence in Pakistan's capital city, Islamabad. (Building the largest US embassy in the region underscored the resolve to consolidate Washington's position in the theater in pursuit of the "War on Terror.")
- This presence would mark the beginning of direct US handling of its "war and peace" diplomacy in the region, together with the forging of a seamless relationship between Pakistan's military establishment and the Pentagon.
- Under the agreement, private security firms (DynCorp aka Blackwater) could set up offices in Islamabad, where they had already rented 284 houses, besides setting up bases in Peshawar and Quetta. In addition, Pakistan was to provide land in Tarbela to the United States for its operations.
- ISI was to set up a syndicated intelligence service under a proxy network to provide information to be transmitted to the CIA predator drones used to target the top Al-Qaeda leadership in Pakistan's tribal areas.

In short, while intense efforts were under way to use the (moderate) Taliban for peace talks, there were comprehensive preparations to tighten the noose around the neck of Al-Qaeda and its Taliban affiliates. And finally, there was a war plan called "Operation Lion Heart" under which the commands of both NATO and Pakistan's armed forces were to devise a format to crush the Al-Qaeda-led militancy from the regions of Bajaur and Mohmand on the Pakistani side, and from Kunar and Nuristan on the Afghan side.

Al-Qaeda had been observing all of these new developments in 2008, but there was no way to confront them. This was a completely new situation. A powerful political alliance was supporting the strongest war machine in the world, and the Pakistan Army was giving them full space and cooperation. The loss of its franchise operations in the Bajaur, Mohmand, Nuristan, and Kunar regions was staring Al-Qaeda in the face. Several of its top leaders, like Osama Al-Kini, Khalid Habib, Abu Laith Al-Libi, and over a dozen of its best brains had been killed in drone strikes. It was apparent that once Pakistan's army was successful in the tribal area it would go with full force into the Swat Valley and Malakand, and the Taliban would not be able to resist. Al-Qaeda had been completely outmaneuvered. It did not have the capacity to play around any more. Inevitably the idea of assassinating the new COAS, Kayani, came up.

Kayani's daily routine was already being closely watched by Al-Qaeda. He was a frequent visitor to a gym. The plan was to plant a man inside the gym who would give Kayani a suicide hug. Had this mission been accomplished Pakistan could have been in total disarray and incapable of carrying out any plan to tighten the noose around Al-Qaeda's neck. But Al-Qaeda's *shura* dismissed the plan. It had a flipside – it could give the United States reason for direct intervention in Pakistan, in which case the Pakistan Army would have no choice other than to support the idea of an all-out war against the militants in Pakistan's tribal areas.

This was when Commander Muhammad Ilyas Kashmiri appeared on the horizon. Born in Bimbur (old Mirpur) in the Samhani Valley of Pakistan-administered Kashmir on February 10, 1964, Ilyas passed the first year of a mass communication degree at Allama Iqbal Open University, Islamabad. He did not continue because of his involvement in Jihadi activities. The Kashmir Freedom Movement was his first exposure in the field of militancy. Then there was the Harkat-ul Jihad-i-Islami (HUJI), and ultimately his legendary 313 Brigade. This grew into the most powerful group in South Asia, with a strongly knit network in Afghanistan, Pakistan, Kashmir, India, Nepal, and Bangladesh. According to some CIA dispatches, the footprints of 313 Brigade are now in Europe, and it is capable of carrying out the type of attack that saw a handful of militants terrorize the Indian city of Mumbai in November 2008.

Little is documented of Ilyas's life, and what has been reported is often contradictory. However, he is invariably described by the world intelligence agencies as the most effective, dangerous, and successful guerrilla leader in the world. Kashmiri left the Kashmir region in 2005 after his second release from detention by the ISI, and headed for North Waziristan. He had previously been arrested by Indian forces, but had broken out of jail and escaped. He was next detained by the ISI as the suspected mastermind of an attack on then-President Musharraf in 2003, but was cleared and released. The ISI picked Ilyas up again in 2005 after he refused to close down operations in Kashmir. His relocation to the troubled border areas sent a chill down spines in Washington. They realized that with his vast experience, he could turn the unsophisticated battle blueprints in Afghanistan into audacious modern guerrilla warfare. Ilyas's track record speaks for itself.

In 1994, he launched the al-Hadid operation in the Indian capital, New Delhi, to secure the release of some of his Jihadi comrades. His group of 25 included Sheikh Omar Saeed (the abductor of US reporter Daniel Pearl in Karachi in 2002) as his deputy. The group abducted several foreigners, including UK, US, and Israeli tourists, and took them to Ghaziabad near Delhi. They then demanded that the Indian authorities release their colleagues. Instead the Indians attacked their hideout. Sheikh Omar was injured and arrested. (He was later released in a swap deal for the passengers of a hijacked Indian aircraft.) Ilyas escaped unhurt.

On February 25, 2000, the Indian army killed 14 civilians in the village of Lonjot in Pakistan-administered Kashmir after its commandos had crossed the Line of Control (LoC) that separates the two Kashmirs. They returned to the Indian side with abducted Pakistani girls, and threw the severed heads of three of them at the Pakistani soldiers manning their side. The very next day, Ilyas conducted a guerilla operation against the Indian army in Nakyal sector after crossing the LoC with 25 fighters from 313 Brigade. They kidnapped an Indian army officer and beheaded him. This officer's head was then paraded in the bazaars of Kotli, in Pakistani territory.

Ilyas's deadliest operation took place in the Aknor cantonment in Indian-administered Kashmir against the Indian armed forces following the massacre of Muslims in the Indian city of Gujarat in 2002. In this, he planned attacks involving 313 Brigade divided into two groups. Indian generals, brigadiers, and other senior officials were lured to the scene of the first attack. Two generals were injured (in contrast, the Pakistan Army did not manage to injure a single Indian general in three wars), and several brigadiers and colonels were killed. This was one of the most telling setbacks for India in the long-running insurgency in Kashmir.

With Kashmiri's immense expertise in Indian operations, he stunned Al-Qaeda leaders with the suggestion that expanding the theater of war was the only way to overcome the present impasse. He presented the suggestion of conducting such a massive operation in India that it would bring India and Pakistan to war. With that, all proposed operations against Al-Qaeda would be brought to a grinding halt. Al-Qaeda excitedly approved the proposal to attack India. Kashmiri then handed over the plan to a very able former army major, Haroon Ashik, who was also a former LeT commander who was still very close to LeT chiefs Zakiur Rahman Lakhvi and Abu Hamza. Haroon knew about an ISI plan for a low-profile routine proxy operation in India through LeT. It had been in the pipeline for several months but the official policy was to drop it. The former army major, with the help of Ilyas Kashmiri's men in India, hijacked the ISI plan and turned it into the devastating attacks that shook Mumbai on November 26, 2008 and brought Pakistan and India to the brink of war.

According to investigations, the attackers traveled across the Arabian Sea from Karachi, hijacked the Indian fishing trawler *Kuber*, killing the crew, then entered Mumbai in a rubber dinghy. The first events took place at around 20:00 Indian Standard Time (IST) on November 26, 2008, when ten Urdu-speaking men in inflatable speedboats came ashore at two locations in Colaba. They targeted the Chhatrapati Shivaji Terminus, the Leopold Café, the Taj Mahal and Oberoi Trident hotels, and the Jewish Center in Nariman House. They held people hostage and then killed them. The drama continued for almost 72 hours. The entire world was stunned by 26/11. It was almost identical to 9/11 in that it aimed to provoke India to invade Pakistan in the same manner as 9/11 prompted the United States to attack Afghanistan. The purpose of 26/11 was to distract Pakistan's attention from the "War on Terror," thereby allowing Al-Qaeda the space to manipulate its war against NATO in Afghanistan.

However, the decision makers in Washington had read between the lines. They rushed to India and Pakistan to calm nerves and prevented a war from breaking out. Significantly though, during the time Pakistan and India stood eye to eye, the fighting between Pakistan's military and Al-Qaeda militants came to a complete halt. While the sword of an Indian invasion was hanging over the head of Pakistan, the militants were saying *Qunut-e-Nazla* (prayers in days of war) that they would not be forced to fight against a Muslim army. They prayed that Al-Qaeda and the Pakistan Army would join and fight India together, instead. Timely US intervention had prevented this, but while the Pakistan military was readying for a showdown with India, the militants availed themselves of the opportunity to mount attacks on NATO supply lines in the Khyber Agency. This left Pakistan with no choice but to close down the transportation link between Pakistan and Afghanistan for several days during December 2008.

This had a devastating effect on the NATO forces in Afghanistan, especially those based in the provinces of Ghazni, Wardak, and Helmand. NATO troops there faced serious fuel shortages and had to suspend operations. Due to the tense situation on its eastern borders with India, Pakistan's participation in "Operation Lion Heart" was tepid, and it was forced to strike a deal with the Taliban, on their terms, in Swat at the beginning of 2009.

Several actions followed, including a new operation in the Swat Valley, operations in South Waziristan and Mohmand, and the killing of Baitullah Mehsud. But these did not faze the militants. Their retaliation came in the form of an attack on the military headquarters in Rawalpindi on October 10, 2009, and a high-profile massacre of some of Pakistan's military officers in Rawalpindi's military mosque during Friday prayers on December 4, 2009.

Behind these events a new Al-Qaeda *A Thousand and One Nights* tale was unfolding which saw an overstretched US army having to send an additional 30,000 troops to the Afghan theater of war. Meanwhile Al-Qaeda was already redrawing the boundaries for the next phase of the war, which was to stretch from the Central Asian republics down to South Asia, along the Hindu Kush mountains, into the cities of Pakistan, and outside the country. Tuned in to this strategy, Kashmiri was appointed the new chairman of Al-Qaeda's military committee. His strategy envisaged new theaters of war in Somalia and Yemen, which aimed at severing the Western trade routes through those countries. His aim was to turn Yemen into the strategic backyard for Al-Qaeda's operation in the Middle East and hence provide support to an Al-Qaeda-led Iraqi resistance, while initiating an insurgency in Saudi Arabia. Kashmiri's war perspective in South Asia was to expand Al-Qaeda's Afghan–Pakistan operation into India. The CIA and ISI were both aware of what Kashmiri was up to, and from February 2009 until September 14 (according to information provided by the ISI) CIA drones targeted him three times. In the last attack he was pronounced dead, with Washington officially celebrating his demise as a defining moment in the "War on Terror."

However, I was invited to North Waziristan by the 313 Brigade and taken to Angorada, situated at the crossroads of South Waziristan and Afghanistan, where on October 9, 2009, Kashmiri gave me an interview which was intended to quash all the rumors that he had been killed.

"Al-Qaeda's regional war strategy, in which they have hit Indian targets, is actually to chop off American strength," he told me. "So should the world expect more Mumbai-like attacks?" I asked. "Mumbai was nothing compared with what has already been planned for India in the future," Kashmiri answered.

Subsequently a number of people, allegedly from Kashmiri's

group, were arrested in the United States. They readily confessed to planning an attack on the National Defense College in Delhi, India, which aimed at killing all of the top brass of the Indian military assembled there. They also underscored that there were targets other than Delhi and Mumbai for the purpose of opening a new theater of war in India. The aim was to keep Pakistan and India engaged in hostilities, which would provide a breathing space to enable Al-Qaeda and its Taliban allies to realize their objectives in Afghanistan. They admitted to pursuing a similar strategy, but at a much lower level, throughout Europe, as well as planning a possible attack on the Danish newspaper *Jyllands-Posten*, which had published allegedly blasphemous cartoons featuring the Prophet Muhammad (Peace Be Upon Him) in 2005.

From 9/11 Al-Qaeda developed a politics of war and peace. It maneuvered through peace accords in Pakistan to create an enlarged space to wage war. It sabotaged the peace process by war. And this remains a never-ending process until a final victory can be announced.

3

FIRST STEP: LEADERSHIP BUILDING AND TRANSFORMATION OF THE "SONS OF THE SOIL" TO "BLOOD BROTHERS"

A picture of a young Dr Ayman al-Zawahiri shows him in Western attire. Beardless, with a golden moustache and black-framed glasses over his eyes, he looks the picture of a budding career surgeon. However, the picture does not tell all. Al-Zawahiri was, in fact, a not an ordinary man but a half-century-long movement. Various authors have documented fascinating facts about him. For instance, as a child, al-Zawahiri looked down on playground activities, unlike the other boys around him, and instead loved poetry as might an adult. Although he pursued a worldly education designed for a future as a surgeon, his real inspiration was Syed Qutb and his revolutionary writings. Qutb was a Muslim Brotherhood ideologue executed in the mid-1960s for writing inflammatory literature.

Syed Qutb's influence on al-Zawahiri was deep. Islamic revolution became al-Zawahiri's credo, and rebellion an imperative against any human-made system which he believed – as did Syed Qutb – to be *Jahilliya* (the age of ignorance, barbarism, and unbelief in Arabia before the coming of Islam). Syed Qutb and some Islamists interpreted Western political systems as *Jahilliya*. Al-Zawahiri joined the Muslim Brotherhood when he was only 14. In the year following Qutb's execution in 1966, al-Zawahiri began to work on developing his own strategies to bring Syed Qutb's vision and ideology to life.

In the following years al-Zawahiri became a surgeon, married, and practiced medicine. At the same time he formed his own underground organization to work together with other underground movements planning coups against the Egyptian government. He was jailed, released, went into exile, on to the Afghan Jihad, was involved in another coup in Egypt, then joined Al-Qaeda in the 1990s for a long war against US hegemony. During this 50-year period he saw each segment of his life as a movement, whether it involved working in his clinic, or for underground organizations, or on his marriage. Throughout this time Syed Qutb remained al-Zawahiri's inspiration and, in the light of Qutb's teachings, al-Zawahiri conducted operations to defeat *Jahilliya* through Jihad (armed struggle) for Islamic revolution in the Muslim world.

In 1979 when the Soviet Union invaded Afghanistan, thousands of young Muslims came to Afghanistan from all over the world (mostly from the Middle East) to join the Afghan resistance movement. The majority of these had welcomed the call for Jihad and had come to fight for an Islamic victory. They were ready to sacrifice their lives for Islam, believing in the saying attributed to Prophet Muhammad that the "End of Time" battles would start from the victory in ancient Khurasan. (The Prophet used the word "East," synonymous in those days with Khurasan, which included present-day Afghanistan, a part of Iran, Central Asia and areas in Pakistan.) The Jihadis had journeyed to Afghanistan as soon as they received confirmation through various religious decrees issued by scholars such as Dr Abdullah Azzam, that the Afghan resistance against the Soviets was actually an Islamic resistance aimed at establishing an Islamic state in Afghanistan to mark a new beginning. Most of these young Arabs who arrived in Afghanistan were qualified professionals like al-Zawahiri. They had the same dedication to Islamic revolution and were ready to sacrifice their lives to ensure victory, not just for the Afghan *mujahideen*, but to initiate the wider struggle. They wanted to establish an Islamic base in South Asia, which would work for the revival of a Global Muslim Caliphate. After the Soviet Union's retreat from Afghanistan, these idealistic, ultra-radical youths were inspired by Al-Qaeda's ideology and became the movement's core fighting force.

That is the simple explanation of events as they were played out – from the Soviet invasion of Afghanistan to 9/11. However, the real story is much more complex. It moves through the lives of individuals like al-Zawahiri, who became the inspiration for others such as Osama bin Laden. Each passed on their ideas to the next generation, and they then moved to wage war as "blood brothers." The process went on uninterrupted and prepared Al-Qaeda's forces to orchestrate a battle across the world. But Afghanistan remained its central highpoint.

There has never been a full picture shown before of Al-Qaeda to a Western audience. Whatever was portrayed was misleading. Thus all the decisions taken after 9/11 were wrongly directed. Intelligence services around the world pre-9/11 visualized Al-Qaeda simply as a disorganized group of mercenaries, not a sophisticated organization capable of orchestrating attacks on the United States. Even when the new awareness of Al-Qaeda's capabilities dawned, the organization's true nature and intentions were a mystery. What remains a fact, however, is that the defeat of the United States has become an obsession with Al-Qaeda and it prepares its game plans accordingly. Ideas play a pivotal role in wars, but ideas alone do not provide results. A fusion of ideas and resources is necessary for success. The absence of either one can lead to failure. Al-Qaeda came into existence in the late 1980s, but it took its real shape when ideas fused with resources in the middle of 1990s: with the alliance of al-Zawahiri's ideas and bin Laden's resources.

Six feet three inches tall, rich, and close enough to the Saudi royal family to be counted a family member, Osama bin Laden was seen as an "angry young man." Fourteen years ago in his native Saudi Arabia he spoke out against the kingdom for allowing Western forces to use its territory after the first Gulf War. The bin Laden family conglomerate was influential in business and highly respected in Saudi Arabia, as well as in the world business community. Family members finally persuaded bin Laden to appear personally before King Fahd and request a royal pardon. Many important members of the Saudi royals, including Prince Turki and Prince Abdullah, tried their best to settle the dispute. But it was all to no avail.

That was the beginning of the false impression presented about bin Laden and his supporters. US intelligence agencies reported him as a Saudi dissident who had fought bravely in Afghanistan against the Soviets in the 1980s, but who was no more than a political nuisance in Saudi Arabia. In fact, bin Laden had become anti-American to the core – and anti the Saudi monarchy soon after they invited US troops to take part in the first Gulf War. But he did not have an ideology or a strategy. Most political analysts believed his initial sloganeering against the United States would not amount to anything, and, had he not met up with al-Zawahiri in 1997 it might not have. But al-Zawahiri indoctrinated bin Laden with the idea of armed opposition to the United States, and gave such a spin to it that bin Laden's uncertain security threat to the United States turned into a deadly reality.

Saad al-Faqih, who heads the Saudi opposition group Movement for Islamic Reform in Arabia (MIRA), is a widely acknowledged

expert on Al-Qaeda. *Terrorism Monitor* special correspondent
Mahan Abedin conducted an interview with Saad in London
on January 23, 2004, in which he gave an explicit account of
bin Laden's transformation after his acceptance of al-Zawahiri's
doctrine of war against the United States. Saad felt that it was
late in 1997 when al-Zawahiri's meeting with bin Laden actually
changed the nature and course of bin Laden's struggle against the
United States towards a new strategy based on global and cosmic
confrontation. Saad explained the word cosmic as:

> Global and full scale confrontation .... Zawahiri and bin Laden
> decided to conduct their actions, relying not just by their own
> resources, but by manipulating those of their enemies: in short to
> turn the enemy's assets into a powerful tool for their own use.

Saad elaborated:

> Let us start from the beginning. When bin Laden started Jihad
> in Afghanistan he was a simple motivated Muslim who wanted
> to assist his brother Muslims in Afghanistan. Of course he
> started learning about international politics and the balance of
> power between the Americans and the Soviets at that time. But
> he was too preoccupied with the military situation. Some of his
> followers have said that he was predicating a future confronta-
> tion with America .... The period in the 1980s was largely taken
> up by confrontation with the Soviet army. When the Royal
> Family invited the American forces to Saudi Arabia or when the
> Americans decided to come – however you like to put it – bin
> Laden was shocked.
>   He had fought in Afghanistan to keep the Russians out, while
> now the most sacred Islamic country was being invaded by the
> Americans, as he saw it. Now, if he wanted to be consistent, he
> would now have to fight the Americans. Bin Laden was stunned
> by the betrayal of the Saudi regime, the religious establishment
> and the scholars. No one seemed to take it seriously that half
> a million American infidels were in the middle of the Arabian
> Peninsula. This had a profound impact on bin Laden's thinking
> and view of the world. He came to the conclusion that the cause
> of Islam could no longer be promoted through the exploitation
> of schisms between states. He had to choose other means. His
> plan then, was to leave Saudi Arabia.
>   At first he went back to Afghanistan to try to mediate between

the warring *mujahideen* factions. He failed and, in fact, was almost assassinated .... Then bin Laden went to Sudan. In Sudan he became aware that the regime there was not very strong .... Bin Laden's interest at that time was shelter, rather than patronage .... He thought they would give him shelter. He also wanted to help the Sudanese with his own expertise in construction. At that time the Saudi regime was not treating him with hostility. Many Hijazi merchants would go to Sudan and consult with bin Laden. Bin Laden encouraged people to invest in Sudanese commerce and finance. But he did not promote Islamic causes in Sudan.

Saad's description of bin Laden shows him as ordinary Muslim concerned about Muslims and their interests worldwide. There was an antagonism towards the United States, but the United States did not feel challenged by him because, although he had resources and ambitions, he did not appear to have any strategy. That situation completely changed with the emergence of al-Zawahiri armed with a plan.

Saad maintained:

The plan was not very complex. It was just to bomb American installations in Saudi Arabia. The Americans understood the significance of bin Laden's calls for the infidels to leave the country, and that is why their response was muted. If you go back and trace American statements you will not find any statement of significance about bin Laden. This did not alter until May 1998 when Zawahiri appeared on the scene and changed bin Laden's outlook. On Zawahiri coming to Afghanistan ... they decided that this idea of confronting the Americans in the Arabian Peninsula was not going to produce results. Zawahiri impressed upon bin Laden the importance of understanding the American mentality. America has a "cowboy" mentality – if you confront them with their identity, both theoretically and practically, they will react in an extreme manner. In other words, Americans with all their resources will revert to being "cowboys" when irritated. They will then elevate you to new heights as the implacable enemy, and this will produce the Muslim longing for a leader who could successfully challenge the West. Zawahiri advised bin Laden to forget about his 12-page statement on the subject as nobody had read it and instead issue a short statement identifying every American as a target. Even though this was controversial from an Islamic perspective, Zawahiri argued it had to be sanctioned on pragmatic grounds. The statement subsequently issued in February 1998, was only three or four lines long, but it sanctioned shedding the blood of every American.

If Bin Laden persisted in attacking the US forces alone in Saudi Arabia, he would have shared the same destiny of those groups in South America and Africa nobody cares to remember any more. This challenge to the American identity itself was a result of a huge transformation.

The attacks on US embassies in Africa in 1998 jolted the US perception about Al-Qaeda, and Washington came to realize that a new terror ring had emerged which was determined to counter US interests. This was confirmed in no uncertain manner by 9/11. Yet US decision makers were still very much in the dark on Al-Qaeda's thinking, despite the outlay of millions of dollars, countless hours, and counter terrorism networks formed across the world. Had the war in Afghanistan been reviewed more carefully from the mid-1980s to late 2000, it would have been easy to assess that Al-Qaeda strategy went beyond its material strength to fight the United States: it rotated its "human resources" around the Muslim world.

A simple-minded but concerned Muslim such as bin Laden then became a strategic asset for al-Zawahiri. Once he had convinced bin Laden on his strategic and ideological objectives, al-Zawahiri's movement automatically became stronger, especially with bin Laden's wealth added. Hence a dangerous armed reality against the US war machine emerged. Al-Qaeda then looked around for more resourceful and concerned young Muslims to sharpen into weapons.

But this is still not the entire picture. There are dynamics not yet mentioned which actually prepared the stage for the Al-Qaeda's *One Thousand and One Nights* tales beyond 9/11, and orchestrated the global battle against the United States. It is worth repeating that the seeds of Al-Qaeda's thinking were planted during the decade-long Jihad against the Soviet occupation of Afghanistan in the 1980s. The Arabs who poured into the country to join the Afghan resistance fell broadly into two camps: Yemeni and Egyptian. The religious zealots who went to Afghanistan after being inspired by local clerics fell into the Yemeni camp. They exercised hard, doing military drills all day long between fighting, cooked their own food, and then slept straight after *Isha* (the last prayers of the day). As the Afghan Jihad tailed off toward the end of the late 1980s, these Jihadis returned to their countries. Those who stayed, merged into the Afghan population, or went to Pakistan, where many married. In Al-Qaeda circles, they were termed *dravesh* (easy-going).

The Egyptian camp comprised those who were extremely politically minded as well as ideologically motivated. Although they were largely members of the Muslim Brotherhood, they were unhappy with that organization for its insistence on bringing about change in their societies through democracy and elections. The Afghan Jihad served as a powerful glue for these like-minded men, many of them educated as doctors, engineers and so on. Others were former military personnel from the Egyptian army associated with the underground Egyptian movement Islamic Jihad, run by al-Zawahiri (now bin Laden's deputy).

This group was responsible for the assassination of President Anwar Sadat in 1981 after he had signed a peace deal with Israel at Camp David. All were united on a single point: the reason for the Arab "doom and gloom" was the United States and its puppet governments in the Middle East. The Egyptian camp was in the hands of al-Zawahiri. After *Isha* prayers they would sit and discuss contemporary issues in the Arab world. One of the strong messages their leaders gave was that they should invest their resources in the armies of Muslin countries and ideologically motivate them.

In the mid-1990s, when then Afghan president Professor Burhanuddin Rabbani and his powerful defense minister, Ahmed Shah Masoud, allowed bin Laden to move from Sudan to Afghanistan, the Egyptian camp drew many members into its fold and ran *maaskars* (training camps) teaching strategies for the future fight. By the time the Taliban had emerged as a force to be reckoned with in Afghanistan in the mid-1990s, the Egyptian camp had settled its strategies, the most important being to:

- speak out against corrupt and despotic Muslim governments and make them targets to destroy their image in the eyes of the common people, who interrelated with the state, rulers, and nation
- focus on the US role, which was to support Israel and tyrannical Middle Eastern governments, and make everyone understand this.

These were years of the Afghan Jihad against the Soviets, in which the Egyptian camp molded the minds of Muslim youths drawn from all over the world. Al-Qaeda itself emerged from another organization. This was the Maktab al-Khidamat, the services bureau that

Abdallah Azzam set up in the early 1980s to facilitate Arab youths coming in from the Middle East to fight the Soviets in Afghanistan. Azzam was assassinated in 1989 and succeeded by bin Laden, one of his leading disciples. Bin Laden transformed the organization into Al-Qaeda. However, his was no more than a structural change. It would not have had much impact had al-Zawahiri and the Egyptian camp's ideology and pattern of struggle not been there for bin Laden to make use of. Al-Zawahiri is the person who made Al-Qaeda into the organization the world knows today.

The Osama bin Laden of the late 1980s was different from the bin Laden of 2009. He was against the United States, but had not fully realized that contemporary Muslim states, including Saudi Arabia, were totally committed to Washington's international policies. During an interview in Amman, Azzam's son Hudayfa, who has spent almost 20 years among Arab militants in Afghanistan and Pakistan, told me:

> Most Yemeni fighters are simple-minded warriors whose only ambition was martyrdom. They left Afghanistan after the fall of the communist government. The Egyptians stayed on because they had ambitions yet unfulfilled. When Osama bin Laden joined them after he left Sudan in 1996, they focused on shifting his thinking from basic opposition to American hegemony in the Middle East, to perspectives which did not differentiate between the contemporary Christian West and the Muslim Middle East.
>
> When I met Osama bin Laden in 1997 in Islamabad, he was flanked by three members of the Egyptian camp: the Somali Abu Obaida, and the Egyptians Abu Hafs and Saiful Adil (all part of Dr Ayman al-Zawahiri's team). I realized how successfully they had instilled their extremist ideas into him. When my father asked him to go to Afghanistan in 1985, he had replied that he would only do so if King Fahd personally granted permission. At that time Osama still referred to Fahd as Wali al-Amr (the supreme authority). After 9/11, when he denounced the rulers of Saudi Arabia, I could see how much the Egyptian camp had influenced him.

The 1998 attacks on the US embassies in Dar-es-Salaam, Tanzania and Nairobi, Kenya, were the start of Al-Qaeda's (as it came to be known) offensive against US interests. In retaliation, the United States launched cruise missiles on Kandahar and Khost in Afghanistan. It was consequent to this that Al-Qaeda formed a special task force to plan for the 9/11 attacks. It took three years for the plan to reach fruition, but discussions continued after 9/11 among members of the Egyptian camp – the then senior members of Al-Qaeda – over broader plans to bring the United States to its knees.

Before October 7, 2001, when the United States invaded Afghanistan in retaliation for the 9/11 attacks, most of Al-Qaeda's top minds had already left the country, their mission focused on several targets:

- to ideologically cultivate new faces from strategic communities, such as the armed forces and intelligence circles
- to bring in new recruits and establish cells
- to have each cell assigned to raise its own resources and devise a plan, but have only one cell implement the plan, while the others served as decoys to "misdirect" intelligence agencies.

Al-Qaeda's real war began after 9/11. Following the US invasion of Afghanistan, their migration to the Pakistani tribal areas was a major milestone in their struggle. The old Egyptian camp had now completely merged into Al-Qaeda, which served to guide it. Osama bin Laden and al-Zawahiri were its leaders.

Al-Qaeda faced a new challenge in its new home of Pakistan. Pakistan was a fertile soil to sow the seeds of its radical ideology. The Afghan Jihad against Soviets from 1979 to 1993, followed by the five-year-long Taliban rule in Afghanistan, had a direct bearing on the social and political fabric of the country, with thousands of Islamic seminaries of Taliban learning springing up in a matter of a decade. To take advantage of the situation the Pakistan establishment fueled Islamic separatist movements in Indian-held Kashmir, rearing several Jihadi outfits like Jaish-e-Mohammad, Harkatul Mujahadeen, Harkat-ul-Jihad-e-Islami, and Laskhar-e-Taiba (LeT).

In addition, General Zia-ul-Haq's eleven-year-long military government had promoted Islamic values in society as well as in the army, and contributed a lot to promoting the Jihadi spirit within the military rank and file. The US invasion of Afghanistan further aggravated antagonism towards the United States and brought about increased empathy for the Taliban and Al-Qaeda. In this buzzing arena, all Al-Qaeda needed to do was to pass on the same sort of indoctrination message as al-Zawahiri had conveyed to bin Laden, in order for him to permeate the whole area with Al-Qaeda's ideology and strategy, to split Islamists into sundry camps and exploit their special skills. That was Al-Qaeda's ultimate weapon to fight NATO in Afghanistan.

The next step was ideological fusion: to spawn Al-Qaeda's ideological genes in *Ibnul Balad* (Sons of the Soil), transforming them into "blood brothers." The whole of the future war was to be fought by the *Ibnul Balad,* from which Al-Qaeda aimed to produce a new generation of al-Zawahiris, with each and every segment of their lives committed to a lifelong struggle. They were to live for the movement and die for it. But before they died they were to leave another generation behind to continue the war against the United States. This was Al-Qaeda's arsenal.

Al-Qaeda next laid the foundation of a media wing, Al-Sahab, which produced state-of-the-art footage on the Taliban and Al-Qaeda attacks on NATO troops in Afghanistan and the Iraqi resistance movement. It broadcast detailed speeches by bin Laden, al-Zawahiri, Yahya Al-Libbi, and other ideologues. It released documentaries based on Al-Qaeda's messages against both the West and its Muslim allies. Arabic literature written by several Al-Qaeda ideologues was translated and published, and thousands of copies were distributed all over Pakistan. This exercise targeted a particular audience: Islamic-minded professionals, doctors, engineers, army officers, soldiers, IT experts, and so on.

The earlier chapters of this book gave a detailed account of how Al-Qaeda motivated the tribal youth to raise pro-Taliban militias, but the purpose of Al-Qaeda's strategy was not to pull in an unruly crowd. In the tribal areas, it hunted for natural leaders like Nek Muhammad, Baitullah Mehsud, Abdullah Mehsud, and Hakeemullah Mehsud, to infuse into them the spirit of Al-Qaeda ideology and the strategies to be employed in the future. The selected leaders were required to raise adherents themselves.

The Al-Qaeda leadership believed that once their message was disseminated among the targeted professional Muslim youths, mobilizing material resources would not be a problem. There would be no need to procure millions of dollars worth of sophisticated weaponry, as once the Muslim soldiers and officers had been recruited and indoctrinated, they would produce weaponry using their own ingenuity. Moreover, if the situation so demanded they could steal arms from their parent organizations' depots. Indoctrinated youths from the information technology and medical sciences fields would be added assets.

To achieve this target, the Al-Qaeda leaders disseminated messages to create disillusionment among Muslim youths and push them to use their acquired skills to move their respective establishments away from Western camps. Al-Qaeda never actually aimed at instigating rebellion against Muslim establishments. The aim from the beginning was to counter US hegemony in Muslim lands.

Al-Qaeda took up arms against Pakistan in 2007 when it became obvious that Pakistan's political and military goals seemed tied to the West. Its strategy was simple, but it worked. From 2003 onwards Al-Qaeda succeeded in sowing the seeds of dissent within Pakistan's armed forces, when Pakistan's tribal youths and formerly pro-establishment Jihadi cadres moved away from Pakistan's ruling establishment and promised allegiance to Al-Qaeda. Fresh plans had to be initiated after the defeat of the Taliban and subsequent retreat of Al-Qaeda to the Pakistani tribal areas in early 2002, but Al-Qaeda had meanwhile succeeded in persuading core South Asian Islamists to subscribe to its ideology and strategy, and begun to orchestrate war games of its choice.

It merits repeating that in Al-Qaeda's *One Thousand and One Nights* tales, characters like the young special forces commando Captain Khurram, his brother Major Haroon Ashik, and their special forces colleague Major Abdul Rahman emerged.

CAPTAIN KHURRAM, THE MARTYR

On December 23, 2005, retired Captain Khurram wrote in an email message to me:

Dear Dr. Sahib [the Taliban refer to any person who is reasonably familiar with the English language as Dr, so Khurram and his friends used to call me Dr because I was an English-language journalist], *Assalam o alaikum.*

I started reading your articles a couple of months back and concluded that you are probably amongst those very few analysts who have real insight into the Pakistani Jihadi cadres.

I read your last article "Armed and dangerous: Taliban gear up," and before making any comment. I would now like to introduce myself.

In 2001, I was serving as an assault commander of the elite anti-terrorist Zarrar Coy from Pakistan's Special Service Group (SSG). 9/11 was a strange volcano. It divided people on strong ideological lines. I was also struck by the Jihadi waves and joined Laskhar-e-Taiba in Kashmir.

Laskhar training in 1998–99 was revolutionized by a former

Zarrar Coy NCO, who on retirement, joined this outfit. His specialized urban assault training proved to be the most important element in the series of fearful Laskhar *fedayeen* attacks on the Indian barracks. The culmination of those attacks came with the deadly attack of the Kalu Chak which brought a furious Vajpayee to Jammu beating the war-drum. Mr Shamshad, known as Abu Fahad Ullah, was martyred in 2000, and suddenly there was a lull and stagnancy in the training of the Laskhar.

My brother, a former army major, hung up his boots right after 9/11. On his release from service, he joined the LeT. One of my unit officers also followed the suit. I joined the outfit soon after, without caring for the consequences. After one year all three of us came out of the Laskhar, dejected after facing the conspiracies of their leadership. There is enough to say about the extreme hypocrisy, luxuries, and evils of these so called Pakistani *mujahideen* leaders, but that isn't the objective of my mail to you. The aim of my writing to you is linked with your article above.

Once inside the LeT cadres, I came to know about their tactics, logistics, and black market activities. Moreover, I learned about the difference in the ideologies and tactics of the different groups, namely AQ, Taliban, and the Pakistani groups. Terrorism is my favorite topic. The last time I wrote a feature article on this was in *The Nation plus* on 31st Oct. 2004. It was about the desperate demonstration of the Chinese hostage rescue. With this background and having studied the tactics of the Tamil Tigers in depth, I would like to make the following comments:

You have quoted senior Pakistani security officials, on the condition of anonymity, as saying the AQ and Taliban are developing new links with the Tamil Tigers for logistic support. I would like to add that most of the security officials in Pakistan do not have any real insight or understanding on these cadres. After 9/11 they have re-molded the pan-Islamist view of world domination by the Pakistani *mujahideen* organizations into a nationalist outlook i.e. liberating Kashmir only. The Pakistani organizations were probably the largest in the world in terms of cadres, logistics, and support base to stop [*mujahideen*] from attacking the US interests, against which they had been raising slogans for years. To break this tide from joining AQ and Taliban inside Afghanistan was a huge task. The officials can claim some success for this but the real credit goes more to the corrupt leadership inside organizations, rather than the security and the intelligence hierarchy.

So, at least I do not believe all they claim. Most of what they say is based on some internet story or book which they have read about insurgency, or a presentation given by them in the past to earn an A grade in a compulsory course.

Two Tamil Tigers headed the group responsible for all their big deals – shipments of explosives from Rubizone Chemicals Ukraine, shipments of LMGs, rounds and guns from Russia, SAMS [missiles] from Thailand and Burma. They chartered ships in the corrupt PAN HO LIB [Panama, Honduras and Liberia] territories. They even bribed an Israeli weapons dealer and diverted a shipment of mortar rounds to their bastion of Jaffna. They forged end-user certificates and in many cases used the end-user certificates of third world armies, e.g. Bangladesh. But all these are memories of the pre-9/11 world, when the US's counter-terrorist forces had their eyes closed.

Where have those happy times disappeared after 2001? What to talk of moving cross borders? I know how many obstacles these cadres faced just moving things city to city. In the given situation, only the Iraqi AQ had the ability to operate across borders. Taliban, I really doubt.

The sudden upsurge in the Afghan resistance, I feel, is due to the changed policy of AQ to exploit Iranian channels from Iraq. If we look at the chronology of attacks in Afghanistan, it doesn't seem that any kind of advanced weaponry is used anywhere. The changed trend is the adoption of the suicide bombings by the Taliban. The downing of Chinook and other gunships may be attributed to the RPG fire, since it has a history.

The only possibility of logistically supporting the Taliban/AQ with SAMS is from Iraq via Iran, with Pakistan out, because of the infiltration of the security agents into these organizations, a fact the AQ has only lately understood.

The Tamil Tigers themselves have been searching hard for the latest weaponry, since the time they were black-listed by Scandinavia, from the Far East, Central America, West Africa to the jungles of Jaffna, in the post 9/11 scenario.

The AQ/Taliban can do anything – from killing people to stoning to death, but the one thing they are very strict about is no hashish, no marijuana! I noticed in my one year with them that printing fake money and smuggling was their favorite all-time pastime, but drug dealing is strictly prohibited through all kinds of *sharee* fatwas issued by the respected Arab Ulema.

Anyhow sir, this mail is for the sole purpose of letting you know that I am a fan of your articles and wanted to give you my views and bit of personal experience on the topic!

I am in the Great Lakes region and importing rice. But I have learned how the Europeans, Americans, and the Israelis are robbing the Congo out of its huge mineral wealth including uranium, which is also an interesting topic!

I also lived from 2001 to 2002 in Sierra Leone, West Africa, as a peace keeper. Once we entered its diamond-rich eastern Kono province to find it was completely out of the control of the capital and the world. How we got weapons back from the rebels, held the elections, made the government, and finally sent the diamond-rich country back into the lap of England. This is also an interesting story which demands your attention.

Thanks and wishing you great writings.

Khurram

D R Congo

Captain Khurram came from a Kashmiri family of the Salafi dispensation. His story is a telling account of how the infusion of Al-Qaeda's ideology and Islamic ideas convinced some middle-ranking officers in the Pakistan army to become "blood brothers" and adopt successful war strategies in the South Asian theater of war.

Ritualistically and otherwise, Khurram was a practicing Muslim. He was clear in explaining his religious viewpoints and political convictions on contemporary national issues. This made him particularly popular among his Special Services Group (SSG) colleagues. When he was deployed to Sierra Leone in 2001 and 2002 as part of the UN peacekeeping mission, he was extremely disturbed about the confusion of the local Muslims there. They were clearly identifiable as Muslims by their names, but they were totally unfamiliar with the details of their faith and obligations as Muslims. Khurram built a mosque and a *madrassa* in Sierra Leone, despite the opposition of his commander, Brigadier Ahmad Shuja Pasha. (Shuja is now a lieutenant-general and the director general of Inter-Services Intelligence, ISI.)

Pakistan's policy turnaround on the Taliban after the US invasion of Afghanistan had disillusioned the whole of the middle cadre of the country's armed forces. But unlike his other colleagues, who remained silent critics of the policy, Khurram and his elder brother Major Haroon decided to take practical steps to rectify this.

Haroon, an equally competent officer, took early retirement from the Pakistan army in 2001 after Pakistan had decided to support the US-led War on Terror. Khurram left the army in 2003 on his return from Sierra Leone. Both brothers then joined the LeT, but soon realized that the LeT was only a civilian extension of Pakistan's armed forces.

The events of 9/11 also brought a change in LeT policies concerning Afghanistan. The LeT advised its cadre to stay away from Al-Qaeda and the Taliban. Haroon and Khurram were not only excellent army officers, but also concerned Muslims. Thus this became a bone of contention. Haroon's inspiration came from the Salafi school of thought, and was the result of his reading habits. He extensively read classical Muslim academics like Imam Ibn-e-Tamiyyah, Ibn-e-Khaldoun, and Muhammad Bin Abdul Wahhab. Among modern-day Islamic scholars, he studied the works of the Muslim Brotherhood ideologue Syed Qutb, as well as the founder of the Jamaat-e-Islami Pakistan, Syed Abul Ala Maududi. Additionally, and even after retirement from the army, Haroon continued to read up on military strategies in military journals and through extensive internet surfing. Haroon never kept his criticism of the Pakistan Army a secret. He was a vocal critic of the country's armed forces. He visited his old military comrades frequently and taunted them on their weak Islamic beliefs, and for serving in Pakistan's armed forces, which he considered a continuation of the old British colonial army. He often cited the example of how the Frontier Corps still showcases its wars against "tribal insurgents" like Haji Saheb Taragzai and the Faqir of Ipi, who had fought against the British Indian forces before independence. Haroon motivated his former colleagues to leave the army, referring to it as a purely mercenary force. He advised them to do something else for a living. Several of his colleagues took his advice seriously and left the army.

In the meantime, Haroon had found a new comrade in Commander Muhammad Ilyas Kashmiri, a veteran Kashmiri fighter, who had been roughed up by Pakistan's armed forces time and again. He decided to sever his ties with the Kashmiri struggle and move to North Waziristan with his family.

Major Abdul Rahman was another officer who resigned from Pakistan's armed forces and joined Major Haroon. Their first and foremost aim at the time was to go to Afghanistan to fight against the NATO troops there.

Khurram and Rahman then went to the Afghan province of Helmand and fought against the British troops. Khurram died in the battle in Afghanistan's Helmand province in 2007. Rahman came back alive, but alone. Khurram's death became a source of inspiration for both Haroon and Rahman. Haroon was by now seriously involved in Afghanistan. He saw the death of his brother as martyrdom and dedicated his life to the Afghan resistance against the NATO forces. By 2006, Kashmiri was part of Al-Qaeda's Shura and his 313 Brigade came under Al-Qaeda's discipline. Soon after, Haroon reduced his business engagements and frequently journeyed to South and North Waziristan to take part in guerrilla operations against NATO in Afghanistan.

Haroon had fought in the Kargil war[1] in 1999 and often cited the cowardice of the Pakistani officers. He was convinced that the Pakistan Army was incapable of fighting any major battle. Haroon's exposure to the Taliban and Al-Qaeda had fired his imagination. The "soldier with a mission" stood up in him. He engaged in extensive physical training and made himself super-fit. His relations with Al-Qaeda grew and he soon became part of its inner circle. The fusion of Al-Qaeda's ideology and his own commitment and capabilities as a professionally trained army officer saw him loom large in the South Asian theater of war.

Haroon began evaluating the Afghan war theater from a new perspective. Thousands of brave Taliban, ready to kill or to be killed, stood before him, but their obsolete guerrilla tactics prevented them from emerging on top. The Taliban made a successful comeback in 2006 in Afghanistan, but their casualty rate was very high. At least 2,000 Taliban fighters were killed in the spring offensive of that year, while NATO's casualties were less than 200. Haroon was convinced that if the Taliban clung to old war techniques, the aerial power and military machine of the United States would eliminate them by 2008. There was need to develop novel guerrilla tactics through new schools of thought with the fighters oriented to new disciplines.

Haroon felt the Arab guerrilla fighters had a better sense of war than the Taliban but their ideas were limited. They did not have the capacity to strategize the war to advantage the Taliban. Rahman and Haroon jointly worked on this. They went to libraries and studied the most successful guerrilla battles against the United States in Vietnam. After extensive reading, both concluded that without more advanced weapons and improved strategy, success in Afghanistan could not be achieved.

Haroon then went to North Waziristan and gave his presentation to senior Al-Qaeda commanders. He laid out two models of insurgencies, one related to Vietnam guerillas operating against the

United States, and the other to the Tamil Tigers operating against the government of Sri Lanka.

He advocated that a start be made in the Afghan provinces of Khost, Paktia, and Paktika, with a three-pronged Tet-type offensive strategy, similar to the one that General Giap had used in North Vietnam in the 1960s to defeat the United States. He proposed that the first phase of operations involve armed opposition to the NATO forces in these provinces. In the second phase, the militants would target isolated security posts and military personnel. Militants would capture and hold these isolated posts for 24 to 48 hours and then melt away. In the third phase, they would spread the insurgency to urban areas and the federal capital.

Haroon emphasized that the central idea of General Giap's strategy was to catch the enemy by surprise, and he placed emphasis on the training of select warriors for special operations. They were to use sophisticated arms acquired by insiders. The Arab militants paid close attention to Haroon's presentation and discussed it with regional commanders such as Sirajuddin Haqqani and Mullah Nazir. (The strategy was later successfully employed in Pakistan's tribal areas against Pakistan's armed forces.) Haroon developed a "guerrilla" mortar gun of a type available only to some of the world's more advanced military forces. The gun was so small it could be hidden in a medium-sized luggage bag. Unlike the normal mortar gun, the length of which makes it difficult to hide, this gun could be transported easily. Haroon also developed a silencer for the AK-47, hitherto available only to a select few internationally. This became an essential component of Al-Qaeda's special guerrilla operations. He then visited China to procure night vision glasses. The biggest task was to clear them through the customs in Pakistan. Haroon called on his friend Captain Farooq, who was President Musharraf's security officer. Farooq went to the airport in the president's official car and received Haroon at the immigration counter. In the presence of Farooq, nobody dared touch Haroon's luggage, and the night vision glasses arrived in Pakistan without any hassle. (Farooq was a member of the Hizbut Tahrir, a fact discovered by the military intelligence as late as nine months after his posting as Musharraf's security officer. After being spotted, he was briefly arrested and then retired from the Pakistan Army.)

Once a level of sophistication had been reached, the militants prepared for special operations. The militants for these operations all emanated from North Waziristan. An attack on the Serena Hotel Kabul in January 2008, a Taliban strike on the national day parade in April 2008 in Kabul, multiple bombing attacks in Khost in May 2009, and an attack on the Kamdesh US base in Kunar in September 2009, are just a few examples of the successful guerrilla operations they launched. In most cases, the Taliban donned Afghan armed forces or Afghan police uniforms, and in almost every attack they had insiders providing them with information on the targeted complexes' entry and exit points.

Neither Haroon nor Kashmiri favored gathering adherents randomly for these special operations. They recruited the best and most ideologically motivated youths to their 313 Brigade. These youths were given special guerrilla training, including swimming and karate lessons, shooting and ambush techniques, and were familiarized with explosive devises as well as reconnaissance. The 313 Brigade fell strictly under Kashmiri's control. The role of Al-Qaeda's Laskhar al-Zil (Shadow Army) was to coordinate with other groups. Several different groups of the *mujahideen* were then inducted into the Laskhar al-Zil.

Haroon had the Taliban widen their war perspectives. He then presented his most important assessment of future operation procedures to Kashmiri and Al-Qaeda's other leaders. This was a comprehensive plan to sever the NATO supply line of containers from the port of Karachi to Afghanistan. Of these shipments, 80 percent go through Pakistan's tribal area to the Khyber Agency and 20 percent use the Chaman–Kandahar route. Haroon next planned a masterstroke, to organize attacks on NATO supplies running through Pakistan into Afghanistan in January 2008. The focal point was the Khyber Agency. This key transit point accounted for most of the NATO supplies needed to battle the Afghan insurgency. Laskhar al-Zil was assigned to execute the plan. Ustad Yasir, an Afghan, was appointed in the Khyber Agency project head. The chief of the Tehrik-e-Taliban Pakistan (TTP), Hakeemullah Mehsud, although then only an ordinary foot solider, was sent from South Waziristan to coordinate the action. Al-Qaeda knew that Laskhar al-Zil operations in the Khyber Agency would not receive any support from the locals as the majority of the population of the Khyber Agency belongs to the anti-Taliban Brelvi school of thought which believes in Sufism. There were several local groups from the Deobandi School (a pro-Taliban Muslim sect in Pakistan), but they had good relations with the Pakistan Army and local tribes who stood against creating a law and order situation. Haroon suggested that Laskhar al-Zil establish its sanctuaries in the neighboring Orakzai Agency and make Dara Adam Khail its base. His strategy aimed at pressurizing the local tribesmen to remain neutral in the Taliban attacks on NATO convoys. Future Taliban attacks were then launched from the Orakzai Agency on daily basis. (Later militants succeeded in establishing their own strong pockets in the Khyber Agency in 2009–10.)

Suicide attacks followed. In one, the warlord Haji Namdar, who had initially been the local facilitator for attacking the NATO supply line, and who had supported the Pakistan Army against the Taliban and Al-Qaeda in the Khyber Agency, was killed. The other powerful warlord of the area, Mangal Bagh, learned from this lesson and remained neutral. The Taliban attacks rose to the point of Pakistan having to close its borders several times in December 2008. Haroon next contemplated widening the attacks on NATO supplies. He was convinced this would be the key to NATO's defeat in Afghanistan. He visited Karachi several times, and set up efficient teams there to monitor the movement of NATO's shipments arriving at the port. These teams were to study how the NATO shipments were passed on to the various contractors. Each and every detail was closely examined, including the companies which had the contracts for the shipments. Several contractors were abducted in Karachi and the rest given warnings to break with NATO, or suffer the consequences. NATO commanders were taken aback by these new developments, and more so when in the last months of 2008, the Taliban virtually stopped their attacks across Pakistan and Afghanistan and shifted their entire focus towards blowing up NATO supply arteries. In Karachi, most of the contractors had been abducted, or were on the run. At the Peshawar terminal, almost every other day the Taliban suddenly appeared, carried out rocket attacks on NATO convoys, and disappeared into the Khyber Agency. Almost every day 20 to 40 NATO convoys were set on fire or looted.

The Pakistani Taliban released a picture to the Pakistani press of a US Humvee being used by the Taliban in the Orakzai Agency. This sent shock waves through Western capitals. The stories published in the international press of missing NATO aircraft engines said to be in the possession of the Taliban added to Westerners' concerns.

The NATO command wondered who was guiding the Taliban. The immediate suspect was the Pakistani military establishment, but there was no hard evidence of this. Western intelligence fully examined the profiles of all the leading Arab commanders in North Waziristan and those who had been commanding the Taliban in Afghanistan, but was unable to track anyone with the required knowledge or skill to successfully pursue this strategy. The rising shortage of supplies in the provinces of Helmand, Ghazni, and Wardak seriously affected the patrol capabilities of NATO forces during the latter months of 2008.

In April 2008, NATO struck a deal with Russia in Bucharest to send its supplies through Russia and Central Asia. On the sidelines of the 45th Munich Summit in February 2009, an agreement was simultaneously reached between Iran and United States for Iran to allow some non-military NATO shipments through the port of Chabahar. Permission for supplies through Iran, however, was given only to individual countries like Italy, France, and the United Kingdom – not NATO as a whole. But neither of these routes proved an economically viable alternative to the Khyber Agency route, through which 70 percent of NATO supplies still moved.

Haroon wrote me an email after the Bucharest conference in April 2008, citing Wikipedia. He also sent a map in another email:

A landlocked country, surrounded entirely by other landlocked countries, may be called a "doubly landlocked" country. A person in such a country has to cross at least two borders to reach a coastline.

There are only two such countries in the world:

Liechtenstein in Central Europe.

Uzbekistan in Central Asia.

Uzbekistan has borders with four countries – Turkmenistan to the southwest, Tajikistan and Kyrgyzstan to the south and east, with Kazakhstan and the Aral Sea to the north – that border the landlocked saltwater Caspian Sea, from which ships can reach the Sea of Azov by using the Volga–Don Canal, and thus the Black Sea, the Mediterranean Sea, and the oceans.

There was no doubly landlocked country in the world after the 1871 Unification of Germany until the end of World War I. This was because Uzbekistan was part of Russia and then of the Soviet Union; while Liechtenstein borders Austria, which had an Adriatic coast until 1918.

DOCTOR SAAB IF U LOOK AT IT IN A SUPPLY ROUTE PERSPECTIVE, IT'S A LAUGH. CAN U FURTHER HIGHLIGHT THIS POINT? ALLAH HAFIZ.

Haroon's assessment was correct. NATO tried to move its supplies on the Central Asian routes to northern Afghanistan, but was not able to transport more than 10 to 15 percent of its requirements because of the much higher cost of transportation cost through the "doubly landlocked" region. Pakistan remained the main supply route.

THE RISE AND FALL OF MAJOR HAROON

Major Haroon was elated. He was playing the role of a general. This was something he could never have achieved in the regular army, given his time of service. He bought a non-custom Pajero off-road vehicle from North Waziristan at the dirt-cheap price of PKR 125,000 and used it to travel through North Waziristan to Karachi. When night fell, he stayed in army messes in the countryside. Being an ex-army officer he was allowed that facility. He always kept his army revolver on him with lots of bullets in case he was obstructed at any checkpoint, but his imposing bearing and unmistakable military accent in both English and Urdu always prevented this from happening. With his success in evading identification and capture, he looked forward to broadening both his, and through him Al-Qaeda's, network. Every visit brought forward new comrades. Most of them were from the LeT, a few from other Jihadi outfits, but there were a number from the Pakistan Army as well.

Through his close connections in the Pakistan Army, Haroon was able to develop an effective intelligence network. In 2007 he became aware that the United States had taken a new view on the South Asian terror war, and had arrived at the conclusion that the problem lay in Pakistan. The United States did not want a partnership with the Pakistan Army to defeat the militancy, it wanted to place US personnel inside the army to fight it. In 2008 the United States took over some bases in Pakistan in order to launch predator drone attacks against Al-Qaeda in Pakistani tribal areas. The same year the United States bought land in Tarbela, 20 km from Islamabad, and allocated US$1 billion for the extension of the US embassy in Pakistan's capital. Earlier, in 2007, US war contractors had arrived in Pakistan. They interviewed and selected a group of Frontier Corps personnel to be trained as an anti-insurgency force. In Pakistan's ISI, a counter-terrorism cell was established with the officers to be trained in the United States. They were to visit to the United States at regular intervals to allow the US administration to assess them and their conviction about fighting the War on Terror. The US establishment focused on making personal contacts at all levels in the Pakistan Army to set the stage for a conclusive war effort against Al-Qaeda.

Haroon was privy to all of this, and busied himself working on a strategy to generate a crisis in the Pakistan Army. His avowed aim was to have the Pakistan Army sever all ties with the United States. Using terror tactics was the only way Haroon knew to jolt the conscience of his former comrades-in-arms. He made a list of the senior ranking army officers involved in anti-terror activities, and decided to make a horrible example of them to deter others from joining the United States. The name of retired Major General Ameer Faisal Alvi came to mind. Faisal had commanded Pakistan army's elite Special Services Group operations in Angor Ada on October 2, 2003, when 2,500 commandos had been airlifted into the village of Baghar, located near Angor Ada, with aerial support from 12 helicopter gunships. According to local residents, some of the helicopters flew from the Machdad Kot US air base from across the border in Afghanistan. Witnesses reported that 31 Pakistani soldiers and 13 foreign fighters and local tribesmen were killed in the action. A large number of militants fled. In that operation several high-profile Al-Qaeda commanders, including Abdul Rahman Kennedy, were killed. Several others were arrested and transported to Guantanamo Bay. The attack was burned into the minds of Al-Qaeda and they mulled over the setback, especially since as, at that time, there had been no open hostility between them and Pakistan.

Tracing the address of Alvi, who was British born, was not a problem. After developing personal differences with the then chief of army staff, General Musharraf, Alvi had been forcibly retired from the Pakistan Army. After his retirement he worked as the CEO and executive director of Redtone Telecommunication Pakistan Ltd, a private telecommunications company in Pakistan. On November 19, 2008 while he was on his way to work, Haroon followed him. His plan was to waylay the retired general when he slowed down at a speed breaker near the PWD colony in Islamabad, where the general's passage would be obstructed by two accomplices. Everything went according to plan. Haroon jumped out of his car and killed Alvi with his army revolver.

The murder sent shock waves through the military rank and file. Intelligence outfits could read the fine print: both former and serving army personnel were to be future targets. But they remained tight lipped. The murder of Alvi was not Haroon's sole mission, he was on the lookout for similar targets. The killing of the retired army official was not purely an act of vengeance, it was to serve as a reminder to the serving military cadre that one day they too would retire and could suffer a similar fate. However, there was more to Haroon than being just an assassin. He was rapidly reorganizing the cadre of the Jihadi militants and changing their mindset to fight a more disciplined war against the United States.

The first time I met Major Haroon was at his Lahore residence in September 2007. He was clearly a religious person from his appearance. He had a long beard and wore a prayer cap and the traditional Pakistani *shalwar-qameez* (a unisex form of dress similar in manner to the shirt and pants worn by Westerners). When I met with him later, I found a different person. He had trimmed his beard, shed some weight, and wore Western attire. But in his private life Haroon was a devout Muslim. At one time he came to visit me at the Avari Towers Hotel in Lahore and said his prayers in my room. There were pictures on one wall of the room, and he covered them all with a sheet as he considered them prohibited under Islam.

Haroon was closely watching developments in Pakistan. He was in touch with all of his former colleagues in the armed forces (except those who were part of the military operations against the militants), including a major general who was the officer commanding the garrison in Peshawar. The general had tried to reach Haroon many times to condole with him on the death of his brother Khurram, but Haroon had not responded. Meanwhile Haroon was getting information on expanding US influence from his old army colleagues. Being an avid internet surfer and book reader, he was well informed about state apparatus procedures, their manipulations and strategies. He focused on altered plans to counter them before the state could use them. He realized that if the United States continued to enjoy the success it had had up till then, Pakistan's army would ultimately have no choice but to bow down to it.

The United States was already promoting a role for India in Afghanistan as a countervailing force to Pakistan. Haroon knew the United States was playing on the existing rivalry between India and Pakistan to encourage Pakistan to engage more fully in the US War on Terror. He saw this as a carrot-and-stick game aimed at luring the Pakistan Army into the trap of committing itself to fight the militants. From 2007 onwards, Haroon worked on a counter-strategy along with his *Ameer* (commander), Muhammad Ilyas Kashmiri. The essence of this strategy was to expand the terror war into India. In the first phase Haroon aimed to conduct a 9/11 type event in India which he thought would surely lead India to declare war on Pakistan. Haroon assessed that once that happened, the Pakistan Army would have no choice but to pull its troops out of the military operations against the Taliban and Al-Qaeda on its western front. Haroon assigned Major Abdul Rahman, the close friend and former colleague of his slain brother Captain Khurram, for the Indian operation. Rahman was a living encyclopedia on Indian affairs. Haroon then set up an India cell and worked to expand the network to its maximum limits.

Haroon had left the LeT but was still in touch with its field commanders. He was aware of the LeT's strengths and weaknesses. The LeT's main strength was its connection with Pakistan's military establishment and its resources. Its weakness was limited vision. Haroon would often discuss these aspects with the LeT commanders, who considered him a totally trustworthy person because he was a Salafi as well as a retired army officer. Haroon used his connections for the execution of Al-Qaeda's plan. He was aware that in late 2007 the ISI had decided on the launch of a new uprising in Indian Kashmir and LeT was to be used for it. Funds were allocated and LeT was given the green light by the ISI to launch the operation. That was the routine proxy war plan.

But after the fencing of the LOC, the infiltration of militants into India became difficult. The LeT then had to use the deserted coastal area of Thatta (in the southern Sindh province of Pakistan) to move its fighters into India. From there they moved on into Kashmir.

Haroon met with a LeT commander, Abu Hamza, and advised him not to waste his time and resources on futile exercises in India. He told Abu Hamza that he would draw up a more effective strategy for the cause. Haroon next turned to his expert on India, Rahman, to brief him more fully on the country. Rahman had visited India many times. He had photographs and maps of all the important targets in India. He identified the areas in Mumbai where white foreigners lived, like Nariman House and the Taj Mahal Hotel.

Haroon informed Abu Hamza they would travel on a Pakistani boat initially and then capture an Indian trawler to land from. He told Abu Hamza that once they were in position to launch a massive operation it would force India to the negotiating table to discuss an advantageous settlement on Kashmir. Abu Hamza forwarded the plan to the LeT commander-in-chief Zakiur Rahman Lakhvi, who immediately left for Karachi to organize the operation. Lakhvi spent two months in preparation before the November 26, 2008 attacks in Mumbai. He worked night and day to select and train the militants who were to carry out the mission. When the selected militants were thought to be fully prepared to proceed precisely along the lines of Haroon's plan, they were launched. Haroon devised the mechanism of indirect communication for Abu Hamza, drawing the guidelines for instructions to the infiltrators, which were conveyed from countries other than Pakistan. The Mumbai attacks stunned the whole world.

The event was a great test for India as the regional superpower. One of the attackers, Ajmal Kasab, was taken alive, and during his grilling he told his Indian captors the whole story of how, where, and when he had been given his training. All links led to Pakistan, and India geared itself for a limited war on Pakistan, which was to include air strikes on LeT camps in Muzzafarabad, in Pakistani Kashmir, the LeT headquarters in Muredkey, in Pakistani Punjab, and its seminaries in Lahore. This could have been the beginning of a fourth Indo–Pak war.

Al-Qaeda's objective in undertaking the Mumbai 26/11 attack was to provoke a war between Pakistan and India. All hostilities between the military and the militants would then come to a halt in the Swat Valley in Pakistan's NWFP, as well as in the tribal areas of Bajaur, Mohmand, and the two Waziristans. Pakistan's militant leaders Mullah Fazlullah and Baitullah Mehsud announced that they would fight alongside Pakistan's armed forces in an India–Pakistan war, and the director general of ISI, Lt.-Gen. Ahmad Shuja Pasha, confirmed this understanding in his briefing to national and foreign correspondents, when he called Fazlullah and Baitullah Mehsud Pakistan's strategic assets.

The stage was all set to change the dynamics of enmity and friendship in the region when Washington put its foot down. Washington hurriedly sent several officials to India and Pakistan to advise their governments that any war between them would only benefit the militants. Washington assured India that Pakistan would cooperate fully in the investigation of the Mumbai attacks and arrest those who had been responsible for their planning.

Watching his plan fail, Haroon advised Rahman to use another approach for the 313 Brigade. LeT structures were now under siege because of US pressure on Pakistan, and hence of little value. Rahman journeyed to India again to acquire more information and photograph sensitive installations. These included India's nuclear research laboratories in Mumbai and Hyderabad. He also took photographs of the National Defense College, India's parliament building, and some other high-profile government offices in Delhi. Rahman always drew up a contingency plans for assaults on different targets. In this case, if the militants were unable to hit India's National Defense College during the day when several senior military officials were present, they were to attack the Indian parliament.

Rahman was arrested after a 313 Brigade militant, Zahid Iqbal, was picked up by the ISI in Islamabad on July 2009 and identified him. But as he had not been involved in any terrorist act in Pakistan, he was released and soon back at work planning the sabotage operation in India using the 313 Brigade. However, information was leaked to the FBI before he could proceed with the action, and the entire team, including Rahman, was captured.

In October 2009 a conspiracy was unearthed in Chicago by the FBI. Two suspects were arrested, David Headley and Tahawwur Rana. Their interrogations revealed that they had been planning to attack the National Defense College in Delhi and India's nuclear facilities. The Danish newspaper *Jyllands-Posten*, which had published allegedly blasphemous cartoons featuring the Holy Prophet (Peace Be Upon Him), was also on the hit list. The conspirators all belonged to the Kashmiri group. Their affidavit exposed the roles of Major Haroon and his aide Abdul Rahman in the recruitment and orientation process.

Kashmiri was optimistic about giving India a far bigger jolt than the 26/11 attack on Mumbai when I interviewed him on October 9, 2009 (see *Asia Times Online*, October 15, 2009). "So should the world expect more Mumbai-like attacks?" I asked. "That was nothing compared to what we have planned for the future," he replied.

Extracts from the FBI's affidavit

After visiting Denmark in January 2009 [David] Headley traveled to Pakistan to meet with Individual A. During this trip, Headley traveled with Individual A to the Federally Administered Tribal Area (FATA) region in north-west Pakistan and met with (Ilyas) Kashmiri. Headley returned to Chicago in mid-June 2009. Following Headley's return from Pakistan, Headley communicated by email with Laskhar-e-Taiba Member A regarding the status of the Northern Project. Because Laskhar-e-Taiba Member A responded that he had "new investment plans," coded language for the planning of a different attack, Headley and Individual A began to focus on working with Kashmiri to complete the attack on the newspaper. In late July 2009, Headley traveled again to Copenhagen, Denmark, and to other locations in Europe. When Headley returned to the United States, he told a Customs and Border Patrol inspector that he was traveling on business as a representative of an immigration business. Headley's luggage contained no papers or other documents relating to such business. Following Headley's return to Chicago in August 2009, Headley used coded language to inquire of Individual A on multiple occasions whether Individual A had been in touch with Kashmiri regarding planning for the attack. Headley expressed concern that Individual A's communications with Kashmiri had been cut off.

In early September 2009, Individual A called Headley to report that Kashmiri might be dead. Headley expressed dismay and concern, and said that Kashmiri's death means "our company has gone into bankruptcy then," and that "the projects and so forth will go into suspension." Shortly after initial press reports that Kashmiri had been killed in a drone attack in Pakistan, Headley and Individual A had a series of coded conversations in which they discussed the reports of Kashmiri's death and the significance of Kashmiri's death for the projects they were planning. Individual A sought to reassure and encourage Headley, telling him, among other things, that "This is business sir; these types of things happen."

According to the affidavit, Headley also talked about A's friend "Harry." A was Major Abdul Rahman, who was in charge of the India cell, and Harry, his friend, was Major Haroon.

ARREST

Before the arrest of Rahman, Haroon had approached his LeT and army friends. He convinced them to take part in the battle against NATO in Afghanistan. He took them to the Pakistani tribal areas and trained them in modern guerrilla warfare. In a matter of a few years the 313 Brigade came to be held in high regard in Jihadi circles for its expertise and resourcefulness. However, as more missions appeared on the horizon, more resources were required.

Money had always been lacking for the war, and Haroon was now facing a situation in which he did not even have enough money to buy fuel for his car, let alone pay hotel bills during his travels. To keep going, he sold his Corolla station wagon and resorted to a modest style of living. At one point he sold his AK-47 silencers in the Dara Adam Khail market, but even that did not generate enough money. Their monetary situation forced Haroon and Kashmiri to think of an alternative strategy. This was kidnapping for ransom. However, they would only abduct non-Muslims. Haroon came to Karachi and contacted an old army friend, retired Major Abdul Basit. The only help Haroon sought from Basit was to spy on Satish Anand, a renowned film producer. Satish is a Hindu, an uncle of the famous Indian actor Johi Chawala and son of the renowned film distributor Jagdaish Anand. With the information he had received from Basit, Haroon came back to Karachi and abducted Satish for ransom, thinking his family to be rich. He took the film distributor to North Waziristan, only to discover that all the estimates about his money were wrong. Satish did not have liquid funds. He owned properties but in captivity he could not sell them. Satish was told to contact his family members and ask them to raise a ransom, but it was to no avail.

The abductors then made Satish an offer: they would release him if he embraced Islam. They did not kill Muslims. Satish embraced Islam and promised to make a documentary on the militants. It is still a mystery whether or not any money was paid for his release, and if so how much, but what is true is that Satish came back safely to Karachi and refused to register any case against his abductors. He was also tight- lipped about their identities. Haroon was eventually arrested in February 2009 in Islamabad while he was trying to abduct Sarwar Khan, a member of the Qadyani sect. (The Qadyanis are considered non-Muslims under Pakistan's constitution.) Several cases, including the murder of Faisal Alvi, were then lodged against Haroon.

Haroon had served under some leading military officers including the chairman joint chiefs of the Staff Committee, General Tariq Majeed (now retired), while his brother Khurram had served under the director general of ISI, Lt. Gen. Shuja Pasha. I am sure that the Pakistan Army command, who knew of their professional skills, would miss these two brothers, very much like the Saudi establishment might have missed Osama bin Laden. These are the stories of Islamists pushed by circumstances onto a particular track, and then indoctrinated. They then became counterproductive, if not useless, for Muslim establishments that decide to go along with the US designs of a new world order in the post-Cold War era.

On March 3, 2009, only a week after Haroon's arrest in Islamabad, around ten gunmen attacked a bus carrying the Sri Lankan cricket team on its way to play in Pakistan's second city, Lahore. The pattern of the attack suggested that the attackers had no intention of killing the cricketers, as they sprayed bullets only on the escorting policemen. When the policemen fled, the gunmen tried to hijack the bus. This was prevented by the bus driver who kept his wits about him and drove the vehicle past the gunmen to safety. Six of the policemen escorting the team bus were killed, and seven cricketers and an assistant coach were injured in the attempted hijack. Rocket launchers and grenades were left on the site of shooting, as were water bottles and dried fruit. Officials said the incident bore similarities to the deadly November attacks in Mumbai. ISI claimed the incident was an action taken by militants trained by Haroon, and that the intention was to capture the cricketers and hold them hostage until they could be exchanged for the captive commander.

MAJOR HAROON'S IDEOLOGICAL JOURNEY

All the Western strategic experts wondered how Taliban's rag-tag militia, which was on the verge of collapse, had in a few short years rehabilitated itself and come up with hugely effective guerrilla tactics. These strategists wondered how the guerrillas' skills, which had been virtually nonexistent till 2005, had suddenly transformed. NATO failed to comprehend that there could be a strategist behind the change. That strategist was Haroon, who had been shuttling continuously between Pakistan's tribal areas in the two Waziristans and Karachi, undetected. In Al-Qaeda circles Haroon is today held in as high regard as Abu Hafs (killed in 2001) for his military operations and strategy.

While walking on the sandy shores of the Arabian Sea near my Karachi sea-view residence with Haroon, it was hard for me to believe that this was the person who had moved the internal dynamics of the war in South Asia from Afghanistan to India. Like al-Zawahiri, Haroon's whole life was the movement. Every part of his mind was focused on formulating a strategy to win the war against NATO. While walking near Karachi's Clifton beach he never once appeared to enjoy or comment on the cool breeze, or the sight of the awesome waves. Instead his eyes were riveted on the oil terminal as he pondered strategies to block NATO's shipment from the port in Karachi to land-locked Afghanistan. Haroon shared his thoughts with me every time he came to Karachi in 2008, when I was living in the city. He said:

> Dr Saab, the victory of Khurasan is near. I am certain that if the *mujahideen* succeed in severing the NATO supply lines from Pakistan by 2008, NATO will be left with no choice but to withdraw by 2009. And, if the supply line is cut by 2010, NATO will leave Afghanistan by 2011. This strategy is of critical importance in this war game.

NATO's claim of an alternative supply route through Central Asia is a joke. It is so long and complicated that the economy of the whole of Europe and the United States would collapse under the financial strain. The only other option is to move the NATO shipments to Iran. But if you study history, you will see that relations between the ancient Persian Empire and Roman Empire were strained. Similarly, in this battle, although Iran facilitated the US invasion of Afghanistan against the Taliban, it is still looking to defeat America and its NATO allies. I don't think that Iran would allow NATO any permanent route for its supplies through its territory.

Haroon saw the climax of the battle coming in 2012:

This is the time the Mahdi [the ultimate reformist leader] will make his presence felt. By all the reckonings and the estimates of Muslim scholars he has already been born. By 2012, he will come forward to command the Muslim forces in the Middle East and defeat the Western forces led by the Antichrist [Dajjal].

I used to spend hours walking with Haroon on the seashore in the evening, trying to understand the Al-Qaeda perspective on various issues. It was doubly perplexing for me that while the West doubted the loyalty of Pakistan Army in the War on Terror in Afghanistan, believing it to be hand in glove with the Taliban, the Taliban were repeatedly attacking Pakistan's armed forces, believing their loyalties were pro-West. Haroon was the perfect source of enlightenment on this, as not only was he a former officer of the Pakistan Army, he had also personally served under the command of several leading generals, including General Tariq Majeed (then chairman joint chiefs of the Staff Committee). Haroon said:

Their [the Pakistan army's] support to the Afghan Taliban is purely tactical. It does not come from any conviction. This kind of support to the insurgencies in neighboring countries is given by states for its nuisance value – and to gain influence in the region. The Pakistan Army also supports Laskhar-e-Taiba, but only as the means of waging a proxy war against India. India does the same with its fifth columnists in Pakistan. If the situation changes, the army will also change its policies on India. For instance, the ISI used to launch LeT men in Calcutta [India] for acts of sabotage. These men were always arrested. Some because of their long beards, some because of the Salafi rituals they practiced, and some because of the language they conversed in. Whenever they carried out an operation, they were found and arrested.

The Pakistani intelligence agencies wondered why ISI operations in India were always exposed while Indian proxy operations in Pakistan never came to light. The reason became clear to them later. The Indian saboteurs in Pakistan were rarely Indian. The Indian intelligence hired Pakistanis as their proxies. Pakistan decided do the same, and in 2007 and 2008 it used the Indian underworld to carry out bomb blasts in Delhi and other places. For the first time the Indian security agencies were clueless about the origin of the saboteurs. Now Pakistan does not need or want to use LeT any more.

"But if that is the case, what prevents Pakistan from completely dismantling LeT?" I asked. He answered:

They still require LeT for many reasons. First, after their U-turn following 9/11, Pakistan lost its Islamist allies one by one. LeT is their only ally in Pakistan. There is one major reason for this. The Pakistan army is culturally Punjabi. Approximately 60 percent of its strength comes from the rural areas of Punjab. LeT comes from the same background. LeT is from the Ahle-Hadith school of thought [the South Asian version of the Saudi Wahhabi school] and in this school of thought *khuruj* [revolt] is not allowed. In other words, LeT is a pro-establishment group. The Pakistan Army does not feel threatened by it.

Comparison between the various Muslim societies and the successes or the failures of local insurgency movements was Haroon's other favorite topic. "Dr Sahib, Islam is a universal message for all of mankind, but it does not ignore local themes, culture and traditions," he remarked when we discussed the philosophy of Michael Aflaq, the founder of Arab Baath Party, and how Islam was practiced by Saddam Hussain in both letter and spirit.

"But isn't against the basic spirit of Islam to paint this great religion in a narrow perspective of Arab nationalism, as did Michael Aflaq and Saddam Hussain?" I argued. He answered:

Dr Sahib, there is no denying the fact that Islam is culturally Arab, but I don't think that there is any harm if somebody supports the Islamic state on the basis of Arab nationalism. That happened in the time of Umar Bin Khattab [the second Muslim Caliph and the

Prophet Muhammad's companion], when he gained the support of some Iraqi Arab tribes on the basis of Arab nationalism during the war against the Iranian imperialism.

"Then what do you think of the Muslim Brotherhood which condemns Arab nationalism and the Baath ideology?" I asked. "I don't know enough about their perspectives, but I do believe that in wars for the protection of an Islamic state, nationalist themes can be used," Haroon replied.

I often confessed to Haroon that I could not understand the rationale of wars in which thousands of non-combatants are killed. His answer was:

Big causes demand big sacrifices. History witnesses that innocent people are often killed in wars and otherwise. In peace they are crushed by the tyrannical systems. Life is only for those who chose to play an active role on one side of the fence or the other. The rest are anyway caught in no-man's land.

Haroon is now in Adyala jail, Rawalpindi. The senior police officer who interrogated him and exchanged notes with me admitted he was impressed with him, and is at a loss to understand how Haroon got himself arrested for a crime like abduction for ransom. He quotes Haroon frequently and is proud he has had the chance to meet such a revolutionary in his lifetime. He wondered why Haroon's life is such an under-reported story.

Haroon continues to share his views on the need to defeat NATO forces in Afghanistan with his interrogators. Sometimes the loneliness and the emptiness of jail depress him, but his convictions bring him back to the world, and he lives for another day. His is another story of Al-Qaeda's *One Thousand and One Nights* tales which lead to the promised "End of Time" battles. Meanwhile his colleagues in Waziristan look forward to his coming back to the tribal theater of war. They are convinced that his ideas and presence would lead them to victory.

THE NEO-TALIBAN IN TALIBAN RANKS

The story of the Neo-Taliban began after 9/11 in Pakistan's tribal areas in the shape of secret organizations. It then went all the way through Pakistani cities to entice people like Haroon and Kashmiri into the Taliban fold through a massive restructuring process, and back to Afghanistan, where the central high point of Al-Qaeda's continuing struggle came with the war entering a new phase.

The United States and its allies have now opted for a troop surge aimed at withdrawal in 2011. This step was taken at a time when the Taliban were winning on nearly every front. Each passing day adds a chapter to their likely victory. According to Western think-tanks, over 80 percent of Afghanistan is already under Taliban control. Analysts, however, still see the troop surge as putting pressure on the Taliban to open negotiations with the occupation forces to leave Al-Qaeda and its closer affiliates besieged and at the mercy of US predator drone strikes and Special Forces operations.

Al-Qaeda's strategy in the next phase of war will be to counter these US moves. Al-Qaeda had in fact read the situation well before the US troop surge plans were announced. It had begun work on a counter-strategy to prevent the Taliban being lured to the negotiation table. This was the most sensitive part of Al-Qaeda's operation. It aimed at restoring power to the Taliban, who stood to lose all their territory in 2001 for having provided safe sanctuary to Al-Qaeda. The plan was a slow and subtle injection of Al-Qaeda's ideology into the Taliban ranks in a way that was designed not to cause fragmentation. Al-Qaeda did not need to reach all the way across to the Afghan Taliban for this. The Haqqani network lay right next to their bases in North Waziristan, where circumstances have naturally evolved to transform Talibanized society into an ideologically motivated, anti-establishment, global Jihadi movement. Al-Qaeda needed to put very little effort into stepping up this natural process of transformation.

THE HAQQANI NETWORK: THE TALIBAN'S REAL STRENGTH

Sirajuddin Haqqani is the son of the legendary Afghan commander Jalaluddin Haqqani. He is considered the most dangerous Afghan Taliban commander fighting NATO troops in Afghanistan. His network is responsible for some of the effective attacks against the occupation forces in Afghanistan.

I met Haqqani in April 2004 at his base in Dande Darpa Khail in North Waziristan. This was the first interview he had ever given to any correspondent (published as "Through the eyes of the Taliban," *Asia Times Online*, May 5, 2004). At that time Sirajuddin was thought of as no more than just a son of the legendary Jalaluddin. His mettle had not been tested in the battlefield as a commander. When I was granted an interview with him, he was sitting in a small room in front of Manbaul Uloom, an Islamic seminary founded by his father Jalaluddin Haqqani. The seminary was forcibly closed by the Pakistani authorities after the Taliban's defeat in Afghanistan in 2001. When I entered the room some youths sitting in the room quickly covered their faces, but I could see from their eyes and their foreheads they were neither local tribesmen nor Pashtuns. I was not surprised to discover they were Punjabis, as Punjabi fighters were known as the real strength of the Haqqani network.

Jalaluddin Haqqani was a graduate of Darul Uloom Haqqania, a religious seminary in Akora Khattak near Peshawar, but he relied largely on Punjabi fighters for his Jihadi ventures. Although he came from the Zadran tribe of Paktia, he drew his strength from Pakistani Jihadi organizations, especially Harkatul Mujahadeen and Harkat-ul Jihad-i-Islami.

Khost is the home town of former President Najeeb Ullah. In North Waziristan, all the credit for its fall to the *mujahideen* in 1991 is given to the Punjabi militants of the Harkatul Mujahadeen fighting under the command of Jalaluddin. The Punjabis led by Haqqani were the first to defeat the communist army in any urban center. At that time the Afghan tribesmen under the command of Haqqani were far fewer than their Pakistani counterparts.

After the fall of Taliban in late 2001, like all other Taliban commanders, Haqqani lost influence in Afghanistan. He had to migrate to North Waziristan to raise another army. Most of his Afghan followers disappeared into the Afghan fabric of society. In North Waziristan, the local tribesmen were organized under their own tribal commanders. Haqqani was thus left with no choice but to fall back, once again, on fighters from the Punjab to wage his war on NATO troops.

Sirajuddin Haqqani's allies, the Punjabi fighters (in Afghanistan all non-Pashtu-speaking Pakistanis are called Punjabis), had survived an ordeal in Pakistan after 9/11. The Jihadi outfits were banned after 9/11 under US pressure, and then after the attack on Musharraf's life in 2003 hundreds of Jihadis were rounded up and detained for several months without trial. Naturally that also influenced Sirajuddin Haqqani's attitude, and he gradually leaned towards anti-military thinking. From 2006 onwards he took a track different from the traditional Afghan Taliban. (Afghan Taliban commanders, like Sirajuddin Haqqani's father Jalaluddin, had always been close to Pakistan and the Arab countries.)

Although Jalaluddin Haqqani had been a favorite of the ISI during the Soviet invasion of Afghanistan, the situation changed dramatically from 2007 onwards. Earlier, the Al-Qaeda-led operation reached its climax in Pakistan, and in retaliation Pakistani security agencies conducted across-the-board crackdowns against militant organizations such as Jaish-e-Mohammad, Harkatul Mujahadeen, and Harkat-ul Jihad-i-Islami. Hundreds of their members were put on the wanted list and were left with no choice other than to seek refuge in North Waziristan. They made Jalaluddin Haqqani's base their home and the Jihad against NATO their mission. They brought an anti-military establishment mindset with them to North Waziristan.

From 2005 to 2007 the migration of Jihadis to North Waziristan was huge. Thousands of Punjabi Jihadis fled to the territory. Although most of them were connected to the Haqqanis' network, Al-Qaeda was the source of their inspiration, even before their arrival in North Waziristan. They had felt privileged to sit with Arab ideologues like Sheikh Essa, Abu Waleed Ansari, and Abu Yahya al-Libbi. They often invited them to their camps, where the Arab ideologues had frequent interactions with Sirajuddin Haqqani.

Interactions with the Arabs had a deep and penetrating influence on Sirajuddin, but this process came about so gradually that perhaps he himself was unaware of the spell they had cast. Jalaluddin fell ill in 2007 and was compelled to hand over his command to Sirajuddin. That was the turning point in the internal dynamics of the Haqqani network. Soon afterwards, Jalaluddin became completely bedridden. He was no longer in any position to give directions to Sirajuddin, who was then in his mid-thirties. Al-Qaeda commanders seized the opportunity and developed strategic ties with Jalaluddin's heir. His assault on Bagram in February 2007, for instance, was recognized as being guided by Abu Laith Al-Libi. This Arab ideologue made all his expertise available to Sirajuddin to carry out the attack. Subsequently, several other operations carried out by the Haqqani network in Ghazni, Khost, and Kabul were coordinated by Al-Qaeda. Within months the Haqqani network was considered the most effective Taliban group in Afghanistan.

His interaction and coordination with the Arab ideologues drew Sirajuddin deeper into the Al-Qaeda net. Pakistan's military operations in North Waziristan, and the CIA's repeated predator drone attacks on the Haqqani home in Dand-e-Darpa Khail in 2008 and 2009, added fuel to the fire. Several of his family members were killed during that period, and this wrecked Sirajuddin's connections with Pakistan's military establishment. Pakistan's military was blamed by the militants for feeding information to the CIA regarding their hideouts. Jalaluddin had always kept at a safe distance from the Al-Qaeda-influenced Pakistani militant groups, but from 2007 onwards, Sirajuddin felt his own interests might be better served were he to develop closer links with Al-Qaeda and its Pakistani associates. His plan was to rise to the position of the most important commander in the Afghan national resistance against NATO forces.

Sirajuddin's main handicap was the nature of relations between the Taliban and his father. Jalaluddin had been on his own during the Taliban-led Afghanistan resistance. For example, although Mullah Omar had appointed him his deputy and commander in chief for the spring offensive in 2006, the Kandahari clan of the Taliban, who came from south-west Afghanistan, fought independently of him. Commanders like the slain Mullah Dadullah kept coming to the two Waziristans to recruit local tribesmen to fight NATO in Afghanistan's Helmand province. This intrusion into Haqqani territory naturally upset Jalaluddin, but he did not utter a word in reproach. Nor, if the truth be told, was he in a position to. After all, he had never been a Taliban in the true sense of the word.

When the Taliban rose in the mid-1990s Jalaluddin was the first *mujahideen* leader to accept them. He pledged allegiance to the much younger Mullah Omar, who was then a little-known Taliban commander. Despite this, and notwithstanding that he was one of the most celebrated resistance figures in Afghanistan, Jalaluddin was not accorded any importance. Only the *Talibs* (students) were assigned important portfolios. After Jalaluddin passed on his command to him, Sirajuddin would have considered these background facts before diving into the waiting arms of Al-Qaeda. Still, his relations with Al-Qaeda were circumspect.

The NATO command in Kabul could see new developments taking place in the Haqqani network. They had been evaluating Sirajuddin's distancing from the Taliban command council, and saw him as an independent operator. They drew the wrong conclusion. In their media releases Sirajuddin was noted as a possible rival to Mullah Omar. This erroneous assessment came from little understanding of the crucial relations between Sirajuddin and Al-Qaeda. In fact, Sirajuddin had always been loyal to Mullah Omar. Al-Qaeda had approved of this as it wanted Sirajuddin to tighten his ties with the Taliban to ensure they did not deviate from Al-Qaeda's broader aims and strategies. Al-Qaeda also did not want him to be disloyal to Mullah Omar. They wanted this most important Taliban commander to sit tightly with the Taliban as their man, and ensure the Al-Qaeda agenda was kept on track. Sirajuddin's network was in a position to do this as it was the most influential Taliban-led group of the Afghan national resistance against NATO. Sirajuddin was seen to move out completely from his father's shadow.

During the Shiite–Sunni riots in Pakistan's Kurram Agency in 2007–08, Sirajuddin sent his men to support the Sunnis. He developed strong ties with the anti-Pakistan commander of TTP, Baitullah Mehsud. In 2009 when the Pakistani security forces arrested Sirajuddin's brother Naseeruddin, he was released only after Mahsud agreed to swap him with Pakistani soldiers he had captured.

Sirajuddin might not have put much effort into wondering how he had been pulled into the Al-Qaeda camp, but factually it had much to do with extraneous factors like his having to take into consideration the views of his Punjabi fighters, all of whom had turned anti-establishment because of the government crackdowns on them, on suspicion of their interaction with Al-Qaeda in North Waziristan. Then there was his father Jalaluddin's illness, and finally Al-Qaeda and its associates' unconditional support of him. In fact, so committed did Sirajuddin become to the Al-Qaeda cause that during Pakistan's military operation against the TTP (an anti-Pakistani government group) in 2009, he not only provided sanctuary, but also helped the militants fight the Pakistan Army.

FROM THE SHADOWS TO THE SHADOW ARMY

Sirajuddin Haqqani was the most important addition to Al-Qaeda's arsenal. This notwithstanding, the situation after spring offensive of 2006 changed so radically in favor of Al-Qaeda that it was in a position to raise its own army from Pakistan and Afghanistan to fight under the command of the Afghan Taliban flying the Al-Qaeda flag. There were multiple reasons for this ultra-radicalization of the Pakistani Taliban, which became a critical opening for Al-Qaeda. These included:

- the unnecessary oppression by the Pakistani military establishment of the Pakistani Jihadi cadre
- killings and arrests of senior Al-Qaeda members and the handing over of them to the United States to be detained in Guantanamo Bay prison camp

- the Iraq war
- the Israeli invasion of Lebanon in 2006.

With all of this added impetus, Al-Qaeda successfully managed to turn the Taliban insurgency into an ideological battle which gave birth to a new generation of Taliban fighters, the Neo-Taliban. The Neo-Taliban are Taliban in essence, but fight under the command of Mullah Omar and owe final allegiance to Al-Qaeda ideology and its goals. Commanders like Sirajuddin Haqqani were already established leaders who simply moved closer to Al-Qaeda, but there were not many other capable commanders of his stature visible in Pakistan's tribal areas. Al-Qaeda looked to find some to train as their regional commanders.

The Al-Qaeda focus was on the Hindu Kush mountains, where new developments were rapidly taking place and creating space for new leadership. This space was found in Pakistan's tribal areas of Bajaur and Mohmand, and the Afghan provinces of Kunar and Nuristan. All of these areas connect to the north-eastern Afghan province of Kapisa, a very long natural corridor which facilitates the passage of fighters from Pakistan's tribal areas and takes them to the doors of Kabul from the north-east. Immediately after the retreat of the Taliban from Afghanistan, the regions of Kunar and Nuristan in Afghanistan, and Mohmand and Bajaur in Pakistan's tribal area in the Hindu Kush mountains, were Al-Qaeda's weakest Taliban links. Warlords linked to the Jamaat-e-Islami Afghanistan of Ahmad Shah Masoud, and former commanders of the Hizb-i-Islami Afghanistan (Gulbaddin Hikmatyar group), who submitted to the will of the Karzai administration, were calling the shots in Afghanistan's Kunar and Nuristan provinces. An identical situation prevailed in the Bajaur and Mohmand Agencies, where the Pakistani administration was in control. A few influential pro-Taliban commanders like Dr Ismail and Moulvi Faqir Mohammad hid a dozen or so Al-Qaeda leaders, but in 2005–06 the Taliban could not move around openly in Bajaur and Mohmand. The will of the Pakistani state was simply too strong.

However, the militants began to flex their muscles near the Hindu Kush range in this period. During my visit to Pakistan's Mohmand Agency and Afghanistan's Kunar province to make a documentary for a Canadian television network, I met a Pakistani militant who had been previously associated with the LeT. His name was Sadiq. He provided the missing links of the circumstances under which Al-Qaeda was able to expand its influence in the region and raise its own leadership. "Three years ago, it was actually a dream, but now the circumstances have changed. Apart from North Waziristan and South Waziristan, the *mujahideen* moved very guardedly in the Bajaur and Mohmand Agencies, as they might have in Karachi or Lahore. We were afraid of somebody spying on us and being arrested," Sadiq admitted to me. (Sadiq has since left LeT and joined the Al-Qaeda camp to fight against the NATO forces.)

> We used to make secret trips to Afghanistan to conduct occasional raids. On the one side the Americans were after us, and on the other the Pakistani army was tracking us. We didn't want to fight the Pakistanis, as they are Muslims. We tried our best to avoid fighting them, and even now no more than 3 percent of the *mujahideen* are opposed to them. However, the Pakistanis did not think of us in the same the way we thought of them. They were cruel and even more ruthless with us than the Americans. We had a companion who had fought alongside us in Kashmir. His name was Umer, and he was deadly opposed to our fighting the Pakistani army. Whenever the military conducted operations against us, he used to desert, saying he could not and would not fight fellow Muslims. One day, however, he was picked up by the ISI. They hung him by one hand from a roof, and carved stars on his thighs with daggers. They humiliated him in many other ways. When he was released, it was thought he was a broken person. But he wasn't. He is now is one of the staunchest advocates of Jihad and a sworn enemy of the Pakistan Army.

"These sorts of incidents have brought the *mujahideen* into our camp. They now understand they were fooled into fighting the Jihad in Kashmir," said Sadiq, referring to Islamabad's sudden de-escalation of the fighting in the Kashmir Valley.

Sadiq said that his real revolutionary zeal came through al-Qaeda:

> [A senior al-Qaeda leader] Abu Marwan al-Suri was killed [in May 2006] by the Khasadar force [a tribal police] in Bajaur Agency. This is a force of peons. Had Marwan been killed by Pakistan's elite commando force, we would not have felt so humiliated. But to see a person like him killed by a third-rate force like the Khasadars was demeaning.
>
> Suri was traveling in bus when he was identified as an Arab and

was asked to step down. He took out his revolver and warned the Khasadars he was a Mujahid and did not want to kill fellow Muslims, so they should not obstruct his passage. The Khasadars laughed at this. You know Arabs. They do not try to escape. They fight until their last breath. But to avoid fighting fellow Muslims Suri sought escape and was killed.

His body was photographed and pictures of him dead were presented to the Americans. The people responsible for his killing received medals. Every Mujahid felt humiliated. Brother ... our blood is not so thin as to be played around with by third-rate persons. The *mujahideen* were furious. They rose from their hideouts. Marwan's death became an inspiration. The spilling of his blood became legend in Bajaur and his graveyard a holy site. Violent reaction swept through Bajaur and in a matter of days all of the Khasadars' posts were wiped out. The army began operations, but it was defeated too.

Our victories gathered all the tribes around us. You know our most important commander in Bajaur, Maulana Faqir Muhammad, was trained by the Pakistani Army against the Soviets [in the 1980s]. But after September 11 his brother was captured by the same army and he was beaten to death. In 2005 the Taliban were limited to South Waziristan and North Waziristan, and in Mohmand Agency there were only a few dozen of them, but now we number 18,000, thanks to the operations of the Pakistani Army.

Al-Qaeda was keeping a close watch on all of these developments. They had a good number of allies among the Pakistani tribesmen, but were looking for an Afghan to be elevated to the position of top commander – someone like Sirajuddin Haqqani – someone who could be the main representative of the Taliban resistance, but would conduct operations under the Al-Qaeda command. Not much later they found the man they wanted, and raised him in the Al-Qaeda camp. His detention by the ISI had turned him a bitter foe of the Pakistan Army. And he was not ready to buy the Afghan Taliban's policy of not fighting against the Pakistan armed forces. His name was Commander Qari Ziaur Rahman.

Ziaur Rahman was a shadowy figure who suddenly began to loom large in the region of Kunar-Nuristan (Afghanistan) and Mohmand-Bajaur (Pakistan) in mid-2008. He inflicted a significant defeat on the NATO forces in Nuristan in November 2009, compelling them to evacuate their bases. Earlier, in 2008, NATO and the

Pakistan Army officials had assessed Ziaur Rahman as no more than a second-string Taliban leader, but he had stealthily been elevated by Al-Qaeda to a standing of influence.

When I met him in the Afghan Kunar Valley in May 2008, he was barely known. He was not the offspring of any legendary *mujahideen* commander, as might have been expected, but the son of a simple yet respected cleric named Maulana Dilbar. His ties were not with the ISI, but with Osama bin Laden. Ziaur Rahman's father had taught bin Laden the lessons from the *Hadiath* (the sayings of the Prophet Muhammad). In his mid-thirties, Ziaur Rahman had been raised in the camps of the Arab militants. They instilled in him the passion to fight against the United States – not only in Afghanistan, but worldwide. Ziaur did not receive his command as any hereditary right. He had to prove himself on the battlefield. He did this by taking on US troops in Kunar and Nuristan. He was the first to mount operations against the United States in the Korangal Valley district of Kunar, and he engineered the second-biggest encounter ever in Nuristan. Following a chase by the NATO forces, he entered Pakistan's Bajaur tribal areas and was arrested by the Pakistani Army, but released soon after in a prisoner exchange deal with captured Pakistani soldiers.

When I met him in May 2008 for an interview I could see he had strong ties with Al-Qaeda. That is why I confidently predicted in *Asia Times Online* (May 23, 2008) that "Ziaur is widely tipped to become one of the most important Taliban commanders in the whole region." Within a few months Operation Lion Heart was launched in the Kunar Valley in Afghanistan, and Operation *Sher Dil* (the Urdu translation of Lion Heart) in the Pakistani tribal areas of Mohmand and Bajaur against the Taliban and Al-Qaeda. Ziaur Rahman emerged as the leading commander. The Pakistan Army spotted him as the commander-in-chief of all the Taliban and Al-Qaeda groups in the eastern Hindu Kush.

He was mercurial. Unlike other Taliban he did not have any regard or sympathy for the Pakistan Army. In September 2008, Pakistani security forces claimed that Ziaur Rahman led hundreds of fighters including Chechen, Arabs, and Afghans from Kunar, and attacked the Pakistan Army positions in Mohmand Agency. In November 2009, the Taliban under his command carried out relentless attacks on US forces and compelled them to leave their bases in the Afghan province of Nuristan. And soon NATO recognized Ziaur Rahman as one of the most dangerous enemy commanders in south-east Afghanistan.

Al-Qaeda required figures like Ziaur Rahman to remain among the Taliban to lead the local resistance movements and operate covertly under the Al-Qaeda command and control system. However, throughout this time, Al-Qaeda strategists had been thinking along different lines. Between 2006 and 2007 they decided to convert this new leadership into an organized background force. Known Taliban leaders and commanders like Mullah Dadullah (died 2006) and Akhtar Osmani (killed 2007) were to remain in the foreground as bait for the Western coalition to speculate over how they might eliminate them. Meantime, the real war would continue to be fought by a dark, shadowy force from behind the scenes about which NATO and its allies would know nothing.

I had interacted with several Taliban commanders in Helmand before, but Ziaur Rahman was a different breed. Al-Qaeda had completely transformed him. He was no longer just a fierce tribal fighter, but a committed Al-Qaeda ideologue. When I met him at his base in Kunar, he hosted a lavish meal for me. He arrived at the base along with several of his men. The men were armed with AK-47 guns and rocket-propelled grenades (RPG). They were Afghans and Pakistanis. Lunch was served, and all sat on the floor around him and began to eat – all, that is, except Ziaur Rahman. "I don't take meals during the afternoon. It brings a forgetfulness of prayers and a weakening of relations with Allah," he said in explanation. His grasp of Urdu was basic, but he was fluent in Arabic. He had learned the language from the Arabs in the Kunar Valley, where they had established an educational center during the Taliban rule in Afghanistan. Ziaur Rahman comes from the Salafi school of thought, and it was he who was responsible for the segregation of command along tribal lines being broken. Earlier, Pakistani tribal members would only join a commander from their own tribe, just like in all the other parts of Pakistan's tribal areas and in Afghanistan. Under Ziaur Rahman these lines were crossed. "We are all one, all the faithful are brothers, whether we come from the east or from the west; whether we are Arab or Pakistani. We are one for all and all for one," he pronounced dramatically.

The dynamics of the region, which had been known for its pro-establishment leanings, were changed. The region had turned against the state of Pakistan and become one of the most powerful bases of Al-Qaeda, able to produce generation after generation like Ziaur Rahman, committed to Al-Qaeda above anything or anybody else. Ziaur Rahman's emergence in the eastern Hindu Kush region turned everything upside down. No longer were the Pakistani tribal areas of Bajaur and Mohmand in the hands of the Pakistani establishment or in the hands of Pakistan-friendly Taliban commanders. They were under Al-Qaeda.

The joint NATO–Pakistan military operation, Operation Lion Heart, was launched in November 2008 to clear these new militants out of the eastern Hindu Kush. NATO operated against them in the Afghan provinces of Kunar and Nuristan, and the Pakistan Army fought them in the Pakistani tribal areas of Mohmand and Bajaur. The operation continued for months. Victory was claimed by the NATO and Pakistan armed forces, but in November 2009, the militants emerged in the region again. They carried out devastating attacks on US forces border posts, killing at least nine US soldiers and dozens of Afghan National Army servicemen, and abducting several of the latter. In the last week of November 2009 militants under the command of Ziaur Rahman seized US bases in Nuristan and invited international television channels to witness their victory. In the Pakistani Mohmand and Bajaur areas, militants loyal to Ziaur Rahman resurfaced again and carried out more deadly attacks against Pakistan's security personnel, forcing them to leave the border villages. The Hindu Kush was under the control of Al-Qaeda when the snow fell in December 2009. However, it remained an unending struggle, and became the reason for another military operation on the both sides of the Durand Line all through the eastern Hindu Kush.

AL-QAEDA'S SOUL IN A NEW BODY: LASKHAR AL ZIL

A senior US intelligence official told ABCNews.com in December 2009 that approximately 100 Al-Qaeda members were left in Afghanistan. This was another example of the US establishment's failure to grasp the real situation. When President Barack Obama decided to send an additional 30,000 soldiers to Afghanistan, his decision was made in terms of subtractions from and additions to Al-Qaeda's numerical strength. Washington missed out on the story of Al-Qaeda's evolution from the period of 2002 to 2009, when it broadened its perspective to bring in new strategies. This saw the end of narrow targets like the 2002 Bali bombing, and it moved on to the higher level of cutting off the Western coalition's supply lines, not only in Afghanistan, but worldwide.

In the picture that emerged with the events of 2007–08 Al-Qaeda went far ahead of its 9/11 mindset and set up a game which did not simply rotate around its ideology. It went well past physical

structures. This is where Al-Qaeda breathed its soul into a new generation of fighters with a new name: the Laskhar al-Zil (or the Shadow
Army). Instead of the basic resistance pattern it had pursued since its
formation through the mid-2000s, Al-Qaeda now made preparation
for a global war through this Shadow Army. Al-Qaeda had developed
several militant structures in Pakistan's tribal areas, such as Jundullah,
but the extent of Al-Qaeda's reach went beyond this with the raising
of the Shadow Army. Local militant structures such as the TTP were
raised to facilitate the passage of Al-Qaeda operations in Pakistan's
tribal areas, Pakistani cities, and Afghanistan. The Shadow Army was
a manifestation of the new Al-Qaeda added to the old.

Al-Qaeda's aims and objectives throughout the mid-1990s focused
on the instigation of war between the West and the Muslim world.
They were are reflected by events like the African bombing attack
on USS Cole in Yemen, and the 9/11 attack on the US mainland. By
mid-2000, however, Al-Qaeda widened the canvas to set up a defeat
for the West. Here the debate begins about why Al-Qaeda, with its
already developed structures like the TTP, did not simply lump them
into an organization and work for a separate dispensation such as
the Laskhar al-Zil. From 2002 onwards Al-Qaeda had put down an
effective networking system to create organizations to perpetuate
its cause in South Asia. It was through this that the TTP had come
into existence. The arrangements were loose, and designed to force
a crisis in South Asia through which Al-Qaeda could prevent a
complete breakdown of its organization and its resources when they
came under attack by the United States and its ally, Pakistan.

The forerunners and operators of those organizations were local
tribesmen and Pakistanis from the plains. But Al-Qaeda's influence
over organizations like the TTP was slanted. Those organizations
were often involved in activities the Al-Qaeda leadership abhorred,
but they were tolerated under the law of necessity, with Al-Qaeda
having to turn a blind eye to such activities. This was a transitional
period for Al-Qaeda in which it was gaining time and gathering
strength, and at the same time collecting adherents to turn into
"blood brothers," believing that under a dialectical process matters
would eventually gravitate towards it.

In the South Asian theater of war, the situation compelled the
Al-Qaeda leadership in the early 2000s and after 9/11 to stay silent
over the Taliban brand of Islam in Afghanistan. This opposed the
modern education system and imposed laws, from the compulsory
growing of beards for men, to the TTP attacking saloons and
bombing the innocent civilian population. The Al-Qaeda leadership

were cognizant of the fact that such actions would eventually turn the local population against both it and the Taliban, but they also appreciated that the Afghan Taliban and the Pakistani Taliban were the only people on earth who would provide them with shelter. They knew that if they interfered in local affairs they would lose the Taliban's support altogether. So Al-Qaeda compromised to accommodate local customs and thereby keep a hold over the local militant groups, but in a very subtle way they were working at moving to a point where they would no longer be dependent on others and instead would have a direct control over affairs.

Al-Qaeda steadily reared a new generation of commanders committed to its ideology, and succeeded in cultivating people like Sirajuddin Haqqani and Ziaur Rahman. One task remained, however, and that was to preserve Al-Qaeda's soul and transform it to a new body for Al-Qaeda's mission to move the struggle up a level. The task of the preservation of Al-Qaeda's soul and its transformation under a new dispensation was delicate and complex.

Al-Qaeda's ultimate aim was to establish an Islamic system under a Caliphate, but it was not an Islamic enforcement movement. Al-Qaeda was a resistance movement against Western hegemony that expected Islamic movements and the Muslim liberation movements around the world to forge a common front instead of fighting independently. This was the basic disagreement between Al-Qaeda and the Muslim Brotherhood. Al-Qaeda's al-Zawahiri believed that until Western influence was wiped out from the Muslim world and the institutions of Muslim countries were rid of this influence, the *Shariah* would never prevail.

Al-Zawahiri drew his inspiration from the founder of the Muslim Brotherhood, Hasan Al-Banna (assassinated in 1949) who had promoted Islamic values in Egypt in 1930s and 1940s, but with the particular perspective of resistance against British colonialism. Al-Zawahiri was also inspired by another Muslim Brotherhood ideologue, Syed Qutb (also slain: he was hanged in 1966), who saw Western society as *Jahilliya* (the state of ignorance of guidance from God) and demanded a complete disconnect with the traits and behavior of Western society for an Islamic revolution to bring forward Islamists as rulers.

Al-Qaeda often cites the example of Saudi Arabia, where Islamic laws are enforced, but the country is still a slave to Western designs and interests. Al-Qaeda aimed at the revival of a resistance movement across the Muslim world against Western hegemony, and in the process the negation of organizations like the Jamaat-e-

Islami Pakistan, the Muslim Brotherhood in the Middle East, and the Islamic Court Union in Somalia, as well as the Hezbul Islami Al-Iraqi, since although these organizations were the so-called flag bearers of Islam, they were, in fact, major forces maintaining the status quo. They survived as a result of a compromise with state institutions and forces working as Western proxies in the Muslim world to safeguard Western interests in Muslim countries. Similarly, Al-Qaeda feels that armies in so-called Muslim countries are there to defend Western interests, and it brands the institution of armies in the Muslim world as the most lethal Western tool against Islamization. Hamas and the Islamic Jihad are similarly categorized as they go along with the arrangements that come under international laws interpreted by the West. Al-Qaeda strives to break the West's hold over Muslim armed forces and West's domination over world politics and trade.

Before 9/11 Al-Qaeda did raise a generation like Khalid Sheikh Mohammad, who was master strategist on sabotage and terror activities, but it did not have any person with the experience to operate high-profile insurgencies. Al-Qaeda had allies like Gulbaddin Hikmatyar, but they had independent policies and thinking. It was possible that these allies would temporarily endorse Al-Qaeda's cause and operations, but there was always the risk they would choose a solo flight at a critical juncture.

Al-Qaeda was looking for a person who was a master of guerrilla warfare with a global perspective, someone able to think over and above his own personal interests. Once again a crisis in the Kashmiri militants' camp provided it with an opportunity to benefit and to breathe its soul into a new order. This came with the attack on the former Pakistani President Musharraf in late 2003, which resulted in a massive crackdown on the militants fighting for the right for self-determination of Indian Kashmir. During the course of investigations, any shred of doubt about a person was enough to nail anybody connected with Jihadi circles, no matter how well connected he was with Pakistan's military establishment. The supreme commander of Jaish-e-Mohammad, Abdullah Shah Mazhar, was one of the people picked by the ISI when it found a person by the name of Asif Chotu financing the attack. Asif had once been a member of Jaish-e-Mohammad. He later joined Al-Qaeda. Abdullah Shah Mazhar gave me this account of his days in detention:

I was picked up from Karachi and taken in a vehicle. The last building I saw was the Sultan Mosque in the Defense Housing

Authority. After that I was blindfolded and taken to a bungalow. I was offered good food and treated with all good manners. I was asked few questions about Asif and how much I knew of him, and my possible involvement in attacking General Musharraf. I told them categorically that although Asif and I had studied together in a *madrassa*, I knew nothing of his activities, and nor was I involved in his purported plot to assassinate General Musharraf. The military officer told me that I had three days to think, after which he would hand me over to people who would not be nice to me. My answer remained the same: I had no idea what Asif Chotu had been up to.

Abdullah said that in next three days he was shifted to another location which was a military barracks:

Nobody came to see me except for a person who used to give me food and water. Then one day I was taken to the airport and to another city, possibly Lahore. There I was not asked a single question. They simply hanged me from the roof as a butcher hangs a chicken before slaughter – my hands and legs were tied together with a rope and I was strung up to a roof. Each muscle and bone of the body cried with pain. After an hour they pulled me down and then took off my *shalwar* (Pakistani trousers) and beat me on my hips with a thin cane. Each hit of the cane ripped off my skin. Throughout this time nobody spoke to me. When I was near unconscious, I was shifted to a small cell. After a few hours a man came, slid the small window in the door open, and asked me to give him my hand. I gave my hand and he put some ointment into it and told me to spread the ointment over my wounds.

Abdullah said that after this there was a brief interrogation session, then he was left in isolation. He was given a chamber pot to use as a toilet. After six months he was declared innocent. A brigadier came to him and tendered his apology for the harsh treatment. He offered monetary compensation, which Abdullah refused with thanks. Abdullah then returned to Karachi and became engaged in routine work, without any thought of revenge. But there were other people like Ibne Amin (real name Bin Yameen) from Swat who were detained in the same detention cells and refused to forget the vicious treatment meted out to them. Ibne Amin later became the most influential Taliban commander in the Swat Valley.

Another person, who, unlike Mazhar, adopted the path of defiance against the state of Pakistan was Commander Muhammad Ilyas Kashmiri. His name still terrifies the Indian military establishment. Among the guerrilla commanders of today's world nobody has attained the type of success Kashmiri had as a field commander. His track record and his complete submission to Al-Qaeda impressed the Al-Qaeda leaders. He was quickly included in Al-Qaeda's *Shura* and later given command of Al-Qaeda's operations. This was Al-Qaeda's turning point. Al-Qaeda was now able to operate independently. It gathered together commanders like Qari Ziaur Rahman and Sirajuddin Haqqani, and its soul shifted into a new organization, Laskhar al-Zil. Its best brains, men like Haroon and Ziaur Rahman, were members of Laskhar al-Zil.

This was the beginning for the next phase of war in Afghanistan, for which the Western coalition forces were prepared and ready to send thousands of fresh soldiers. This was the phase in which India was preparing to support the Western coalition in Afghanistan. It was also the phase when it was intended that, under immense pressure from the West, Pakistan would wage an all-out war against the militants.

Thus begins another story from the Al-Qaeda *One Thousand and One Nights* tales. In this phase, although Afghanistan remained the central front, Al-Qaeda decided to plan its revival in Iraq and open up new fronts to conclusively engage Western resources. As in the earlier strategy it had successfully applied in Pakistan of taking advantage of a situation and splitting the Islamists to bring them into its cadre, Al-Qaeda now gathered former officers from the Iraqi Republican Guard, together with Islamists from Yemen and Somalia, to march towards its new goal.

The initial purpose of Laskhar al-Zil was to provide support through expertise to various Taliban factions in Pakistan and Afghanistan against NATO and Pakistan's armed forces. In 2008 and 2009 Laskhar al-Zil played a critical role in the Taliban's successes in south-east Afghanistan and Swat in Pakistan. However, later on it was geared to move towards the broader Al-Qaeda aim, which was to handle the war zones of Afghanistan and the Middle East in keeping with its ideology and strategies. In this new set-up, people like Ziaur Rahman and Haroon were no longer required to look to the Taliban for coordination. Through Laskhar al-Zil they could devise independent strategies, which would also eventually benefit the Taliban against NATO.

The formation of Laskhar al-Zil was the step to take Al-Qaeda's program ahead. Al-Qaeda's step forward was intended to gather under one umbrella all of the Muslim guerrilla outfits and strategic experts previously working separately for the Islamist cause, and transform them into "blood brothers." Al-Qaeda's ultimate aim is to control the dynamics of all the local Muslim armed resistance movements, including the Taliban, Iraqi and Palestinian resistance, and create an environment in which local agendas are surrendered to synchronize with Al-Qaeda policies. At the same time, Al-Qaeda also aims to put pressure on countries like Pakistan, Saudi Arabia, Egypt, and Jordan through Laskhar al-Zil to change their pro-US stance.

Still completely in the dark, the Obama administration declared Afghanistan its primary focus in 2009 and announced a surge of 30,000 additional troops in this theater of war. The United States also appealed to its European allies for more troops to eliminate the Taliban and Al-Qaeda. While the Obama administration was worked to implement its new policies, Al-Qaeda explored new areas to confront NATO, and went on to the new destinations of Yemen and Somalia to counter the United States through "shadow strategies."

AL-QAEDA'S BLOOD BROTHERS SAGA: SOMALIA AND YEMEN

A message posted on http://www.alqimmah.net/ says:

> May God protect the beloved Shaykh Abu Yahya al-Libbi who advised his brothers in Somalia to invade by land and sea. The spoils of war from the sea are legitimate and are divided in the same way as bounty from the land. The spoils from the sea, in our time, are even greater and more blessed and worth invading for. This is because what might be captured from one infidel ship can be much more than the spoils obtained by dozens of land raids. Ships have increased in size and some of them are as large as a small village. They all carry valuable and expensive cargos that might benefit the people. Some infidels are ready to pay many millions as a ransom in order to get their ships back. I believe that those who deserve and need these spoils the most are the *mujahideen*. Many of them weep in sadness because they cannot find money to spend.

This is Al-Qaeda's justification for its Somalia operation. Al-Qaeda's existence in Somalia was weak until 2004, but after it had applied the same methods it had learned from its experiences in Pakistan's tribal areas – transformation of indigenous Islamists into Al-Qaeda "blood brothers," without mobilizing its own human or material resources – it succeeded in gaining control of Somalia. This put even more pressure on the Western coalition fighting in Afghanistan against the Taliban and Al-Qaeda, as it severed a very important sea route from Europe to Asia.

The peculiar circumstances in Somalia during 2006 provided Al-Qaeda with plenty of room to implement its agenda. These included the emergence of the Islamic Court Union (ICU) – a regime identical to the Taliban regime in Afghanistan – its fall within six months, and subsequent chaos and war with Ethiopia. In fact, Al-Qaeda mobilized Laskhar al-Zil in 2006–07, soon after the emergence of the ICU, to establish a branch in Somalia. As soon as Somalia had plunged into chaos after the fall of the ICU government in late 2006, Laskhar al-Zil's members, Kashmiri and the Al-Qaeda leader in Waziristan, Saleh Somali (killed in 2009), orchestrated the formation of Harkatul Shabaab to spread further chaos. Al-Qaeda made sure the several hundred youths whom it funded and organized under the name of Harkatul Shabaab would work exclusively on marine operations near Somalia. The purpose, as mentioned earlier, was to cut off the Western trade arteries going from Europe to Asia.

In the same year Al-Qaeda regrouped itself in Yemen. Laskhar al-Zil was once again in charge of the regrouping operations. Under Laskhar-al-Zil, Al-Qaeda pooled militants from various countries, including Iraq and Saudi Arabia, to help its revival in Yemen. Yemen is an exceptionally important land for the broader aims of Al-Qaeda as it is the strategic backyard for the whole Arab world. Al-Qaeda needs it to control the liberation movements of Palestine and Iraq. It intends to apply the same approach it did in Pakistan, Saudi Arabia, Jordan, and Egypt: to neutralize their support for the United States in the Middle East, and to mend its broken networks in those countries.

The actual reason for wanting control over Yemen and Somalia, however, is again connected to Al-Qaeda's war in Afghanistan. On June 12, the *New York Times* quoted US officials as saying that Al-Qaida operatives were moving from Pakistan to Somalia and Yemen in what Washington feared was a systematic redeployment to exploit the chaos in the Red Sea states. This was a true reportage of Al-Qaeda playing for major strategic gains. Somalia and Yemen straddle the Bab el-Mandeb Strait at the southern end of the Red

Sea, a key oil supply route between the Gulf and the West. The scourge of Somali pirates preying on shipping in the Gulf of Aden underlines the growing concerns for the region.

"Yemen is strategically important, not only for Saudi Arabia, but for the world, because it is the only country on the Arabian peninsula from which oil can reach the open seas without passing through a narrow strait – either the Strait of Hormuz or the Suez Canal," Mai Yamani, a Saudi analyst who is a visiting scholar at the Carnegie Middle East Center in Beirut, wrote to United Press International. "To endanger this passage is to endanger the world economy's energy lifeline," she added. This was actually a re-run of Al-Qaeda's 2007–08 strategy to cut off NATO's supply line through Pakistan to Afghanistan for a victory in Afghanistan. In the eye of storm in the Middle East, Al-Qaeda's focus is the West's defeat in Afghanistan.

Geographically speaking, Yemen is identical to the tribal belt situated between Afghanistan and Pakistan at the heart of the Arab world. Politically, very much like the Pakistani tribal areas, the local tribes actively participated in the Afghan Jihad in the 1980s. Therefore, they allowed Al-Qaeda room for its new Middle Eastern operations. Laskhar al-Zil was required to send its expert teams to again train the *Ibnul Balad* on strategy. The atmosphere is ready for conflict engagement.

Al-Qaeda's core operations before 9/11 emanated from Yemen. The bombing of USS *Cole* in October 2000, logistical preparations for the "Black Hawk Down" operation, the killing of US soldiers in Somalia in 1993, the attacks on Jewish properties in Mombasa, Kenya in 2002, and the Al-Qaeda 2003 attacks against Saudi targets, were all conducted from Yemen.

Al-Qaeda took five years to reach the turning point in Afghanistan and Pakistani tribal areas, but the Al-Qaeda leadership was convinced that its Yemen and Somalia operations would take only a year or two to reach fruition. The immediate dividends of those operations would be obtained in Afghanistan, where maintaining the presence of Western troops would be difficult when the entire region came under siege both politically and militarily. With their supply lines cut, they would be completely choked from the Red Sea zone. Defeat for the West would thus become inevitable. Al-Qaeda leaders in Pakistan's tribal areas believe there will be rapid development in this direction by 2012. They are convinced the theater of war will be ready in the Middle East for orchestrating the "End of Time" battles by then. In the meantime, under the traditional black flag with the inscription of the *Kalma* (the first word of faith) the downtrodden Afghans, the Arab–Afghans, and Central Asian Muslim tribes would emerge through the mountain passes to announce a most unexpected victory. Then they would start the new journey of their struggle to the Balad Al-Sham (Syria, Iraq, Lebanon, and Palestine) under the command of the promised messiah, Al-Mahdi, for a final showdown against the Western forces, for the defeat of the anti-Christ and for the revival of a global Muslim Caliphate.

4

TAKFEER AND *KHURUJ*: AN IDEOLOGICAL THESIS FOR THE SEPARATION OF ISLAMISTS AND STATES

Do Muslim ruling elites whose external policies support a non-Muslim government against another Muslim state remain Muslim according to Islamic tenets? Or are they expelled from Islam? Can an army comprising Muslim soldiers but committing atrocities against fellow Muslims who are fighting a war against an invasion by a non-Muslim army be called Muslim? Do Muslim masses who deny the Muslim political order of a Caliphate and instead follow Western liberal democracy, monarchy, socialism, or any other human-made political systems remain Muslim? Or, after adopting any such non-Islamic political system, are they driven out of the Islamic faith? Can Muslim individuals or Muslim masses who adopt a Western lifestyle giving up Muslim rituals still be called Muslim, or are they non-Muslim?

There have been many publications over the 20 years in which these questions have been raised and discussed at length. The conclusion arrived at by one strain of this debate is that barring small clusters in Muslim societies, the majority of the people who call themselves Muslims have in fact given up Islam. This has not come from purely academic debate, or sectarian discussion of a particular clerical order, but is factually the basis of Al-Qaeda's ideology which today paradoxically aims at the polarization of society in the Muslim world and is strategizing its future struggle in line with that.

The continuing debate and the conclusions reached spring from the rediscovery of a thought process drawn from classical Islamic academic work on the situations in which the Muslim world has

124

found itself in the post-Caliphate era. But what brought the matter to a head was the little publicized siege of the Grand Mosque of Mecca in 1979, when a small band of Muslims briefly gained control of the commanding mosque to instigate a rebellion against the Saudi regime. The revolt was brutally crushed by the Saudi Arabian monarchy, but it fired the imagination of many a Muslim youth who had gone to fight the Soviet invasion of Afghanistan. While fighting the war against the "godless" Soviets in Afghanistan, their understanding of the contemporary world sharpened, and their struggle to revive the Muslim Caliphate intensified, drawing inspiration from the 1979 Mecca siege.

Al-Qaeda ideologues mark this siege as the first true *khuruj* (rising against a Muslim ruler of un-Islamic governance) in the twentieth century. Muslim youths drawn into Afghanistan had already began working on procedures to change the dynamics of the Muslim world through reading books written by classical Muslim jurists, as well as modern Muslin academics, and the Mecca siege spurred them on.

After the withdrawal of Soviet Russia from Afghanistan, these young militants who had fought in Afghanistan, laid the foundations for the Al-Qaedatul Jihad, a global Muslim resistance movement for the liberation of all Muslim-occupied lands from Western presence and/or influence, for the revival of the Muslim Caliphate. However, they realized that before the West could be confronted effectively there was need to ignite controversy over whether contemporary Muslim states should be recognized as Islamic in their collective thinking and practices. This was the beginning of Al-Qaeda's maneuvers to polarize the Muslim world and then restructure Islamic society under the Al-Qaeda umbrella after gaining control of the resources available to ensure their rise to the helm of affairs in the Muslim world. Al-Qaeda anticipated three possible results emerging from this ideological spin:

- Pressure on the ruling Muslim elite, Muslim armies, and the Muslim masses to break their alliance with the West and support the Islamists' cause of a global struggle for the freedom of occupied Muslim lands and establishment of a Global Caliphate.
- Muslim societies so polarized that their governments' support for Western forces against Muslim resistance movements would weaken and ultimately become inconsequential.
- Islamist elements of society emerging victorious and launching a direct confrontation against the West's hegemony over the

world order for the liberation of Muslim territories through the establishment of a global Muslim political order under a Caliphate.

Any one of the above mentioned situations was acceptable to Al-Qaeda. Al-Qaeda sought to bring the contradictions between Muslim states and societies, and the differences in their approach to international affairs, under a single dialectic for a common pattern of struggle, but in fact this dialectical process had emerged as the natural consequence of situations which had developed in the post-Caliphate era.

The institution of the Muslim Caliphate after 661 AD (when the fourth Caliph, Ali Bin Abu Talib, was assassinated and the Caliphate became controversial) was symbolic rather than a model of righteousness. Yet until the last Ottoman Caliph, it had united Muslims as the vanguard for their collective interests, especially for the defense of Muslim lands. On the demise of the Ottoman Caliphate, however, the majority of Muslim states were conquered by Western powers, and even after they had been liberated, they followed Western models of governance with their foreign and defense policies subservient and aligned to Western interests.

Although most Arabs welcomed the end of the Ottoman Caliphate because of its strong Turkish, rather than Arab, identity, the single largest population of the Muslim world in British India took exception to the Caliphate's demise. In that period Dr Muhammad Iqbal was one of the few who aroused feelings through his poetry to remind Muslims they were one nation and spelled out resistance against foreign occupation forces through Jihad. Iqbal also voiced opposition to a Western form of democracy, even for the modern Muslim state.

Islamic movements such as the Muslim Brotherhood in the Middle East and Jamaat-e-Islami in South Asia, in the 1920s and 1930s respectively, endorsed Iqbal's message. Thus when several Muslim majority states were carved out subsequent to the Ottoman Caliphate, questions relating to their Islamic identity were raised, albeit on a milder note than Al-Qaeda's with heresy decrees not easily issued.

The founder of Jamaat-e-Islami, Syed Abul Ala Maududi, one of the most important Muslim ideologues of the Islamic movements in the world at the time, ruled that:

If an Islamic society consciously resolves not to accept the Sharia, and decides to enact its own constitution and laws or borrows them from any other source in disregard of the Sharia, such a society breaks its contract with God and forfeits its right to be called "Islamic."

(Islamic Law and its Introduction)

Ideologues of Islamic movements like Maududi and Syed Qutb stated unambiguously that Islamic laws should be enforced in absolute form in Muslim societies, yet their approach was not as direct, harsh, or as frontal as began after the Mecca siege in 1979. Before this, the issues facing Islamic movements were the revival of the Muslim political order with a Caliphate, the imposition of Islamic laws, and the liberation of Muslim territories from foreign occupation. But the 1970s Egypt–Israeli peace agreement and the subsequent suppression of Palestinians in Jordan and Egypt shook the Muslim world. Resentment grew as several Muslim countries forged diplomatic ties with Israel and suppressed Muslim resistance groups, especially after Saudi Arabia struck a defense agreement with the United States in 1990 and invited US forces into the country. The Saudi government then rounded up all the Muslim scholars who stood in opposition to this. The climax of the controversy came with the US invasion in 2001 of the Islamic Emirates of Afghanistan, which is recognized by a majority of Muslim scholars as an Islamic state. The US invasion of Afghanistan was approved by many Muslim countries including Afghanistan's neighbor, Pakistan. The United States next invaded Iraq in 2003, and was supported by Muslim countries like Saudi Arabia, Qatar, and Kuwait, which further aggravated the situation.

Al-Qaeda never considered Juhayman ibn Sayf al Otaibi, the leader of famous siege of Mecca on November 20, 1979, as an ideologue or a leader. Neither did they approve of Muhammad bin abd Allah al-Qahtani, whom Juhayman declared as al-Mahdi, as the real al-Mahdi, or the redeemer of Islam. However, this almost forgotten twentieth-century siege is accepted by the Al-Qaeda leadership as the event that fired the imagination of Islamists everywhere and revived the long quiescent Islamic tenet of *khuruj* (revolt against a deviant Muslim ruler). Hussein bin Ali, the grandson of the holy Prophet, launched the first *khuruj* against the Umayyad ruler Yazid Bin Mauvya after Yazid took over the Caliphate under a hereditary arrangement, against the will of the majority of Muslims. The *khuruj* continued throughout the periods of the Umayyad and Abbasid Caliphates, but failed to remove the governments.

Al-Qaeda examined a strategy for the breaking of ties between the

West and the ruling Muslim elite in the modern day, and organized a powerful Muslim backlash against Western culture, civilization, and the West's influence in the Muslim world. Although Juhayman's *khuruj* was suppressed by the Saudi regime (with the help of French commandos), this first day of the fourteenth century of the Islamic calendar marked the revolt as a unique event which left an indelible imprint on the minds of Muslim militants and reminded them that Muslim regimes in the post-Ottoman Caliphate era were the first line of defense of Western interests, and therefore were to be eradicated.

The literature prepared for the revolt against the Saudi regime thus became the basis of Al-Qaeda's analysis of the contemporary Muslim world and its relations with the West, and Al-Qaeda subsequently developed a dialectical process which would ultimately create the circumstances required for the "End of Time" battles.

The siege, in fact, came at a critical juncture. This was the period when the writings of Muslim ideologues had inspired Islamic movements to rear a new generation of young Muslim radicals divorced from the prevalent orders in nearly every Muslim majority state. These radicals read Syed Qutb in the Middle East, Syed Abul Ala Maududi in South Asia, and Dr Ali Shariati in Shiite majority Iran, and although they appeared divided on the micro issue of jurisprudence (Shiite, Sunni, and Salafi and Sufi Islam), neither the ideologues nor their adherents differed on the need for a united Muslim world.

For instance, Syed Qutb was an Egyptian but was impressed by Syed Abul Ala Maududi, a South Asian, and his writings reflect a strong impression of Maududi's analysis written in the 1930s and 1940s. Similarly Dr Ali Shariati, a Shiite from Iran, drew inspiration from Syed Qutb's work, as well as from the Indian Sunni Muslim Dr Muhammad Iqbal's poetry.

At the crossroads of the new Islamic century, these half-century-long ideological struggles fused into the powerful events in the twentieth century, which actually turned the historical course and jolted the fundamental dynamics of Muslim majority states and their foreign policies.

The siege of Mecca occurred between the Iranian Islamic revolution in February 1979 and the beginning of the Afghan national Islamic resistance on December 27, 1979, when the former USSR occupied Afghanistan. The fusion of all three developments in Iran, Afghanistan, and Mecca in the same year came at the time of the new Islamic century, and set the next stage to a point from which the armed struggle in Afghanistan had attracted Muslim youths from all over the world, while Iran's Islamic revolution presented itself as a model anti-Western Islamic government. In short, by the end of 1979, the world had drastically changed and new forces were emerging on the international horizon to challenge the Western hegemonic order. The catalyst for this change, turning it into a dialectical process, was the Mecca uprising of 1979. This failed uprising against the Wahhabi Saudi government simultaneously instigated an academic debate within the circles of Muslim brigades fighting in Afghanistan about the credibility of Muslim regimes. These brigades now began to debate whether the incumbent Muslim governments would promote Islamic values only to the level where those values would not harm their own interests, leading them to sponsor a disconnect with Islam while harmonizing with Western interests.

The siege of Mecca on November 20, 1979 did not instigate a revolution as the rebels only numbered 400 to 500 and thus did not have the strength to topple the Saudi regime, but it did bring connecting questions into the foreground. At the same time it established the intellectual grounds for the next generation of Al-Qaeda activists to orchestrate the future struggle.

After the failed uprising and subsequent execution of Juhayman, his *Seven Letters,* which had been printed and published in booklet form in 1978, were distributed widely in the Arab world. The basic tenets of *Saba Rasail* (the Arabic title) were to model procedures along the lines of the Prophet Muhammad's struggle for Islam. This included inviting people to join Islam, organizing them, and then migrating to a secure base to launch the movement for Islam's domination. Juhayman traced classical Muslim literature which called for the overthrow of corrupt leadership. He believed that the Muslim leadership should come from the Arab tribe of Quraish and must be elected by Muslims. He emphasized the practice of the Islamic faith according to the Quran and the *Sunnah* (the revelations and practices of the Prophet Muhammad) and not the rigid interpretations of scholars and their incorrect teachings. He also advised his followers to move away from the prevalent sociopolitical systems and refuse official positions.

Juhayman believed in the advent of the Mahdi (the promised reformer) from the lineage of the Prophet Muhammad to lead the revolt against corrupt leadership, and targeted taking Saudi Arabia towards the teachings of Muhammad Bin Abdul Wahhab (1703–1792), the Muslim scholar who had in fact backed the Saud family to seize control of Hijaz. Wahhab placed particular emphasis on monotheism by rejecting all the Shiite rituals of worshiping the Prophet Muhammad's family members, including Ali, Fatimah, Hassan, and Hussain. Juhayman also condemned music and television, and last but not least, proposed establishing an Islamic state in Saudi Arabia which would disclaim all alliances with non-Muslim states.

Juhayman's teachings were not new. There had been hundreds of Muslim organizations in the twentieth century that put forward identical views. What distinguished the Juhayman-led uprising of 1979 from the other Islamic cleansing movements, however, was that he developed it to the point of issuing literature, and organized a team before launching his operation. The *Seven Letters* were of special interest to young Arab Muslims who fought in Afghanistan in the 1980s. Copies were distributed in the Arab *mujahideen* camps and became their most important political guide – as important as Chairman Mao's *Little Red Book* for the Communist movement – to prompt political discourse on affairs in Muslim majority states. Brought under instant review were prevalent corruption, non-Islamic practices, and alliances with Western governments.

At the same time, Arab militants were critical of Juhayman on several counts. For example, they objected to his recognizing Muhammad bin abd Allah al-Qahtani as al-Mahdi, and criticized his ill-prepared operation, which had been organized in haste. But it remained a fact that this rebellion, especially because of its ideological moorings, had a huge impact on Arab fighters and their future political strategy. The uprising was considered crucial to highlight the existing contradictions in Muslim societies and thus heighten polarization in Muslim states.

Palestine has been the main schism between the West and the Muslim world in the post-Ottoman Caliphate era. It is at the same time a critical rallying point for Muslims the world over, as Palestine is considered the second most sacred site in Islam after Hijaz. This makes it as important a legacy as the Caliphate at the various Islamic forums, especially the World Islamic Congress (Moatamar Alam-e-Islami), the Rabita-e-Alam-e-Islami (International Islamic Coordination Committee), and the Organization of Islamic Countries (OIC).

The political and strategic policies pursued by Arab rulers on the Palestine issue over the years are denounced by Islamic militants as corrupt for the defeats suffered by the Arabs in successive Arab–Israel wars, while the peace agreement signed by Egypt with Israel in 1979 which established diplomatic relations between the two countries is a festering sore. The militants read these developments through the prism of Juhayman's *Seven Letters* which denounce the ruling apparatus of the apostate Muslim majority states. They then draw out prospective retaliations against them from the Mecca uprising under *khuruj*.

There has been a long history of bloodshed between Islamic militants and the rulers of Arab states. After the Egypt–Israel peace agreement and restoration of diplomatic ties, a new wave of agitation erupted in Egypt. This was not restricted to a few events of sporadic violence. The Islamic Jihad of Egypt planned a coup for the removal of President Anwar Sadat, whom the militants branded an apostate after he had signed the peace agreement with Israel. The consequential coup plan included the capture of key strategic points in Cairo and President Sadat's assassination. Different cells were assigned to different jobs. But the reports of the revolt were leaked and hundreds of militants were rounded up before the coup could be launched. Despite this, a secret cell of the militants led by Khalid Islamboli killed Sadat during a military parade.

By the mid-1980s the contradictions in the Muslim world had broadened further. The ruling elite of the Muslim majority states was Arab nationalist, monarchist, and tilted towards Western models of governance: dictatorships or democracy. By and large they had lost their charm with their corrupt practices and bad governance. At the same time, Muslim groups, who had been badly mauled in the Middle East, and to some extent in South Asia, regrouped. The Muslim Brotherhood leadership was in exile in Saudi Arabia, Qatar, Kuwait, and UAE, and its middle cadre, comprising astute professionals such as doctors, engineers, and teachers, migrated to North America and Europe and began working for the Islamist cause from fresh perspectives.

In Afghanistan Islamic militants were rapidly gaining ground, and in Pakistan the Islamist military general Zia-ul-Haq had taken over after executing his rival, the former premier Zulfikar Ali Bhutto, in 1979. Zia then proceeded with the Islamization of the country, and promoted ultra-radical Islamist resistance factions like Gulbaddin Hikmatyar's Hizb-i-Islami which had operated in Afghanistan against the Soviet invasion. Pakistan had been the strategic backyard of the *mujahideen*'s resistance against the Soviets. It now became the strategic backyard of the militants. Zia established an International Islamic University in the country, where he invited scholars affiliated with the Muslim Brotherhood and known to be ultra-radical. One of those scholars was Dr Abdullah Azzam, a Palestinian, who later established Maktab Al-Khidamat, a services bureau, for the recruitment and deployment of Arab youths in Afghanistan.

By the mid-1980s young Egyptian Arabs from the Muslim Brotherhood, Palestinian resistance movements, and Muslim separatist groups from the Philippines as well as Burma (Myanmar), had been admitted to the International Islamic University for enlightenment on Islam. Their real objective, however, was to join the circles of Dr Abdullah Azzam and other teachers in pursuit of an international Islamic struggle against Western domination. From the Islamic University these students went to Peshawar's Services Bureau and then on to the militant camps in Afghanistan. That way thousands of Muslim youths acquired hands-on training in the art of war, a refined worldview from the Islamic perspective, and the political strategic insight to raise the struggle to the next level.

In this highly charged ultra-radical political atmosphere a new generation of radical Muslims were reared. Several other events then developed on the international front which strengthened the argument of the militants against the ruling elite in Muslim majority states. The most important of these was the Iraqi invasion of Kuwait in 1990. This invasion added fuel to the fire. Saudi Arabia sought the help of the United States and deployed US soldiers in Saudi Arabia, fearing a possible Iraqi attack. All the smaller Arab states, including Kuwait and Jordan, supported the US counter-attack and invasion of Saddam's Iraq, and international economic sanctions against his regime. The US invasion of Afghanistan followed after 9/11, and was supported by Pakistan through the provision of vital logistic help. This set the stage for a broadening of the division between the Muslim state apparatus and the Muslim militants.

All of the events from 1979 onwards were being analyzed in international militant camps in Afghanistan, while the Mecca uprising and the *Seven Letters* of Juhayman were the essential components of the analysis on strategy. However, the analysis was conducted at a different level, as the militants in Afghanistan were living in a freer environment than Juhayman. They had a lot more time and space to expand arguments for a full-fledged war strategy. They had bases, arms, and ammunition, and with these resources their dialectical process was much more advanced and better thought out than Juhayman's. Then their perspective was not restricted to one state. They had the entire Muslim world in sight for the global battle against the West.

The former USSR had been defeated in Afghanistan and forced to withdraw its forces in 1989. It left behind a weak communist government which collapsed in the early 1990s. A *mujahideen* government followed. All of the Muslim radical groups around the world waited to see what would follow. The world environment was primed for Islamic radicalism. A new Islamic front, Hamas, was forged in 1987. It resurrected the Palestinian resistance movement under an Islamic banner. From 1989 onwards, Islamist factions trained in Afghanistan launched a separatist movement in Indian-held Kashmir. The Abu Sayyaf group, trained in Afghanistan, stirred things up in the Philippines. Chechen separatists, again trained in Afghanistan, regrouped under the Islamic flag and resurrected their all but dead separatist movement. Similar separatist movements sprang up under the green crescent in Eritrea and Burma. Thousands of youths fell into line over Jihad in Pakistan, India, and Bangladesh. Within a few years, Islamic seminaries popped up all over Pakistan and Bangladesh. Students poured in from the newly liberated Central Asian Muslim majority republics, Malaysia, Indonesia, and Europe. Different Islamic groups like Hizbut Tehrir surfaced in the Central Asian Republics.

Pakistan, previously a strategic backyard of the Afghan resistance against Russia, was the country most affected by the new wave of the Islamism. Islamic seminaries in Pakistan were traditional, but the new Islamic trends reared a different generation of students who had been given the opportunity to fight against the Soviets and so were fully blooded. These students became the faculty of the Islamic seminaries and turned the seminaries from seats of Islamic learning into ultra-radical Islamic nests. One example is the Jamiatul Islamia, Binori Town, in Karachi. The Binori Town seminary had always been considered one of the most respected seats of Islamic learning of the Deoband school of thought. It had produced several leading Islamic jurists and scholars. However, in the 1990s the seminary became associated with the ultra-radical Islamic thought process. This was not because it had altered its syllabus, but because some of students from there had gone to fight against the USSR in Afghanistan and accepted the influences of students from more radical seminaries present there. Many of these students later became teachers in the Binori Town seminary and influenced the minds of their students accordingly. For instance, Mufti Nizamuddin Shamzai joined the Binori Town seminary as teacher and changed the dynamics of the seminary, turning it into a Jihadi hotspot. After his assassination in 2004, the Binori Town seminary once again became a seat of learning rather than a Jihadi breeding ground. The Jamia Farooqia in Karachi, another top Islamic seminary, recorded an identical history, as did the Akora Khattak seminary in the north and other larger or smaller Islamic seminaries around the country.

By 1994, Afghan students in the Islamic seminaries had taken a firm stand against Afghan warlords and their vandalism in Afghanistan. By 1996 they had raised the flag of the Islamic Emirates of Afghanistan. This upped the radicalization of Islamic seminaries and mosque networks in Pakistan. However, all these developments from the late 1980s to the mid-1990s did not necessarily directly benefit Al-Qaeda, albeit they were there for them to manipulate. Pakistan's military establishment was quick to act, and vied for the control over the Afghan Taliban (student militia) and its government in Kabul.

Pakistan's military establishment then built bridges with Islamic seminaries, while the ISI assigned special cells to control Jihadi organizations and streamline their activities exclusively for its "bleed India" plan. Pakistan's establishment declared Afghanistan to be its "strategic depth" zone, and established training centers for Kashmiri separatist groups to implement its national security agenda.

Iraq's Saddam Hussein regime, Iran's Islamic government, the Syrian government, and the Saudi monarchy all developed close ties with Palestinian Islamists such as Islamic Jihad and Hamas. The nexus of Islamic groups and the Muslim countries' ruling elites, and their strategy and designs from the developments since the Afghan Jihad against Soviet Russia, were seen by Al-Qaeda as narrow strategic gains by the ruling regimes of the Muslim majority states to consolidate their hold. That situation necessitated a strategy that would separate all the newly propped-up Islamic factions from statecraft and bring them under Al-Qaeda. *Takfeer* (declaring them apostate) was the best way in which to serve this cause. From the mid-1990s carefully crafted literature was published and circulated. The basis of this new literature was classical Islamic concepts based on Quranic teachings, the Prophet Muhammad's sayings and practices, and the traditions of the Prophet Muhammad's companions. The verdicts and opinions of Muslim academics and jurists over the last 1,400 years were also taken into account. The literature applied these concepts to contemporary issues of the post-Ottoman Caliphate era, analyzing the secular democratization of the Muslim world, the personal pursuits of monarchial regimes, and their doctrines on the foreign policy front.

Interestingly, and contrary to the literature promoted by the Islamic movements in the twentieth century, whose target audience was the educated urban youths of the Muslim society, Al-Qaeda's target audience was not the commoner but the cadre of society that already practiced Islam. Al-Qaeda worked to convince these Islamists of the heresy of contemporary beliefs and systems and the prevalent foreign policies in the Muslim world, and incite them to revolt against their rulers. At the same time, this new literature did not aim to promote basic monotheist values in tune with the ritualistic perspectives of Muhammad Bin Abdul Wahhab, the Muslim scholar from Arabian Peninsula and ideologue of the House of Saud who helped found the Saudi dynasty. Instead, the new literature developed, combined the ideas of Muhammad Bin Abdul Wahhab with the thoughts of Ibn Taymiyya (1263–1328), a Muslim academic, reformist, and the leader of resistance against the Tartar invasion, in a broader political context.

A natural characteristic of the Islamic resistance is that its strategy and struggle have always been interlinked with ideological writings. During the Ottoman decline, Muslim intellectuals like Muhammad Abdahu of Egypt, Syed Jamal al-Din al-Afghani, and Dr Muhammad Iqbal from India, worked for the promotion of pan-Islamism which gave birth to new Islamic movements. The literature they produced indirectly turned the cycles of the events after 50 years of struggle to shape the Islamic revolution in Iran, the Afghan Jihad, and the Mecca uprising.

Similarly, after the decline of the Mughals in South Asia, the writing of Shah Waliullah (1703–1762) had analyzed the causes for the social and political decline of the Muslims in South Asia, and now provided a strong base for Syed Ahmad Brelvi's revival of the Jihadi movement against the Sikh dynasty in the Muslim majority regions of Pakistan's Punjab and former North West Frontier Province (now Khyber Pakhtoonkhwa).

Shah Ismail (Syed Ahmad Brelvi's lieutenant, the grandson of Shah Waliullah, and the ideologue of the movement) wrote his book, *Taqwiyat-ul-Iman*, before the battle against the Sikh dynasty. The book redefined the Islamic faith, culture, and traditions, creating considerable controversy in a section of the Muslim society at the time it was written. There was a special reason for writing this book: the Muslims of India had always been considered as foreign invaders from Central Asia. Their indigenization and acceptance began during the Mughal era at the time of the Emperor Akbar. A newly evolved Hindustani language, Urdu, was introduced beside Persian.

Urdu was influenced by local languages such as Sanskrit. Similarly Muslims became influenced by the Hindu and Sikh cultures. This influence penetrated the orders of Muslim minorities, and rituals like the *qawali* (religious song), which was similar to the Hindu *bhajans* (devotional music), became part of Muslim tradition. The lines of demarcation in thought and culture between the Muslims and the other inhabitants of India became thin.

Shah Ismail, the ideologue of the Tehrik-e-Mujahadeen, had to create ground among the Muslims to fight against the Sikhs. In his book *Taqwiyat-ul-Iman* he redefined the faith, negated all the influences which had permeated from Hindu society, and tried to explain to the Muslims of India how different they were from Indian society at large. This feeling of distinctiveness has always been necessary to pitch one nation against the other. Shah Ismail accomplished this mission by stressing Muslim monotheism in polytheist Hindu India. Through this strategy he was able to persuade thousands of irregulars who went to Punjab to fight against the Sikh dynasty.

In pursuit of similar objectives, Al-Qaeda was no different from past Jihadi movements. Syed Qutb's literature provided a base for Al-Qaeda, but before it could initiate its struggle, the flashpoint of which was 9/11, its ideologues redefined faith. The situation, however, was different from the time of Brelvi's movement. The Mughal Empire was close to collapse at the time – its writ virtually non-existent. Al-Qaeda operates in the middle of strong states. It follows, therefore, that Al-Qaeda would employ the tougher tactics of Ibn Taymiyya, a Muslim academic of the thirteenth century who was the ideologue and the commander of the Muslim resistance against the Mongols. Tayamiyya also redefined faith even as he emphasized the monotheist values of Islam to bring Islamic distinctiveness under the spotlight against Mongol traditions, to inspire Muslims to fight the Mongol occupation of Baghdad.

Initially Al-Qaeda made use of Muhammad Bin Abdul Wahhab's literature with its emphasis on Islam's monotheist values. But there was a flaw in Wahhab's writing, in that while it provided some basic themes like the concepts of *wala wal bara* (the benchmark for friendships and foes – in the context of alliances and treaties with non-Muslims), Wahhab was the ideologue of the House of Saud which fought against the Muslim Ottoman caliphate. Nobody could ignore that fact that Wahhab was used against the Ottoman Empire to incite the Muslim masses against Sufi-oriented Islam, which he thought close to polytheism. Thus Wahhab, perhaps unintentionally, facilitated the fall of the Caliphate and paved the way for colonial rule. Al-Qaeda thus felt the need for a different form of text which would document Islam's monotheist distinction from modern secular and/or polytheistic orders of democracy and monarchy to promote its dialectic in the battle against the West.

This redefinition of the Islamic faith began after the collapse of the communist regime in Afghanistan. The new literature documented the distinctiveness of monotheist values against polytheism as well as the secular Western political order. It aimed at drawing Muslims away from the Western cultural ethos and values. As a result, polarization was imminent in those Muslim societies which had been seriously influenced by the West. By the time of 9/11, which marked the beginning of the war, the foundations of an ideological perspective for Islamic renaissance had already built through new Al-Qaeda literature.

9/11 created friction around the globe and initially divided the world into two camps: those who were with the United States and those who were anti-American. This divide impacted Muslim societies where the ruling classes were still close to the West, and after this defining moment, the Muslim ruling classes and the broad masses stood divided. In the coming years Al-Qaeda worked to sharpen this divide to pave the way for revolts in Muslim societies in order to weaken the support of Muslim establishments for the US war against Al-Qaeda.

On the strategic front, Al-Qaeda had successfully stung the United States with 9/11. The United States invaded Afghanistan and, according to Al-Qaeda, the trap was sprung. However, the strategy would have failed had Al-Qaeda not explored the dialectic of events beyond 9/11 which was to reinforce the ideological divide in Muslim societies. It embarked on this mission by enlisting the services of Islamic-minded officers in the armed forces and influential clerics in the religious parties and religious schools in Muslim countries. It then looked to gather resources to launch a long war against the United States in Afghanistan.

Academics associated with Al-Qaeda-authored literature laid down the rules of faith and heresy for a Muslim, but there were other brains at work on the dialectical front. Al-Qaeda aimed at creating a Muslim backlash against the anticipated Western retaliation to the 9/11 attack, but was equally cognizant of the fact that even in the Muslim world, there would be divided reactions, because of the political, military, and economic dependency of Muslim regimes on the West. In countries like Saudi Arabia, Jordan, Pakistan, and Kuwait, this became a flagrant reality. Thus there was never any belief in the Al-Qaeda camp that once the United States reacted to 9/11, pro-Western Muslim regimes would be able to remain "non-aligned." Al-Qaeda was 100 percent sure that once Washington decided on war against Al-Qaeda, the ruling regimes in the Muslim world would have no option but to align themselves with Washington.

The 9/11 attacks were organized for a particular purpose: to provoke the United States and bring it into the Afghan trap. A Muslim backlash was certain to follow, and eventually this would lead to a direct confrontation between the West and the Muslim world. Al-Qaeda also understood that bringing the US war machine into the vastness of the hostile Afghan mountain wilderness was an imperative. But it was equally aware that this would not signal victory. Victory against the West required a long struggle, planning, and a winning war strategy. This in turn would require resources, but all the known resources were under the control of the West-aligned Muslim regimes. Therefore the second most important objective of Al-Qaeda's strategy in the wake of the 9/11 attack and the retaliation to it was to discredit the ruling Muslim regimes by bringing up the contradictions inherent in their political alliances with the West.

Once these Muslim regimes' real allegiance towards the West was exposed, *takfeer* would be the weapon Al-Qaeda employed to isolate them from the Muslim masses. Sympathetic sections of the armed forces, religious parties, and Islamic seminaries would then be activated against the ruling elites and more easily moved to join forces with Al-Qaeda in its fight against the West globally.

Takfeer also aimed at gathering in and employing all of the Muslim world's resources against the Western occupation forces. But Al-Qaeda well understood that it would be a slow and tedious process, and a long-term academic exercise, to topple the ruling regimes in Muslim majority states. Still the goal was clearly to bring about Islamic revolution and pave the way for the revival of the Muslim Caliphate to orchestrate the global Jihad. The struggle for the revival of the global Muslim Caliphate that ran from the 1920s to the 1970s was the first phase of an ideological movement to purge Western thought from Muslim minds. However, by the 1970s Islamic revival movements in Muslim countries had started to succumb to the persuasion of Western "democracy." Earlier, the ideologue of the Islamic movements, Syed Abul Ala Maududi, had declared democracy the best vehicle for Islamization. He felt that once the Islamic forces seized power through the electoral process, they would make fundamental changes in the constitution to enforce Islam, leaving only Islamists to participate in politics. Thus secular democracy would purged from the system. The Muslim Brotherhood in Egypt subscribed to a similar thought process in the 1970s.

The siege of the Grand Mosque in Mecca in 1970 ended this, and revived the ideas of *khuruj* (revolt against the deviant Muslim ruler). This finally matured in 1980s and 1990s in the camps of the militants of Afghanistan, where the sum of the post-Caliphate-era dialectic was put to the test.

In the Introduction and Chapter 3 of this book I narrated the ideological developments in Arab militants' camps during their fighting against Soviet Russia in the 1980s. I also mentioned the Egyptian camp. The Egyptian camp comprised those who were both politically and ideologically motivated. Though most had belonged to the Muslim Brotherhood, they disagreed with that organization for its insistence on trying to change society through the democratic processes and elections. The Afghan Jihad served to bind the like-minded, many of them doctors and engineers. Others were former personnel of the Egyptian Army associated with various underground Egyptian movements like the Islamic Jihad of al-Zawahiri (now Osama bin Laden's deputy). As mentioned earlier, this group had been responsible for the assassination of President Sadat in 1981 after he had signed the peace deal with Israel at Camp David. All were agreed on a single point: the reason for the fall of the Arab nation was the United States and puppet governments in the Middle East. This Egyptian camp was in the hands of al-Zawahiri. After *isha* prayers those assembled would sit and discuss contemporary issues in the Arab world. It bears repeating that one of the messages the leaders drummed home was that members should invest their resources in the armies of Muslim countries, and ideologically motivate the best brains to be found there.

In the mid-1990s, when then Afghan President Professor Burhanuddin Rabbani and his powerful minister of defense, Ahmed Shah Masoud, allowed Osama bin Laden to move from Sudan to Afghanistan, the Egyptian camp drew in several of its better strategists from across the world to Afghanistan. There they ran *maaskars* (training camps), studied, and taught strategy for the future fight. By the time the Taliban had emerged as a force in Afghanistan in the mid-1990s, the Egyptian camp had settled on their strategy, underscoring the following two points:

• to speak out against corrupt and despotic Muslim governments

and make them targets, as this would destroy their image in the eyes of the common people
* to focus on the role of the United States, which was to support Israel and tyrannical Middle Eastern countries, and make everyone aware of this fact.

However, identical ideas had been projected by the Muslim Brotherhood earlier. The Arab militants in Afghanistan were reading Syed Qutb's literature, with his book *Milestone* featuring foremost. (Syed Qutb was an ideologue of Egyptian Muslim Brotherhood who was executed by Nasser's regime in 1966 for writing rebellious literature including *Milestone*.) Also strongly featured were the books authored by Wahhab.

Wahhab's writings were still the basic source of monotheist Islamic thinking, and while the militants argued that Muslim regimes like the one in Saudi Arabia were not abiding by the rules he had laid down for an Islamic state, the bigger problem was that Wahhab's books were written during the period of the Ottoman Empire and were thus less likely to be effective in the twentieth century.

Similarly, Syed Qutb's literature was a fair foundation for revolutionary ideas, but the militants felt that a redefinition of Islamic thought through new writings was required to spell out more clearly the distinctions between Islamic and unIslamic policies. This would then be presented as the benchmark for future friendships and enmities, to negate through *takfeer* the existing Muslim regimes' practices of friendship with the West and enable the new construct to complement Al-Qaeda's strategy as and when the time of an inevitable split in ideas materialized.

After the defeat of the USSR in Afghanistan, the Arab fighters looked for the leading role in the Muslim world. They started compiling their thoughts, and ideas and books like *Qawaid Al-Takfeer* (Rules of expulsion from Islam) were published in 1994.

THE *TAKFEER*: ORCHESTRATING A CLASH

Under the Caliphate all Muslims were one *ummah* (nation) irrespective of caste, creed, and ethnicity. The Caliph was the head of the state. Under that political order, there were only two nations in the world: Muslims and non-Muslims. The interests of Muslims were as of one nation and different from other nations in the world. That mindset prevailed in the Muslim world for over 1,300 years, but broke in 1920s after the complete collapse of the Ottoman Caliphate.

During the decline of the Ottoman Caliphate, an era of prolonged Western colonialism was begun for the purpose of dividing Muslim states into several larger or small countries to be governed under the colonial order. Even after their independence this colonial order persisted. Muslims were never to be allowed revert to their old political order. In most of the Muslim countries Western colonial powers like France, England, and Italy handed over power to leadership of a Western mindset. As a result, newly independent Muslim nations adopted systems of governance inspired by Western political models, whether dictatorial or democratic. By the end of the twentieth century Islamic political orders, in any shape or form, were considered relics of the past.

In the new world order, all countries were to be "nation states" founded on the basis of ethnicity. International relations were to be based on bargains of mutual interests. This new global order drew in subscribers from the Muslim world. These subscribers to modernism in the Muslim world were backed by the international community, with the traditionalist Islamists labeled outcasts. Islamic states all the way from North Africa to the Asia–Pacific compromised and adopted Western democratic practices to remain in the international political mainstream. However, an influential segment of Muslim academia continued to believe in the concept of the Caliphate, and separated itself from the "democratic" content.

The siege of the grand mosque of Mecca in 1979 gave them a boost of confidence, and the subsequent Afghan Islamic resistance movement against the Soviet invasion provided them with the opportunity to promote a return to the Caliphate. For ten years, the militants joined in discussions, and compiled thoughts on ways to counter post-Caliphate "innovations." With that a stream of new literature was published in the 1990s, following the fall of the communist regime and subsequent to the rule of the *mujahideen* government in Afghanistan.

LITERATURE THAT CHANGES THE MIND

Several issues have confronted the Muslim world. Amongst them the one that stands out is the *takfeer* of others (declaring people heretic) .... However, those who do not fulfill the criterion set by the classical Muslim scholars for (rightfully) casting the verdicts of *takfeer* only follow the paths of the classical Kharijite sect which emerged at the time when the Muslim Caliphate was divided between Ali and Mauviya when both were embattled against each other. The Kharijites emerged in those days and specified tough and rigid rules to be followed, and denounced both Ali and Mauviya as heretic and issued a verdict for the killing of both. Kharijites marked *takfeer* on all non-practicing Muslims and those who indulged in punishable sins, and then waged battle against them. They adopted the belief of *wala* and *bara* (friendship and enmity with anybody should be on the basis of Islam), and on that basis gave a blanket ruling that a number of conventional practices were immoral. However, this was not the belief of the majority of the Prophet Muhammad's companions who were the true flag bearers of the Prophet Muhammad's traditions.

The Prophet Muhammad had earlier identified this deviant sect and warned that they would fight against every Muslim, yet raise no objection to idol worshippers. The Prophet had said that if such a sect surfaced in his time he would denounce them as the Nation of Aad (a pre-Islam nation destroyed because of its sins). A companion of Prophet Muhammad later stressed that the sect (identified by the Prophet) would apply Quranic verses meant for heretics against true believers. On the one side now we have groups like Kharijites who would inflate the issue of *takfeer*, and on the other there were groups and sects like the classical sects of Jhmiya and Marjna, who did not believe in *takfeer* at all, and accepted anybody with a Muslim name as Muslim, even if they believe in secularism or communism, and mock Islam and Muslims. Such people, once their national identity cards are issued showing their religion as Islam, work for anti-Islamic forces, and nobody dares expel them from Islam.

(Abu Baseer al-Tartusi in the Foreword of *Qawaid Al-Takfeer*)

Sheikh Abd-al Mun'em Mustafa Halima Abu Basir aka Abu Baseer al-Tartusi is a Syrian Islamist living in London. He has been described as a "primary Salafi opinion-maker" guiding the Jihadi movement. His book *Qawaid Al-Takfeer* is part of Al-Qaeda's syllabus, and was one of the first books which laid down the rules of *takfeer* and hence *khuruj* (revolt against deviant Muslim establishments). Written in London in 1994, Tartusi's book redefines the Islamic faith. It explains the distinction between Islam's monotheism and the polytheism of Western philosophies, encompassing Western democracy, secularism, and secular monarchies which reject any divine guidance and depend on human-made laws. The book aims to stir up polarization in Muslim majority states. It declares as *takfeer* all the modern political systems in Muslim majority states, along with their foreign and the defense policies.

Tartusi goes through all the basic terminologies. For instance *al-kufur* (heresy) is defined in the traditional abstract form, but the explanation comes in the lower-level definitions of *kufur akbar* (the bigger heresy), *kufur amad* (deliberate heresy), *kufur takabur* (heresy with snobbery), *kufur jahud* (venom against Islamic heresy), and *kufar tahli* (contradicting Quranic orders). He interprets these categories of heresies in the political context, and discusses the role of states that are involved in all those heresies and are therefore not entitled to be called Muslim states or Muslim societies. Similarly, *shirk* (polytheism), *fisq* (debauchery), *zulm* (injustice and abuse), *nifaq* (hypocrisy), *zindaqa* (irreligion), *irtidad* (going back from Islam to heresy), *hawa* (vagary), *mawalat* (supports, alliances), and *iman* (faith) are enumerated, and definitions of all those Islamic terms are presented in detail, with each aspect explained in the light of the *Quran*, the Prophet Muhammad's sayings, and through the interpretations of classical Muslim scholars, to connect the dots in the contemporary world. For instance, he cites Quranic Al-Toba's verse number 44 and 45 and then presents Ibn Taymiyya's interpretation: "In this verse God says to his Prophet that whosoever asks to leave Jihad are not believers, though this Quranic commandment is for those people who actually sought permission to leave Jihad. The commandment is harsher on those who abandoned Jihad on their own without seeking any permission."

Tartusi adds the spice to Taymiyya's interpretation in the modern-day world context:

what is supposed to be the commandment against those who are against Jihad? ... the commandments about those who call the *mujahideen* terrorists, criminals, and gangsters .... Those who put pseudo conditions for waging Jihad, for example, Jihad can only be waged by the state authority – a state authority which is established on a democratic system of governance which is itself based on un-Islamic and ignorant percepts ... undoubtedly these people are hypocrites and deprived of faith. Those who prevent people from Jihad should make themselves accountable, restrain themselves from supporting the enemies of God by any mean, whether by the tongue or by creating obstacles in front of *mujahideen* [they must] renew their faith because if such persons were Muslim (once) now their faith is damaged.

Tartusi's manual on *Takfeer* and other literature written in the mid-1990s and onwards was timely, as the militants were victorious in Afghanistan against the Soviets and they had bases to operate from. Similar ideas were developed by Takfeer Wal Hijra, an underground movement organized in Egypt in the 1960s when Nasser used brute force against the Muslim Brotherhood and carried out the execution of its leaders and workers. Islamists were portrayed as villains by the Arab socialist regimes of Syria, Egypt, Iraq, and Libya. The Islamists then took refuge in Saudi Arabia, Kuwait, and sheikhdoms like UAE and Qatar, and even the United Kingdom and the United States, but the refuge provided in those places was restricted to living theree. There was never any question of their being permitted to engage in dialectical debate.

The Mecca uprising in November 1979 popularized ultra-radical thinking which questioned:

- Can a person be called Muslim for being born into a Muslim family without actually believing in Islam?
- Can a state really called a Muslim state where the majority of its population has registered itself as Muslim but politically lives under a non-lslamic constitution?
- Can a state still be called an Islamic state, when though it practices Islamic ritual, it has effectively become the most important instrument of non-Muslim forces against the Islamic cause?

The erstwhile ideas that Takfeer Wal Hijra and other underground Islamic organizations in Egypt, Syria, Iraq, Tunis and Libya had tried to promote in the 1960s came to new life with the Mecca uprising in 1979. Coincidentally, the Islamists gained a base to operate from when the Soviet Union invaded Afghanistan on December 27, 1979 and there was a worldwide call, led and facilitated by Pakistan and Saudi Arabia, to Muslim youths to join with their Afghan brothers against godless communism.

In a matter of few years, thousands of young Muslims from across the world had established independent camps to revive a Muslim political order and explore the dialectic of their struggle in Muslim societies where they aimed to reorganize, resurrect, and imbue the Islamist core with a new spirit of purpose through a new thought process. They then sought to establish their nuisance value

against the ruling classes of the Muslim world and force their respective Muslim rulers to move away from their allegiance to Western
societies and governments. The ultimate purpose of this struggle,
however, was and remains a global war against the West's presence
in Muslim lands, guided by Al-Qaeda.

By the time Tartusi and other Arab authors had compiled books
on the modern definition of faith and heresy, thousands of Muslim
youths had journeyed from Pakistan, the Philippines, Palestine,
Egypt, Syria, Saudi Arabia, Yemen, and other Muslim countries
to join the Afghan Jihad, and developed anti-American and anti-
establishment views. When, in 1994, these youths either had left
or were about to leave Afghanistan, *Qawaid Al-Takfeer* provided a
very strong ideological dimension to continue with a post-Afghan–
Soviet war struggle.

ROOTS OF THE IDEOLOGICAL EVOLUTION

The Mecca uprising in 1979 was also a major turning point in the
analysis of Muslim societies by various Muslim reformers in various
areas. In the 1,400 years of the Muslim history there were several
occasions when Muslim reformers challenged Muslim establishments on the ideologies that prevailed in their domains. However
after events starting with the 1979 uprising, continuing to 9/11 and
onwards, a unique line was followed and a unique analysis of the
situation was made. It was assumed that all the Muslim countries
in the world were allied with the West and their societies were
operating on non-Islamic beliefs, and they were urged to change
their positions. Those who refused to do so were declared heretics,
and war was declared on them. This was most extreme line ever
taken in 1,400 years, ever since the Islamic faith had been defined
from the perspective of contemporary events and issues. And, with
that, the majority of the Muslims living in the new world order were
effectively declared heretics. However, the basics of this thinking
were not alien. It actually reflected an evolving view of new analysis
in the minds of Muslim scholars drawn from a long run of reformist
movements since the advent of Islam.

During the time of Umayyad and then the Abbasid Empire in
the Muslim world, following the initial 40-year rule of the Prophet
Muhammad and his companions, Muslim monarchs had been
inclined towards maintaining a status quo interpretation of Islam.
This status quo arrangement was intended to counter revolutionary
interpretations of Islamic laws on emerging issues in politics, the

economy, and social life, to enable rulers to manipulate statecraft in their personal interests. The emergence of the four Muslim jurists, Imam Abu Hanifa, Imam Shafai, Imam Malik, and Imam Hanbal, at different periods of the Abbasid Caliphate era aimed to deny this status quo arrangement to the ruling classes. They worked in their individual capacities, researched and interpreted new issues despite the opposition of monarchs, and compiled Islamic laws adapted to contemporary governance needs.

Similarly, the promotion of Greek, Roman, and Eastern philosophies in the Umayyad, Abbasid, and Turkish empires was a challenge confronting the Muslim intelligentsia. Dozens of debates on Islamic tenets began in the light of those philosophies. New schools of thought sprang up in Sufism, heavily blended with ancient Zoroastrian traditions or Greek philosophies. New Islamic literature surfaced which took in Greek philosophies. Some Muslim scholars opposed these trends and some favored them. As a result, verdicts of heresy were issued randomly and sectarianism rose sky-high in the Muslim world. Muslim monarchs were the main sponsors and promoters of these sectarian schisms as they helped them divert the attention of the masses away from the real issues concerning statecraft and politics.

The renowned Muslim academic and jurist of that time, Imam Ghazali, confronted these challenges. He documented the spirit of Islamic thought and explained how it might be at odds with other philosophies. He also sorted out and refined the issue of heresy as it had developed according to Islamic tenets, so that Muslims should not unduly issue heresy decrees against each other on sectarian grounds.

IBN TAMIYYAH, AN IDEOLOGUE FOR THE NEXT 1,000 YEARS

The ideological evolution for the reform of the Muslim society following the era of the Prophet Muhammad reached its climax during the invasion of the Tartars who ransacked the Abbasid Caliphate. This was the worst period of Muslim history. Muslims had been the dominant world power, but they faced a sudden fall following the Tartar invasion. The Abbasid Caliphate was abandoned and so were the Muslim political order, Islamic laws, culture, and traditions. Everything became subservient to the Tartar perspective. Different parts of the Muslim world remained free from the Tartars, but the local rulers did not have the courage to stand up against them. They were terrified of the Mongol power and its brutalities, and they did not want to face the fate that had been witnessed in Baghdad, where the people were ruthlessly butchered and an entire civilization destroyed.

This submissive attitude of the Muslim ruling classes and sections of Muslim society towards one of the momentous events in Muslim history, which came with the elimination of the Abbasid Caliphate and the fall of Baghdad, gave birth to a Muslim resistance movement manned by volunteers. The ideologue and commander of that Muslim resistance against the Tartars, and their attempted imposition of Tartar law on Muslim society, was Imam Ibn Tamiyyah (1263–1328).

Tamiyyah was considered the model of ideological resistance in the Muslim world, and his ideas are still the direct source for Islamic revolutionaries, who for the first time aggressively practiced the principle of *takfeer* to reorganize Muslim resistance against the Tartars – and against those who, although they claimed to be Muslims, placed obstacles in the way of the Islamic resistance against the invaders. Tamiyyah aimed to shock deviants by declaring them non-Muslims, and he discredited them in front of the common Muslims, so that the Muslim resistance against the Tartars focused on the expulsion of the Tartars from Muslim soil.

Tamiyyah was a strong critic of the logic of Greek philosophers like Aristotle. He wrote a critical analysis of their writings and presented a model of Islamic thought as a plausible counterweight. He drew a comparison between Islamic thought and the Greek philosophies, and argued for the superiority of Islam through logic.

Tamiyyah was born at the time the Tartars had conquered Muslim territories from the Indus River to the River Tigris. Although the Tartar invaders later accepted Islam, they introduced their native traditions and cultural arrangements into Muslim society. The Tartar rulers took complete control over Muslim religious institutions, and the Muslim religious elite succumbed to their will. They declared Halaku Khan as a righteous ruler, and issued the verdict that a righteous infidel ruler was better than a tyrannical Muslim ruler. The newly converted Tartar rulers had enforced two different laws. Personal laws, like marriages, were interpreted under Islam, but public laws concerning the economy, politics, and the judiciary were interpreted under their traditional Yassa code.

Tamiyyah declared that Jihad against the Mongols was obligatory, and based this ruling on the grounds that the Mongols could not be true Muslims despite the fact that they had converted to Sunni Islam because they subscribed to human-made laws (the traditional Yassa code) rather than Islamic law or *sharia*, and thus lived in a state of *jahiliyya*, or pre-Islamic pagan ignorance. He simultaneously refuted many schools of Sufism, calling them un-Islamic. He declared Shiites to be heretics and fifth columnists against the Islamic *sharia*, and advocated action against them. He announced, "Every group of Muslims that transgresses Islamic law ... must be combated, even when they profess to subscribe to the Islamic credo." His decree of *takfeer* went all the way through to the era of Syed Qutb and on to the ideology of Al-Qaeda.

The Mamluk ruler Nasir Al-Din Qalawun tried to prevent war against the Tartars and proposed neutrality. Tamiyyah forced this Muslim ruler of Egypt to fight against the Tartars, and threatened that if he continued his policy of neutrality and stopped the war against Tartars, he would launch a revolt against Qalawun himself first, and on capturing power, he would resume the fight against the Tartars. His were the first actions of any Muslim academic working on three different fronts as commander of the resistance, academic, and reformer.

Tamiyyah's mindset focused on the struggle against the Tartars, for which he laid ideological grounds by emphasizing the monotheist values of Islam against the polytheist values in Mongol culture. And, in emphasizing monotheism, Tamiyyah aggressively confronted anything and everything he believed to be polytheist, declaring as heresy even the faith of the Khusrawan-e-Shiites of Lebanon, the Sufi schools of Asha'ira Jahmiyya, and the Mu'tazila creeds. Al-Qaeda's interest was in Tamiyyah's ideology of resistance. They used Tamiyyah's work to support their arguments. The larger part of the Islamic movements of the post-Caliphate period in the twentieth century were the flag-bearers of Tamiyyah's ideology.

The founder of Jamaat-e-Islami in South Asia, Syed Abul Ala Maududi, and the Muslim brotherhood ideologue, Syed Qutb, converted Tamiyyah's teachings into contemporary Islamic thought. They employed the *jahilliya* definition Tamiyyah had applied to the Greek, Roman, and Tartar philosophies and their traditions and rules. These twentieth-century Muslim ideologues extended the same rulings to encompass socialism, secularism, and democracy.

Maududi argued against Western democracy, socialism, and the Western social system. He had argued for the Islamic way of life in its entirety. However, he believed in an evolutionary approach. He did not believe in violence to enforce Islam. He researched and studied ways whereby the Islamic system would not clash with modern thinking and institutions. For instance, he approved the adult franchise election system to enforce Islam and did not insist on the revival of the institution of the caliphate. Syed Qutb, on the other hand, while expanding Maududi's earlier arguments against Western democracy and socialism, urged Muslim nations to abandon the West's social, economic, and political system altogether, and advocated Islamic revolution.

Al-Qaeda's ideological discourse starts with the interpretations of Tamiyyah and ends at Syed Qutb. But after that, it does not deliver any modus operandi, or any clear policy or guidelines, to define the onward struggle on contemporary issues. Thus neither Tamiyyah's nor Syed Qutb's thoughts and ideas fully find expression in Al-Qaeda's practiced philosophy. After the execution of Syed Qutb in 1966, the entire Muslim Brotherhood leadership was either terminated or put in exile. The lower cadre of the organization was dismembered or moved into other underground organizations. Jamaat-e-Islami, Pakistan and its founder, Maududi, played a lead role in mediating between Nasser's government and the Muslim Brotherhood leadership, and urged the Muslim Brotherhood to follow the election process to bring change to Egyptian society. From the late 1960s onwards, the Muslim Brotherhood in the Middle East and Islamic movements worldwide were seen to have taken to election politics and in that way become part of the establishment.

All this time the Al-Qaeda Muslim radicals operating in underground organizations in the Middle East were looking for the missing pieces to fuse their ideology into a movement. The Mecca uprising in November 1979 and the immediate beginning of the Afghan Jihad as a result of the Soviet Union's invasion of Afghanistan on December 27, 1979 provided them with the opportunity.

The Mecca uprising set the stage for *khuruj* to clearly define that no matter how much the Saudi monarchy might claim an Islamic identity, since its foreign policies were attached to Western interests, it was to be seen as an instrument of Western powers in the region. Its claim of being an Islamic state was not acceptable.

The Afghan Jihad, meanwhile, provided pre-Al-Qaeda Muslim radicals with the opportunity to establish a base in Afghanistan and an equally strong base over the border in Pakistan's tribal territories. From there Al-Qaeda developed new ideas and strategies through a dialectical process, first in the tribal areas of Afghanistan and Pakistan, and from there all across the Muslim world.

5

ANTITHESIS: DEBATE ON THE LEGITIMACY OF THE RESISTANCE

The twin towers attack on 9/11, 2001 marked the beginning of open hostilities between Al-Qaeda and the West. The United States invaded Afghanistan in October 2001, and by December 2001, the Taliban were defeated and forced to disperse. Washington announced victory in Afghanistan and began work towards establishing a democratic government there.

The Taliban and Al-Qaeda then moved to safer places in Afghanistan, Iran, and Pakistan's tribal areas, and began preparations for a resistance against the new foreign occupation forces in Afghanistan. Afghanistan was the main battleground and Pakistan was to be its strategic backyard. However, the resistance faced challenges on two fronts: from the foreign occupation forces stationed in Afghanistan, and the Pakistani security forces, with Pakistan a major ally in the US-led War on Terror. As a result, Al-Qaeda needed to develop a strategy that could address both the challenges.

The Taliban-led resistance in Afghanistan began in 2002, but was very weak. Al-Qaeda then prepared the grounds for its reinforcement, to include new recruitment, training, and motivation, and a new dialectic to identify the Islamic cadre of Pakistani society, including Islamic-minded officers in the army, Jihadi organizations shaped after the Afghan Jihad against the Soviet Union, Islamic seminaries, and that section of the masses who truly believed in Islam and would join with the resistance. In this process Pakistan was classified as Al-Qaeda's backyard, and under US pressure, Pakistan was forced to wage a war on Al-Qaeda, which had expanded the theater of war so much so that the United States would call the war in Afghanistan its Af–Pak strategy.

Al-Qaeda faced an identical situation when the United States invaded Iraq in 2003. Al-Qaeda and the Iraqi resistance faced challenges from the foreign occupying forces stationed in Iraq, as well as the security forces of Jordan and Saudi Arabia. Therefore, after the Iraq war in 2003, Al-Qaeda decided to replicate its Afghan strategy throughout the Muslim world. As in the case of Afghanistan, Al-Qaeda then made Iraq as a central theater of war, and neighboring countries like Saudi Arabia, Jordan, Syria, and Egypt, all allies of the West, were identified as the enemy. As Iraq's neighbors these countries were to serve as the strategic backyard of Iraqi resistance – which led to a serious confrontation between Al-Qaeda and these Muslim majority states.

Al-Qaeda next expanded its presence into Yemen and Somalia, with the aim of severing Western supply lines to the battlefields. In essence, by 2006 the larger part of the Muslim world had become the theater of war. Revolts, clashes, and suicide attacks became routine. The establishments in the Muslim majority states could clearly see that the roots of the problem lay in Iraq and Afghanistan, and although those establishments were in principle against the US invasions of Afghanistan and Iraq, they were politically and economically compelled to come out in support of the United States.

State-sponsored religious decrees were then issued against rebellions inside the Muslim-majority states. Religious scholars in Pakistan and Saudi Arabia held a dialogue with militants and assured them that if they keep their focus on the US invasions in Iraq and Afghanistan, they would pose no problem to them, but as countries such as Pakistan, Jordan, Kuwait, and Saudi Arabia were gradually compelled to coordinate with and facilitate the United States in its war, they became a target. Al-Qaeda was not an organization which would accommodate the argument that a Muslim majority state had been "compelled" by a non-Muslim invading force, and therefore was not ready to allow such a concession. On the contrary it considered Muslim majority states who supported the West as heretical and thus enemy states. It carried out more attacks on them than on the United States and its Western allies. This forced these Muslim majority states to initiate a debate on the legitimacy of Al-Qaeda for running the theaters of war in Afghanistan and Iraq.

The first round of this ideological battle began in the Middle East. Nasiruddin al-Albani called the Muslim radicals *Neo-Khawarij* – the Muslim sect in early Islamic centuries who had declared the then Muslim rulers heretic on the basis of their unIslamic practices and instigated revolt against them. He said:

History repeats itself. A new generation of Khawarij who have a limited knowledge about Islam has emerged. They think that rulers do not represent the entire Islamic system. Therefore, without any consultations with Muslim scholars, jurists, and learned academics, this new generation have launched an armed rebellion and created serious chaos and crisis. They have carried out bloodshed in Egypt, Syria, and Algeria. Earlier, they attacked the Grand Mosque of Mecca [in 1979]. Therefore, they are the Muslims who oppose the authentic sayings of the Prophet Muhammad which, except the (classical) Khawarij, every Muslim practices.

الأ حا د يث سلسلة   author Nasiruddin al-Albani

A Saudi Salafi scholar expanded on this debate when he was asked whether there were still people who follow the deviant Muslim sect of Khawarij. He narrates:

What else was the ideology and practice of the Khawarij? It was about declaring Muslims as heretics, the worst form of which is the killing of Muslims, and using oppressive tactics against them. The following is the actual belief of the Khawarij:
• declaring Muslims as heretics
• challenging the political order and writ of the state by armed rebellion
• announcing the killing of Muslims as permissible.
If somebody follows the above mentioned things he is a Khawaraji, whether he associates himself with that deviant sect or not.
(Sheikh Saleh Bin Fawzan, *Rules and regulations of Jihad*)

Nonetheless, in the state-sponsored discourse against Al-Qaeda the fact was completely ignored that Al-Qaeda's battle in the Muslim majority states was not the result of any internal political or ideological conflict. This battle was directly linked with international relations in which Muslim majority states stood beside Non-Muslim occupation forces. This helped Al-Qaeda to develop its argument of heresy against them.

The occupation of Muslim territories such as Palestine, Iraq, and Afghanistan has been the root cause of the Muslim insurgency. The reason for the recent troubles in Saudi Arabia, Jordan, Pakistan, and other Muslim countries spins off their support of the West in its invasion and occupation of countries such as Iraq and Afghanistan.

After 9/11, Pakistan provided bases to the United States for its air strikes against the Taliban regime in Afghanistan. Pakistan also provided an inland route for NATO supplies to landlocked Afghanistan. In addition, Pakistan has arrested several hundred Al-Qaeda members and handed them over to the United States.

Jordan, Kuwait, Turkey, Saudi Arabia, and even Iran to an extent provided logistic and intelligence support to the United States to dislodge Saddam Hussain's government for the US occupation of Iraq. The backlash in Muslim countries, especially in Saudi Arabia and Pakistan, has been enough to destabilize the ruling regimes in these states. Militants attempted to assassinate former Pakistan President General Pervez Musharraf and former premier Shaukat Aziz, and assassinated Pakistan's pro-Western leader, Benazir Bhutto. From 2004 to 2006 Saudi Arabia has faced more extreme violence than ever before.

By 2007 the Muslim establishment realized that as long as the wars in Iraq and Afghanistan continued there was no way of stopping Islamist revolts and rebellions in Muslim countries. To counter this, state-sponsored articles and television talk shows were arranged in which pundits discussed the key Islamic principles for a "true" Islamic renaissance. Through these measures, there was an attempt to establish that in neither Iraq nor Afghanistan was armed resistance justified.

Different scholars cite the following rules from the Quran and the sayings of the Prophet for a true Islamic resistance:

- There should be an Imam (leader) to lead the resistance. The Quran narrates "don't you see a group from the children of Israel after Moses, and they urged their prophet to appoint a emperor, so we shall fight for Allah" (Al-Baqara).
- There should be adequate resources for the battle.
- The Prophet Muhammad did not allow Jihad (armed struggle) until he founded a state in Medina and migrated there. Hence no Islamic resistance is justified before a fort or a state is erected to justify a struggle.
- The strength of the Muslim army should not be less than half of the enemy forces.
- Without fulfilling these four conditions any battle cannot be considered Islamic resistance.

These ideas were repeatedly projected on television stations, over the radio, in newspapers, and through religious decrees. But they meant nothing to Al-Qaeda. Each and every Al-Qaeda member was convinced that Al-Qaeda's dialectical process had in fact been developed under strict Islamic principles.

To render "null and void" the establishment's campaign:

> Do you realize now the sea difference between you (Muslim majority states), who obstruct the people from Jihad, and the Taliban? Do you understand the difference between the commander of Jihad [Mullah Omar] and the contemporary ruling elite who are terrified of Israel and America? You must have realized why we have pledged our allegiance to Mullah Muhammad Omar? Indeed we are under his command and his command is our pride. We invite the Muslims of the entire world to pledge their allegiance to this sincere and great warrior of Islam.
>
> (Dr Ayman al-Zawahiri, 2005)

This was part of al-Zawahiri's speech in September 2005 to defeat the argument of the anti-Al-Qaeda Muslim academics that the Afghan and Iraqi resistance did not have any leader and therefore had no legitimacy according to Islamic tenets. The speech was published with the title "if you turn your face against Jihad." Al-Qaeda's aim was not to convince non-practicing Muslims. Its target audience has always been the practising Islamist. So it meticulously modified its arguments thus:

> With the blessing of Allah the structure of the Islamic Emirates of Afghanistan is still intact and very much under Taliban control in the eastern and southern regions of Afghanistan. It is waging a guerrilla war against crusaders and heretics.

Al-Zawahiri emphasized in the same speech that with the establishment of the Emirates of Afghanistan the second requirement for Islamic resistance had also been fulfilled.

After the establishment of the Islamic Emirates of Afghanistan, which includes shadow governorates for all Afghan provinces, Al-Qaeda struggled for years to convert all of the Pakistani tribal areas situated between Pakistan and Afghanistan into an impregnable fortress for the Taliban to conform to the Islamic principle of a base to justify armed resistance. From 2002–05 Al-Qaeda launched an aggressive recruitment drive to raise at least 60,000 men in these areas. The indigenous strength of the Afghan Taliban was no less than 20,000 and with the new recruits from Pakistan's tribal areas the Taliban's strength now numbered the same as the 80,000 NATO troops in Afghanistan at the time. That fulfilled another condition for Islamic resistance: that of not numbering less than half the opposing force.

Bringing together all the militant groups fighting in Afghanistan, Iraq, Somalia, and Yemen to pool the resources of the Muslim groups and utilize them effectively was Al-Qaeda's forward strategy. The strategy turned out to be a vital asset in both Afghanistan and Iraq, and changed the strength of the resistance by 2009. It forced the United States into a troop surge on one hand, and offered a dialogue to the Taliban on the other. At the same time, this strategy was able to raise enough resources to wage war against NATO forces and dispel the argument that Al-Qaeda did not have enough resources to fight against superpowers, thereby answering the question of the resistance's Islamic credentials of having to be resourceful.

As a matter of fact, the state-sponsored debate turned out to be counterproductive. It only exposed the weak grounds the Muslim majority states stood on, and thus attracted more Islamists into the Al-Qaeda embrace.

6

THE SYNTHESIS

In the most difficult terrain of North Waziristan is based Abu Amr Abd al-Hakim Hassan, popularly known as Sheikh Essa, who has been the most visible and accessible Al-Qaeda figure for the Punjabi, Pakistani Pashtun, and Afghan militants. He believes that all the Muslim struggles begin with defiance and *takfeer* (declaring somebody non-Muslim) of the established un-Islamic authority, because this clarifies the rules of the game: who is on whose side in the battle for Islam.

Following the Taliban defeat in Afghanistan in 2001, Al-Qaeda struggled to survive. At the operational level Sheikh Essa pioneered the dialectical process in Pakistan in order to strategize the South Asian theater of war. That dialectical process aimed to orchestrate a clash between the secular forces and the Islamists of Pakistan, to arrive at a point where the Pakistani state apparatus would either remain completely neutral in the US war in Afghanistan or be forced to support Al-Qaeda's resistance against the United States. Al-Qaeda's targets were to gain a complete hold over two Pakistani provinces, the Khyber Pakhtookhwa (formerly NWFP) and Balochistan, both bordering Afghanistan, and to fight the NATO alliance.

Sheikh Essa's 70-year-old body is riddled with injuries. The last one he sustained was during the Pakistan army operation in Angor Ada in 2003. He is known as an ocean of emotions (perhaps the reason for his suffering a stroke in 2007). Essa was the aide of Abdul Qadir al-Audah, an ideologue of the Muslim Brotherhood in Egypt. Al-Audah was executed in 1960s by the Nasser regime. The young Sheikh Essa, a graduate of the College of Commerce in Cairo, then turned against Egypt's ruling establishment. He developed theories on the heresy of Muslim regimes and personally suffered at the hands of the Egyptian government, but his suffering strengthened his resolve and hatred for the existing rulers of Muslim countries.

Sheikh Essa was one of the conspirators in the coup against Anwar Sadat's government in Egypt in 1980, and after Sadat's assassination he was imprisoned. On his release, he was admitted to Al-Azhar University in Cairo and emerged with a degree in theology. In 1986 he went to Afghanistan for the Jihad against the Soviets, and remained close to Abdallah Azzam and Sayyid Imam (aka Dr Fadl). In 1992, he went to Yemen to teach in religious schools but returned to Afghanistan in 1996 on the Taliban's ascendancy to power. When the Taliban regime was defeated by the United States in Afghanistan he migrated to North Waziristan.

The aging factor coupled with sciatica (lumbago) may have contributed to Sheikh Essa's stroke as well. Sheikh Essa was thus unable to take part in combat operations, but he was the source of singular inspiration for the youths coming from the tribal areas for the Jihad. Sheikh Essa was also held in high regard by the militants coming from the Punjab. They listened to his interpretation of *takfeer*, mesmerized. They read his most famous book, *Al-Wala Wal Bara*, "an Islamic benchmark for friendship and foes," which laid down some of the rules and paved the way for the dialectical process in Pakistan which urged a war between diverse segments of Muslim society. His book completely rejected democracy as a system because it brought all political and religious schools of thoughts together and streamlined the liberal Muslim state which he held in contempt. He believed that under the democratic form of governance, even if Islamists were to dominate parliament, as they do in Turkey, they could not establish the totalitarian type of governance or system that is the essence of political Islam. He thus felt that Islam's influence would not transcend borders and would be restricted to the nation-state's boundaries, when the call was for a global Islamic order. His book presents a detailed declaration of heresy for those who support non-Muslims or an unIslamic system, and documents the principles under which Sheikh Essa clearly identified Pakistan as *darul harb* (an abode of war) because it was supportive of the US war on a Muslim Afghan army that was fighting against US-led NATO forces.

Soon disgruntled elements of Pakistani Jihadis, more especially the anti-Shiite Laskhar-e-Jhangvi members including the brutal Qari Zafar (died 2010) from Karachi, Muhammad Afzal of Khanewal, Doctor Umar of Kror Lal Essan, Lyah, Faraz Ali Shami of Faisalabad, Shoaib Ishaq of Faisalabad, Saeed of Jhang, Attock, Doctor Hamid of Lahore, Haji Tariq of Karachi, Hakeem Tahir Abdullah of Lahore who resides in Attock, Ishtiaq of Chunian, Sanaullah of Warbarton, Sheikh Nisar of Sotar Mandi, and Iftikhar Qureshi of Madina Town, Faisalabad, became his disciples. Simultaneously, in North Waziristan two prominent clerics and commanders, Sadiq Noor and Abdul Khaliq Haqqani, became his followers.

Sheikh Essa raised the question first in the Pakistani tribal areas, "Is it sufficient to be a born in a Muslim family or should there be a benchmark on which basis a person, group or country should be labeled as Muslim or heretic?" He compiled the required standards of being a true Muslim in his book *Al-Wala Wal Bara*, which was translated and circulated around the country. The target audience, however, was not ordinary commoners but practising Islamists in the country. Sheikh Essa wanted them to clash with the secularists in the country. He believed in the strategy that the Pakistan Army had to be won over first, before the war in Afghanistan against NATO forces could be won. In *Al-Wala Wal Bara* he cited Ibn-e-Tamiyyah's statement:

> Even when a person is forced into the battlefield against fellow Muslims it is incumbent on that person that he should not take part in hostilities against fellow Muslims, no matter if that person risks execution if he does not obey orders. Similarly, it is completely prohibited for a Muslim to kill another Muslim no matter how much pressure he might be under."

After quoting this, Sheikh Essa commented, "It is clear from Ibn-e-Tamiyyah's statement that those who side with non-Muslims against the Muslims are heretics and have no relationship with the Muslim nation. They are fighting for money and therefore I have no hesitation in declaring them heretics."

Sheikh Essa's literature was a compilation of recognized quotations from the Quran, the sayings of the Prophet Muhammad, and classical Muslim scholars' renderings. He applied all of these to Pakistan's support for the US-led "War on Terror." Sheikh Essa's eyes were on the Islamists in Pakistani armed forces, religious parties, and the Jihadi organizations. He was optimistic that once the Islamists in Pakistan were convinced that Pakistan could no longer be considered an Islamic state while its rulers were allied to the US war and against the fellow Muslims, a revolt (*khuruj*) would follow, whereupon the militants would receive at least one of three benefits.

- Pakistan would not be able to support the US war in Afghanistan.
- Pakistani Islamists employed in the key strategic positions would turn their resources over to the militants.
- If the *khuruj* was successful and Jihadis seized power, they would make available bases in Pakistan to provide the best launching pad for a global Jihad against the West.

Sheikh Essa was wanted by all the intelligence agencies in the country. Being an Arab, although fluent in Urdu and Pashtu, he could easily be spotted as an Al-Qaeda member. Yet he took the risk and traveled all the way from North Waziristan to the major Pakistani cities of Multan, Faisalabad, and Lahore. Sheikh Essa took several copies of his book along with him when he traveled to Lahore. He met Dr Israr Ahmed (who died in 2010), an academic who believed in Islamic revolution and the revival of the caliphate. He also met with the then chief of Jamaat-e-Islami Pakistan, Qazi Hussain Ahmed, and with the chief of Laskhar-e-Taiba, Hafiz Muhammad Saeed. He read out parts of the book and asked whether they were wrong or right. None of these men rejected the contents.

"If all of this is true, why don't you declare as heretic the Pakistan army which undertakes operations in South Waziristan only because the local tribes are supporting the Muslim resistance in neighboring Afghanistan and providing shelters to the Arab Muslim *mujahideen*?" Sheikh Essa questioned. "In principle you are right, but your theories in the present circumstances would only benefit enemies like India and America," Qazi Hussain Ahmed replied. Such responses could not break the will of Sheikh Essa. He continued his interaction with the top religious leadership of the country, and this pursuit took him into the heart of the Pakistani capital city of Islamabad to meet with the prayer leader of Islamabad's Central Mosque, more commonly known as the Lal Masjid (the Red Mosque).

In a modest house attached to the Lal Masjid, hardly 1.5 half kilometers away from ISI headquarters, Sheikh Essa raised the same question again before Maulana Abdul Aziz, the son of the slain Maulana Abdullah who had actively taken part in the Afghan national resistance against the Soviets in the 1980s. Aziz was a simple and straightforward man. Sheikh Essa's sermon and his book had inspired him. Sheikh Essa was desperately looking to get Aziz on his side for obvious reasons. Aziz was not an ordinary cleric or religious scholar. He was a favorite of Pakistan's military establishment because he had raised hundreds of young recruits for the Kashmiri insurgency. Every year Commander Fazlur Rahman Khalil, the head of a Kashmiri militant outfit Harkatul Mujahadeen, came to his door, and within few days of a call by Aziz, hundreds of youths from the *madrassas* were readied to join the Kashmiri struggle.

Many of the religious-minded civil and military bureaucrats based in Islamabad and Rawalpindi used to send their girls to the women's Islamic seminary run by Aziz who, together with his brother Abdul Rasheed Ghazi, headed a citizens' rights committee in Islamabad. Unsurprisingly then, Aziz was a vital asset of Pakistan's military establishment sitting in the heart of Islamabad.

But Sheikh Essa felt that a revolt by the Lal Masjid would be the beginning of the Islamic revolution in Pakistan. "After reading this (Sheikh Essa's book *Al-Wala Wal Bara*) do you still believe that the Pakistan Army is a Muslim army?" Sheikh Essa asked, while reminding Aziz of his duties as a Muslim scholar. "If you refuse the call of *takfeer* on the Pakistan Army, God will never forgive you," Essa emphasized.

Aziz was an emotional person of deep religious conviction. The call of *takfeer* on the Pakistan army amounted to losing all his honor, prestige, and connections with Pakistan's military establishment. But retaining his closeness with the military despite its operations against Islamic militants meant discarding his faith. Abdul Aziz decided to go against the military. Under a pseudo identity he had a letter posted to his own *darul ifta* (an office for issuing religious decrees) asking about the faith status of the Pakistan Army after it had mounted an operation against Muslims in South Waziristan. In response to the query he concluded in a religious decree, "Pakistani soldiers killed while fighting against the *mujahideen* in South Waziristan do not merit a Muslim funeral or a burial in Muslim cemeteries."

Aziz issued this *fatwa* (religious edict) in 2004. The *fatwa* had a huge impact. Dozens of soldiers in the Pakistan Army defied the orders of their seniors to fight, and hundreds of officers and soldiers applied for retirement from service. The situation compelled the army to surrender and strike a deal with the militants. The *fatwa* was the beginning of a new ideological war between the military and the militants. That ideological war aimed to discredit the Pakistan Army's faith and belief, and was more damaging than its military defeats in the tribal areas. The Musharraf regime had invested millions of rupees to hire clerics to support Pakistan Army operations in the tribal areas and to speak against the religious beliefs of the militants, but the Al-Qaeda ideologues sitting in South and North Waziristan launched an organized campaign against them.

The leader of the Islamic Movement of Uzbekistan, Qari Tahir Yaldochiv, who was living in exile in South Waziristan, took the thread from Sheikh Essa and started contacts with Aziz. He sent Uzbek men to Aziz with written notes appreciating the initiative of his *fatwa* against the Pakistan army. "This is the right time to turn this *fatwa* into an organized campaign. Use the network of your *madaris* [Islamic seminaries] and urge the *talibs* [students] and *ulemas* [scholars] to stand in support of *mujahideen* for the Islamic revolution against this infidel army which helps the American assaults to continue in Afghanistan," Tahir urged Aziz in a written note. Sheikh Essa also advised Aziz that instead of sending youths to Kashmir, he should encourage them to play a role in the Islamic revolution.

It was April 2007. I was sitting with Maulana Abdul Aziz on a bedstead woven of jute under a tree in Aziz's residential compound adjacent to Lal Masjid. He was instructing the students to let an Islamic seminary know that he would speak to its students in the evening. "It has been my routine to address the students at Islamic seminaries on a daily basis," Aziz told me. "Maulana, do you want to instigate a Taliban (student) movement on the pattern of Afghanistan for the enforcement of Islam?" I asked. "Indeed I do. And this is the only way to protect Pakistan's integrity which is rapidly plunging into chaos and disintegration due to its ethnic and political polarization," he replied.

Nonetheless, Pakistani intelligence sources were reporting to the presidency that Lal Masjid was demanding the enforcement of Islamic *sharia*, but in fact it was playing mind games under instruction from Al-Qaeda. Whenever the Pakistan Army launched an operation in South Waziristan, Lal Masjid created some mischief which diverted attention from Al-Qaeda's machinations. The intelligence report was partially correct. But that was not the only role delegated to Lal Masjid by Al-Qaeda. Al-Qaeda aimed to promote the Lal Masjid prayer leaders as the leaders of a movement to reinstate Islam, and through them to use Pakistan's Islamic seminaries' structures.

There are approximately 13,500 Islamic seminaries from the Deobandi school of thought adhered to by the Taliban. They are situated all across the country and house 1.8 million regular students. Lal Masjid aimed to use these structures to defy and revolt against Pakistan's policies supporting the US-led War on Terror. That is why its leaders were not primarily interested in the enforcement of Islamic *sharia*. Rather, their aim was to create maximum friction between the Islamists of the country and the Pakistani establishment, so that the Pakistani establishment would eventually succumb to pressure and withdraw its support for the War on Terror.

Al-Qaeda thinkers in North Waziristan wrote and published extensive literature on *takfeer* simply to impress academics like Maulana Abdul Aziz. They did not expect Aziz to pass on those notes in pure academic form in his sermons, but rather to resort to actions and turn the *takfeeri* ideology into a cogent strategy. From 2004 to 2007 – the year when the Pakistani military establishment finally conducted a crackdown on Lal Masjid – Aziz continued to issue defiant religious decrees against Pakistan's military establishment while carrying out such acts as had never before been practiced by any Islamic scholar. For instance, Lal Masjid vigilantes started busting brothels. The Pakistani military establishment advised the Lal Masjid clerics not to take the law into their own hands, and to let Pakistan's law enforcing agencies carry out crackdowns against them instead. To prove a point the Pakistani police carried out massive raids on those guesthouses in Islamabad that had been supplying prostitutes to their clients.

Lal Masjid should have appreciated these efforts of the administration, but this was not what they were looking for. Their aim was to undertake more actions to generate friction. Lal Masjid vigilantes then raided Islamabad's markets, took obscene movies from the video shops and burned them. In the meantime, Aziz continued to address Islamic seminaries all across the country every day. He spoke out against democracy and Pakistan's support for the War on Terror and, without fear or apology, termed the Pakistani style of governance *kufr* (heresy) and claimed that the operations of the Pakistan armed forces against the Pakistani tribes, Al-Qaeda, and the Taliban, were *kufr* too.

What exactly Lal Masjid was up to in the middle of Pakistan's capital was beyond the comprehension of almost everybody, including the top religious leadership of the country. Only Al-Qaeda ideologues understood the undercurrents and real motives behind the defiance.

Pakistani officials, like the minister of religious affairs, Ejaz-ul-Haq, the son of the late president, General Zia-ul-Haq, visited Maulana Abdul Aziz frequently. This was not surprising as Aziz's father, Maulana Abdullah, and General Zia had been very close, and this relation had continued down to their sons. "Maulana, I beg you, please stop all this. I know it will ultimately cause a serious

clash. I am seeing an ocean of fire," Ejaz-ul-Haq was reported to
have said as he held Aziz's feet (a gesture of humility and submission). But all his pleas to Aziz failed. Ejaz-ul-Haq did not have any
idea that Aziz was actually aiming to create more friction to generate
fire. He coldly replied that he would not retreat a single inch from
his position.

Religious-minded ministers in the federal cabinet like Ejaz-ul-Haq
and the leader of then ruling Pakistan Muslim League, Chaudhary
Shujaat Hussain, urged General Musharraf to make special efforts
to reduce the tensions. The outcome of this was an invitation to
Mufti Taqi Usmani, a renowned Islamic scholar and the spiritual
guide of Maulana Abdul Aziz, to come to Islamabad to pour oil
on the troubled waters. Usmani flew from Karachi and reached
Islamabad.

"What are you up to?" Taqi asked Aziz.

"I want an Islamic system of life in Pakistan," Aziz replied
respectfully.

"But what model would you follow – the model of the Prophet
Muhammad (Peace Be Upon Him) or your own?" Taqi inquired.

"Of course, the Prophet Muhammad's model is the only one to
be followed." Aziz answered.

Taqi asked, "Can you please elaborate on the justification for
occupying a children's library [see page 44], kidnapping prostitutes,
detaining cops in the mosque, and creating a law and order situation
in the city by putting video films on fire? Are there any such
instances from the time of the Prophet Muhammad's struggle? Did
we find such modes of struggle in *salaf* [classical Muslim scholars]?
Do you see any difference between a struggle for the enforcement of
Islamic laws and creating chaos in the country?"

Aziz put his head down but did not reply. "Abdul Aziz, I need an
answer," Taqi insisted.

"You are my teacher and my spiritual guide. I do not dare argue
with you," Aziz said.

"Do you then promise me that you will refrain from such
practices in future?" Taqi demanded.

"I will continue to practice what I have been doing because I
think that is the right path," Aziz persisted.

"You intend to do this despite the fact that you don't have any
justifications for such actions in the Quran and the Sunnah [the
Prophet's traditions]?" Taqi asked.

Aziz was silent.

"Abdul Aziz, I hear you still say to the people that you and I have a relationship of guidance, but I now tell you this relation no longer exists. Don't say to the people you take guidance from me," Taqi said furiously. This was the biggest punishment any teacher could have meted out to a disciple, and it meant that Taqi Usmani had expelled Abdul Aziz from his circle for spiritual guidance.

Aziz had tears in his eyes but remained silent.

Taqi did not say another word and went out. Abdul Aziz did not try to stop him.

The Musharraf administration was then left with no choice but to play its last card by inviting the prayer leader of the Mecca Mosque, Sheikh Abdur Rehman al-Sudais, in the hope that his argument would be respected by the Lal Masjid prayer leader. However, al-Sudais's meeting with Aziz also turned out to be an exercise in futility. Finally, Musharraf's military regime decided to take action against the Lal Masjid people on its own. The Rangers and the police were sent to cordon off the area, and demanded that the Lal Masjid students and teachers surrender. Maulana Abdul Aziz and his brother Abdul Rasheed Ghazi refused and delivered fiery speeches in retaliation. Although there were only 11 AK-47 guns in the mosque, the prayer leaders announced to the media over their cellphones that they had guns and suicide bombers ready to confront the establishment forces. The military next sent the chief of the banned Harkatul Mujahadeen, Maulana Fazlur Rahman Khalil, to Lal Masjid as a final effort to win over the clerics. He warned them that their rants had already brought Lal Masjid into the international spotlight, and that the military was bound to follow. He emphasized that the only way to avoid such a military operation was to surrender. He guaranteed that they would be treated with respect during their arrest, and legal bail would be arranged for them within a few months.

With the noose thus tightened around Lal Masjid, Maulana Abdul Aziz finally realized that a prolonged stay would not be possible. He understood that once he had left the place, surrender for his supporters would be easier and he could still command the movement from outside. He put on a *burqa* (a woman's complete covering that hides the face as well as the body) and tried to sneak out of the mosque. But he was spotted by the law-enforcement agencies, arrested, and humiliated on the state-run Pakistan Television in the same *burqa*.

Aziz's attempt to escape outraged the Al-Qaeda ideologues in Waziristan. The chief of the Islamic Movement of Uzbekistan, Qari Tahir, personally called Abdul Rasheed Ghazi and his deputy Abdul Qayyum and warned them that as of now they would have to stay till the last bullet, because that would be the turning point of their struggle, and if they surrendered so easily in future, the whole Islamic revolutionary movement could collapse. Ghazi abided by the instructions. He and his accomplices, his mother, and Maulana Abdul Aziz's son were killed in a military action that followed.

However, the Lal Masjid operation changed the dynamics of the country forever. It laid the foundations for a fresh military struggle, the exit of General Pervez Musharraf from power (one of the reasons for the assassination of Benazir Bhutto, who had approved the Lal Masjid killings), and the discrediting of the religio-political parties of the country (which chose to attend an All Parties Conference in London instead of pressing to prevent the military operation against Lal Masjid). Notwithstanding all of this and contrary to the expectations of Al-Qaeda and Maulana Abdul Aziz, not a single student of the Islamic seminaries from whom they were expecting a Taliban (student) revolt for the enforcement of Islam or/and in favor of Lal Masjid stood up – not even the 18 Islamic seminaries in Islamabad and Rawalpindi.

THE BEGINNING OF REVOLT

Al-Qaeda did not give up. When the funeral prayers for the Lal Masjid students and clerics were being conducted, Al-Qaeda was in communication with its man from the scenic Swat valley. The valley was now in hands of the Tehrik-e-Nifaz-Shariat-e-Mohammadi's Mullah Fazlullah. Fazlullah was the son-in-law of Maulana Sufi Mohammad, the cleric arrested by Pakistan's security agencies for illegally having taken thousand of youths to Afghanistan to fight against the US invasion in 2001.

The little-known Mufti Aftab was then sent by Al-Qaeda from Miranshah, North Waziristan to guide the Al-Qaeda man in Swat on how to pursue the pattern and style of the future struggle. However, the story goes that the purpose of the movement in Swat following the Lal Masjid massacre was not the establishment of Islamic courts, as projected, nor was Mullah Fazlullah Al-Qaeda's real leader there. The real Al-Qaeda leader was Bin Yameen. People who had spent time with Bin Yameen (also referred as Ibn-e-Ameen) during his detention in ISI cells or had worked under his command in Swat, or who had known him from early childhood, agreed on two things about him: his short temper, which stretched to the limits of madness, and his strikingly good looks. Bin Yameen was 6 feet 2 inches tall, had a broad chest, was fair in complexion, and had

a full head of hair. His looks were God's gift, but his short temper
was not inbuilt.

Circumstances were responsible for making an extremely polite
young man into an ideological fanatic. Mufti Aftab used to document
reports on Bin Yameen and send them back to Al-Qaeda ideologues,
and they were convinced that in coming years Bin Yameen would be
the man in Swat to create the maximum friction between the state
authorities and the general public. He was expected to take the
confrontation to the level where the Pakistan Army would not be
able to provide support to the US war in Afghanistan. Al-Qaeda's
instructions and Bin Yameen's fanaticism worked well together,
and turned the movement for enforcing Islamic laws in Swat into a
revolt against the state.

I am not sure whether I should call it his fate that he was born in
Peochar Valley of Swat, the hub of militancy. Legend has it that in
the early nineteenth century the area was the headquarters of Syed
Ahmad Brelvi, the pioneer of the nineteenth-century Jihad in South
Asia against the Sikh dynasty in Punjab and the northern parts of
the present Pakistan. Bin Yameen came from Wanai Namal village,
in Matta in the Peochar valley. Born as a Behloolzai, a subtribe
of the Youzufzai tribe, Bin Yameen was never the playboy of his
village or a poet. He was a school dropout at the matric (high-
school certificate) level. While he was still in his teens he went to
Afghanistan and fought alongside the Taliban against the Northern
Alliance forces of Ahmad Shah Massoud. He was arrested in his
first battle and then spent seven long years in the inhuman jails of
the Northern Alliance. Bin Yameen often remembers how his fellow
Taliban detainees died in the jail. Sometimes he witnessed their swift
deaths while they were talking or cooking. After the Taliban defeat,
he was released by the United States.

But it was not his seven years in the Northern Alliance jails
that had embittered him. After his release from Pansheri prison,
his manners were still extraordinarily polite. He always stood up
to welcome any guest. The marriage and love life of any Pashtun
has always been a very private business. No Pashtun from a village
background would ever confide in anyone over matters of the
heart. But Bin Yameen used to proudly say that his wife (also his
relative) had fallen in love with him and that before their marriage,
when they were only engaged during his prolonged imprisonment
in Afghanistan, all the family members had pressed her to break
her engagement to him and marry somebody else. But against all
Pashtun traditions, the girl defied her family and said that her name

would be tied to Bin Yameen's forever, whether he lived or died. When Bin Yameen was released and went back to his village the first thing he did was to marry her, proud that this was the girl who had steadfastly stood by him despite all the pressures put on her by her family to forget him.

Bin Yameen always said that all the pain and agony of his days in the Afghan prison disappeared after the marriage. It was as if nothing had happened. He started his new life with a loving wife. His wife delivered a son and they moved to Peshawar. Bin Yameen joined Jaish-e-Mohammad, the militant group later banned by Musharraf's regime. Since he was the most knowledgeable person on the Afghan prison system among them – and there were hundreds of Pakistani prisoners languishing in Afghan jails following the defeat of Taliban in Afghanistan in 2001 – he was placed in charge of Jaish's jail affairs. His responsibility was to look after the interests of those who were in Afghan jails and work for their release.

December 2003, when Musharraf was the target of two failed assassination attempts, was the major turning point in the lives of Pakistani Jihadis. They were rounded up like criminals. The state which had been the main supporter and perpetuator of the Pakistani Jihadis turned its back on them. Several Jihadis gave up their struggle and several turned against the state. Bin Yameen was the most prominent of those who came in the later category.

On August 21, 2004, Pakistan's security agencies raided Bin Yameen's house in Peshawar. He was sleeping with his wife. In the next room were two prominent Jihadis, Asif Chakwali and Mufti Sagheer (now in Adyala jail in Rawalpindi). Both Asif and Sagheer broke the police cordon and escaped, but the police who had broken into the house captured both Bin Yameen and his wife and literally dragged them to their vehicles. Bin Yameen was half sleep and half awake, but he saw strangers touching his wife. He attacked them like a wounded lion. He tried to snatch their guns. It took dozens of security personnel to overwhelm him. Both his wife and he were imprisoned. Later his wife and son were released, but Bin Yameen, who had been injured during his transportation, never forgot the humiliation suffered by his wife at the hands of Pakistan's security personnel. He was completely unaware of any plot to assassinate Musharraf, and during the interrogation refused to answer the questions thrown at him. In response, he would either spit in the faces of the inquiry officers, or threaten that on his release he would destroy them and their families. This resulted in a vicious cycle of torture. His inquisitors hung him upside down and beat him, but he only yelled one thing in response, "If I stay alive I will return and avenge all of this." They tied and shackled him but his rage remained unabated. After two months of torture and interrogation, the prison guards and inquiry officers tired of him and sent him to solitary confinement in an ISI detention cell, without a police case being presented against him and without a court trial. He spent two and half years in solitary confinement without further torture or interrogation, but his venom against the Pakistan Army remained high. His prison guards were used to his verbal assaults on them and the Pakistan Army, and sometimes retaliated to his threats with jokes. Just days before his release when he was collecting his clothes and belongings, a corporal asked him in a light vein, "But Bin Yameen, what if you found me walking on the road one day?" Bin Yameen's face turned red and he said in a cold voice, "I will slit your throat."

In an exclusive interview in 2010, a senior Taliban leader reminded me that North Waziristan's environment is so weird it can turn any person into a *takfeeri* within 20 days. As soon as Bin Yameen was released from the ISI's cell, he was summoned to North Waziristan where his hatred of Pakistan's military establishment gained ideological flavor. Mufti Aftab from North Waziristan was Al-Qaeda's emissary in Swat. He took Bin Yameen to North Waziristan. For the Al-Qaeda ideologue, Bin Yameen's life meant nothing. He was a militant who was born for Islam and would sacrifice his life for Islam, although his knowledge of Islam was basic. But his hatred of the Pakistan Army was unbelievable, and this was exactly what Al-Qaeda was looking for. Bin Yameen was given money and Uzbek and Arab fighters to set up his own *maaskar* (training camp). His first task was essentially simple. He was to hijack the Tekrik-e-Nifaz-e-Shariat-e-Mohammadi (TNSM) founded by Maulana Sufi Mohammad, after whose detention it was controlled by Fazlullah. Thousands of people were associated with the TNSM and committed to the enforcement of Islamic laws in Swat and Malakand divisions. Bin Yameen was silently planted in this group.

Al-Qaeda was frustrated after the Lal Masjid operation. Dozens of people had been killed and the most useful Al-Qaeda asset in Islamabad sacrificed without the main purpose being served: not a single person stood up in revolt. Maulana Abdul Aziz had been detained and humiliated. Abdul Rasheed Ghazi and others were buried among tears. This was when Osama bin Laden put his foot down and appointed an *ameer-e-khuruj* (commander for revolt) in

Pakistan. This was Abdul Hameed, alias Abu Obaida al-Misri. Bin Laden instructed him to organize a revolt in the country as soon as possible, and Al-Qaeda urged its Middle Eastern donors to arrange funds on an urgent basis. When these funds were received they were hurriedly distributed amongst all the Al-Qaeda associates including Baitullah Mehsud and Bin Yameen. Targets were then identified to stir up maximum friction in the country, with the aim of making the state ungovernable.

One of the targets was Benazir Bhutto, the only politician in the country to have supported the Lal Masjid operation. However, for a prolonged engagement against the Pakistan Army, a revolt in the Swat Valley (400 kilometers away from Pakistan's federal capital, Islamabad) was essential. Immediately after the Lal Masjid operation, Al-Qaeda mobilized its cadre to provide the logistics for a revolt in Swat. This came on the third day after the burial of Lal Masjid's dead. In Imam Dheri in the Swat Valley, Maulana Fazlullah (known as the Radio Mullah) and his fellows were sitting sadly. "What differences do you have with the government?" I asked him. (Immediately after the Lal Masjid operation I had packed my bags and arrived in the Swat Valley, which I understood would be the next theater of war.)

"The government objects to my FM radio stations. I reject those objections. Mine are non-commercial stations from which I only broadcast Islamic programs. There are other FM stations which are also illegal, but since they broadcast music and vulgarity, the government does not pay any heed to them," Fazlullah protested to me. However, Fazlullah's explanation appeared bizarre. There had been repeated incidents of violence in the Swat Valley. Militants were blowing up video shops in the valley and the state's writ was a question mark. And, the first reaction to the Lal Masjid operation had come in the Swat Valley where the militants carried out an attack on military convoys. Fazlullah said that he had differences with the Pakistan Army as he considered it a continuation of the colonial British Army, but he categorically denied that he was behind any violence.

When I mentioned the attack on the military convoy the day I met Fazlullah, he explained, "Even today's attack on the military will be blamed on me. I tell you, I was with Maulana Abdul Aziz and I am still with him. But I am convinced that implementing *sharia* is the duty of the government, not of an individual. We just demand that the government implement *sharia*, and nothing beyond that." During the interview, when I tried to blame him for instigating the violence, he claimed there were several other groups operating in Swat beyond his control. Fazlullah then got up, apologized to me, and left. "I need to go to my FM radio station this very moment to announce first, that I am not behind any of the attacks, and second, people should not be outraged by the presence of the military in the area. I need to be in constant contact with the people of the area to ask them to restrain themselves from counter-attacks and violence," Fazlullah said as he departed.

After spending a few days in Swat with the militants I became convinced that Fazlullah's and his group's vision of Islam was indeed limited to the demand of implementing Islamic laws in the Swat Valley, an old demand of the people of Swat since the princely State of Swat was annexed by Pakistan in late 1960s when the courts, in any case, were run under Islamic laws. But it was clear that beyond Swat, the militants supported the Taliban resistance, like all other Pashtuns in the former NWFP and parts of Balochistan.

Notwithstanding the rising tide of violence, a revolution in the Swat Valley remained questionable. It nevertheless prompted a military operation. The Fazlullah-led TNSM scattered during the first military push by December 2007, but as soon as the snow had melted the dynamics of the Swat Valley changed again.

This group was the largest of all militant groups in the Swat Valley, and the Pakistani intelligence apparatus labeled it the Tora Bora Group, as it comprised local Pashtuns, as well as Uzbeks and Arabs, led by Bin Yameen.

After the defeat of Mullah Fazlullah in December 2007, Bin Yameen emerged as the top leader, and by January 2008 people were wondering what happened to the easy-going people of the Swat Valley. Bin Yameen's group ambushed military convoys and brutally slit their throats. They took camera footage of this and forwarded it to television channels. Waziristan's Qari Hussain Mehsud, a former leader of the anti-Shiite Laskhar-e-Jhangvi, together with Qari Hussain and Bin Yameen, established a reign of terror there. Defiance meant a very painful death. Within few weeks, the entire police network in the Swat Valley had collapsed and army recruits avoided postings to Swat like the plague. Pakistan's government tried to arm the locals against the militants, but whoever took up arms against them met a horrible fate. Pir Samiullah, a distinguished Brelvi spiritual guide, and his disciples were armed by the Pakistan army with sophisticated weapons, but before his followers could take any action his *darbar* (shrine) was attacked. Pir Samiullah and dozens of his disciples were killed. Bin Yameen frantically searched

for the spiritual leader's body but did not find it. Finally he found
that the Pir had been buried. Bin Yameen had the body exhumed
and hanged it on a pole for several days as an example to those who
would defy him. Bin Yameen's men looted all the banks of Swat and
attacked the vehicles which came from Peshawar with the salaries of
local government employees. He was thus able to enlarge his arsenal
and look after his men's daily rations.

By late 2008 Swat was completely in the hands of the insurgents
and the government had lost all control, with the insurgents having
severed its supply lines. The army then abandoned most of its
ground checkpoints and maintained only a limited presence on some
of the mountain tops where at least the soldiers could be supplied
with food and ammunition by helicopter. For the Pakistan Army the
situation had reached a dead-end. The international media played on
this by running stories of the Swat Valley being lost to the Taliban.
Stunned senior military officials at the military's general headquarters in Rawalpindi did not know what to do next. There was a
consensus, however, that fighting the militants was impossible unless
a much larger force was used, and for that the military would have
to remove some its forces from the Indian border. Pakistani armed
forces think tanks brainstormed and arrived at the conclusion that
the solution lay in accepting the demand of the militants for Islamic
laws in Swat.

ISI's internal security section was convinced that this task could
be achieved through Maulana Sufi Mohammad. ISI had a long
standing arrangement with Sufi Mohammad, so while he was in jail
he was lodged comfortably. The reasons for his being kept in jail
were to show that action had been taken against him after he had
led thousands of youths to Afghanistan following the US attack in
2001, and because two ISI agents wanted to keep him under wraps
as an ace up their sleeve to be played at a time of need. But Sufi
Mohammad was not an ISI proxy. He was really a simple man who
wanted to revive the Islamic laws previously enforced in the Swat
Valley when it was a princely state. Nonetheless, he was loyal to the
military establishment and so was cunningly manipulated by it in the
1990s to destabilize the then premier Benazir Bhutto's government
in the mid-1990s by blocking the Silk Route.

The colonels and majors from the Pakistan Army, who had visited
him frequently, next persuaded Sufi Mohammed to issue a statement
condemning the violence in the Swat Valley and distancing himself
from his son-in-law, Maulvi Fazlullah. As the radical had been
raised by his father-in-law, and the fighters in the entire Swat Valley

including the militants were his devotees, the ISI was confidant that once Sufi Mohammad had retaken charge the situation in Swat would change dramatically.

The Al-Qaeda camps of North Waziristan saw it differently. TNSM had effectively been hijacked by Al-Qaeda and its ideas had been implanted in the Swat militants' minds. Pakistan's armed forces would find themselves in a quagmire. Sure enough the military soon ran so short of supplies and resources with their supply lines cut, that they could not prevent the militants from regrouping and launching new operations inside Afghanistan against the NATO-ISAF forces. As matters deteriorated, ordinary people found themselves obliged to think along different lines for their own survival. They accepted the lasting reality of the militancy and urged Pakistan's military establishment to change its policies on supporting the US terror war. Sufi Mohammad's release and activation could have guaranteed peace and given a breathing space to the military to come up with a fresh strategy to right matters, but Al-Qaeda, which could not oppose Sufi Mohammad, could equally ill afford to see him emerge as an ideologue operated by Pakistan's military establishment.

Al Qaeda then worked on a dispensation to encircle Sufi Mohammad and so isolate Swat. In January 2009 Swat was like a ghost valley where almost every nook and cranny was occupied by militants. But with Maulana Sufi Mohammad launched, the situation abruptly changed. Yesterday's criminal was brought to Peshawar with all government protocols, and there the agreement for the enforcement of Islamic laws in the Swat, Malakand, and Kohistan areas was signed. "We will soon open dialogue with the Taliban. We will ask them to lay down their weapons. We are hopeful that they will not let us down. We will stay here in the [Swat] Valley until peace is restored," Sufi Mohammad told reporters. The military apparatus in Rawalpindi breathed a sigh of relief after the agreement had been signed. They had successfully played their ace and the situation was under control. Mullah Fazlullah announced a ceasefire.

Normal life returned to Swat. People thanked God for peace in the valley. But the international press mounted a campaign against the Pakistan government for its agreement to enforce Islamic laws in the Swat Valley. They saw it as a harbinger of things to come. Pakistan's government discussed the situation with its allies in the War on Terror and convinced them that was the only solution if peace was to prevail in Swat. It then disengaged Pakistani troops from the valley and relocated them to Pakistan's tribal area to use against the militant networks operating from there across the border to fight NATO troops. The international community supported this move.

However, Al-Qaeda was ever-vigilant to the rapidly normalizing situation in Swat. What aspect of Islam was being enforced in the valley was irrelevant to them. The issue was that peace would disengage Pakistan's armed forces from the valley and enable them to start operations in the tribal areas again, which would affect Al-Qaeda's fight in Afghanistan. Once again Al-Qaeda's emissaries were activated. Bin Yameen was asked to play his role. At a juncture when everything had been going according to the plan of the US and Pakistani authorities, militants under the command of Bin Yameen stormed Buner, only 65 miles from Islamabad, in the first week of April 2009.

The ceasefire agreement broke and the media flashed banner headlines that Pakistan was only 65 miles away from capture by the Taliban. The situation which had improved in February 2009 had deteriorated dramatically by April 2009. The government put its foot down and tried to approach Sufi Mohammad again, but he was not to be found. His phones were answered by young men who denied any communication with the man who had started the radical movement in Swat.

Everything had changed, especially when Sufi Mohammad announced an end to his support for peace. The government looked for ways to reach Sufi Mohammad through different channels but was unable to find him. Despite all the pressure on the liberal and secular government of the Pakistan Peoples Party and the Pakistan Army, the president of Pakistan, Asif Zardari, signed the ordinance for the enforcement of Islamic laws in Malakand, Swat, and Kohistan, as a last resort to win over Sufi Mohammed. For Al-Qaeda this had never been the object. Their real aim was to create friction, to arrive at a situation in the theater of war in which the Pakistan Army remained entangled until they withdrew their support for the US war in Afghanistan.

When Sufi Mohammad finally appeared people covered the grassy ground in Mingora Swat in their thousands to listen to his address. The people of Swat as well as the Pakistani military establishment rested their hopes in Sufi Mohammad – that he would diffuse the situation of confrontation after the Taliban's capture of the Buner district. But when Sufi Mohammad emerged onto the stage he was not alone. He was accompanied by eight suicide bombers. Bin Yameen came to Sufi Mohammad and gave him a written speech, saying, "This is from the *mujahideen*. Please read this speech." Sufi Mohammad nodded in assent. Then he started speaking to the crowd. Every word was a bomb. The speech mercilessly butchered the peace accord.

"There is no room for democracy in Islam," Sufi Mohammad said. He called Western democracy a "system of infidels" which had divided Islamic scholars and Muslims into factions, "The Supreme Court and the high courts were two other house of idol worshippers which are strengthening this system of heresy based on the betrayal of God." He gave a deadline for all the judges from Malakand division – including the Kohistan district – to withdraw within four days and set up a *darul qaza* (Islamic court) to hear appeals against the decisions of the government's Qazi courts. He also demanded the appointment of Qazis at the district and *tehsil* (lower administrative units) levels throughout the division (that is, the higher administrative level in the province).

"The government will be responsible for all the consequences if our demands are not implemented," he warned. The cleric then said the Islamic system must be established throughout the world because the world belonged to God, and the existing laws were unacceptable. He said it was impossible to implement the Nizam-e-Adl ordinance – promulgated on the nod of the president and the National Assembly – without support from the army and the police.

Sufi Mohammad's speech changed everything. The international media publicized his address and depicted it as Swat's rule by the Taliban and the beginning of a global Caliphate. The fiercest reaction came from the United States. "The biggest challenge for the US is fighting the Taliban in Pakistan," US Senator Ted Kaufman said. "Pakistan is a big problem right now," he told reporters near the Afghanistan border. The US senator said he had been troubled by Pakistan's recent truce with the Taliban in Swat. "I thought a lot of the problem was that the Pakistani government just didn't have the will [to deal with the Taliban]. ... But now that I've been over there, I'm not sure they have the capacity." Richard Holbrooke, the US special envoy to the region, added, "The Swat deal between the Taliban and the government of Pakistan could affect Islamabad too, which is only 100 km from the troubled valley."

Al-Qaeda had successfully applied its dialectical process to spin the situation in favor of its strategy. In May 2009 came the second battle of Swat, when Pakistan's military launched a ruthless operation against the militants called *Operation Rah-e-Rasat* (Operation for the Right Path). Approximately 2.2 million people in the Swat and

Malakand divisions were displaced as a result, and housed in the refugee camps all across the country. The Pakistan Army deployed its elite Mangla Strike Corps, otherwise used in battles against India. The military also used air cover to advance and bombed the militants' hideouts. Special Services Group (SSG) commandos also took part in the Swat action. Hundreds of militants were rounded up and immediately killed without arrest or trial. The battle continued until the last week of July 2009, when the militants finally retreated to the Hindu Kush mountains and the Afghan provinces of Kunar and Nuristan.

From the Al-Qaeda viewpoint, its strategy was a success as it diverted the Pakistan army's Operation Lion Heart from Mohmand and Bajaur. Militants regrouped in the tribal areas and launched powerful strikes on the two neighboring Afghan provinces. As a result, NATO was forced to flee its border checkpoints in Kunar and left all its main bases in Nuristan unattended. The Swat operation appeared a complete success for Al-Qaeda's dialectical process as the Pakistani nation stood completely divided on ideology.

Pakistan's secularists then boldly stood up against the Islamization of Pakistan. They called for the wings of Islamic seminaries in the country to be clipped. The government arranged religious conferences led by Sufis who spoke out against the Taliban. The Taliban retaliated by killing prominent Islamic scholars like Sarfraz Naeemi. It seemed at first that the situation had turned against the militants, but behind the scenes Al-Qaeda had succeeded in exploiting the ideological contradictions in Pakistan's society, and deepened the ideological divide. With this clash between Pakistani Islamists (mostly from seminaries and religious parties that did not support Al-Qaeda) and the secular forces of the country, Al-Qaeda's dialectical process aimed to create a situation where Pakistan would remain non-governable until Al-Qaeda ideologues and fighters successfully seized control of two provinces, Khyber Pakhtoonkhwa and Balochistan. These two provinces were then intended to become the hub of Al-Qaeda activities to provide recruitment and training for their battle against the NATO troops in Afghanistan.

In pursuit of this, Al-Qaeda's dialectical process, thousands of people were displaced, hundreds of people were killed, the national economy of Pakistan was on the verge of collapse, and Pakistan became completely dependent on US aid. But from all of this, Al-Qaeda could claim only limited success. It had succeeded in gaining a measure of control over parts of Pakistan's tribal areas, parts of its urban centers such as Bannu, Lakki Marwat, and

Peshawar, but was well aware that its control over even these areas would last no more than few weeks at best.

However, during this time Al-Qaeda took advantage of the situation and carried out attacks on NATO's supply line, regrouped its members and launched attacks on the NATO troops in Afghanistan, and succeeded in establishing control over 80 percent of Afghanistan and forcing a situation where Washington had to bring in additional troops. That application of the dialectical process might have seemed brutal, but for Al-Qaeda this was the only way to confront the world's richest and most powerful nations, and to bring this war to a winning conclusion.

7

BUILDING THE EAGLES' NEST

The Taliban made a successful comeback during the spring of 2006 to stun a world that had predicted the total demolition of the movement following the US invasion of Afghanistan in 2001. They had taken refuge in the Pakistani tribal areas situated inside the Hindu Kush and adjoining mountain ranges, where they recruited new blood, organized extensive training progams, and built a new mechanism for generating resources. Over the next five years they were in a position to confront the United States and its allies. On becoming aware of this, the Western allies realized a new strategy was called for. This strategy came to be known as the Af–Pak strategy – a neologism used within US foreign policy circles to define Afghanistan and Pakistan as a single theater of war for future operations. This was a realistic appreciation of the fact that the real theater of war lay in the mountain ranges situated on the both side of the Durand Line, and that war would have to be waged over the whole area if militancy was to be eradicated from South and Central Asia once and for all.

The term 'Af–Pak' was coined by the astute American diplomat and US envoy for the Pakistan and Afghanistan region, Richard Holbrooke, in March 2008 (a year before he officially assumed that post).

> First of all, we often call the problem AfPak, as in Afghanistan–Pakistan. This is not just an effort to save eight syllables. It is an attempt to indicate and imprint in our DNA the fact that there is one theater of war, straddling an ill-defined border, the Durand Line, and that on the western side of that border, NATO and other forces are able to operate. On the eastern side, it's the sovereign territory of Pakistan. But it is on the eastern side of this ill-defined border that the international terrorist movement is located.

This realization formulated US policy from 2008 onwards, which was to have NATO forces operate on both sides of the border. A new mechanism for cooperation in the field of human and technical intelligence was then developed together with the military strategy to be employed against the militants in their Hindu Kush and other mountain retreats. This was first to cut the supply lines the militants had developed on both sides of the Durand Line, then wipe out their hundreds of safe sanctuaries.

There followed the killings of several high-profile Al-Qaeda leaders using Predator drone strikes inside Pakistan's tribal regions, after a secret accord had been signed with Pakistan on the future war strategy. According to a report, this secret accord came after the September visit to Washington by Pakistan's new president, Asif Ali Zardari. It provided new mechanics for the coordination of Predator attacks on a jointly acknowledged list of high-value targets. Behind the agreement was clear recognition by the Zardari government and by Pakistan's new military chief, General Ashfaq Kayani, that the more imminent threat to Pakistan's security came from Islamic terrorists rather than from arch-rival India (David Ignatius, *Washington Post,* November 4, 2008).

From May 2004 to August 30, 2008 there were only 13 drone attacks launched in Pakistan's tribal region, but from September 8, 2008 to April 16, 2010 there were 86, with several drones used to carry out attacks against multiple targets. The drone strikes were complemented by simultaneous US and Pakistani military operations, known respectively as Operation Lion Heart in the Afghan provinces of Kunar and Nuristan, and Operation *Sher Dil* (the Urdu translation of Lion Heart) launched by Pakistan's Army and Air Force in the tribal areas of Bajaur and Mohmand. All four regions of Afghanistan and Pakistan fall in the Hindu Kush mountain ranges.

The Sher Dil operation dislocated 300,000 inhabitants on the Pakistani side and continued until February 2009, when both NATO and the Pakistani armed forces announced the rout of the Taliban and Al-Qaeda in these regions. But as the snow melted on the mountains and the spring set in, the militants were seen to re-emerge, displaying even greater resilience. Their attacks in Afghanistan in the months of August and September shook NATO, with the October 4, 2009 attack on the US base in Kamdesh, Nuristan recording eight US troops dead, a large number of Afghan National Army soldiers killed, and at least 30 Afghan soldiers captured. The United States was then forced to evacuate three of its four bases in Nuristan, and by the last week of November the Afghan Taliban invited the international media to show they had re-established control over Nuristan.

In Pakistan, after February's Operation Lion Heart, the Pakistan Army joined with NATO intelligence and deployed ground forces throughout the Bajaur and Mohmand tribal areas. But the situation continued to deteriorate until April 2010, when the United States had to vacate the strategic Korangal Valley in Afghanistan's Kunar province. That reminded *mujahideen* circles of the evacuation of the Korangal valley by the Soviet Army in 1986, which had marked the beginning of the Soviet defeat in Afghanistan, as it had prompted a stream of militants to pour unhindered into Kunar and then on to Kabul through the strategic Tagab Valley. They reckoned they had carried out so many attacks on their way to Kabul that they had forced the Soviets to withdraw from Afghanistan within three years.

From August 2008 US predator drones unleashed fire on tribal areas while the Pakistani security forces and NATO carried out intensive ground operations to cause a humanitarian crisis. Almost 1 million people from South Waziristan, Bajaur, Mohmand, Khyber Agency, and Orakzai Agency were displaced, yet the world's best armies could not defeat the rag-tag militias of the Taliban and Al-Qaeda. In fact, the attacks presented the perfect opportunity for Al-Qaeda after 9/11 to entrench itself deeper in the Hindu Kush and adjoining mountain ranges, and prove that it was able to confront the most technologically advanced armies in the world without incurring much damage.

Dr Muhammad Iqbal, the great poet of the East and Muslim ideologue of the freedom struggle against British colonial rule in India, wrote that it was not material resources alone but exceptional circumstances, geography, and a spirit of the bird, as free as the mountain eagle, that were the special ingredients for successful resistance. Iqbal recited in his famous poem *Shaheen* (Eagle):

I have cut myself aloof from this vale of dust
Where bread and water constitute man's major quest
Seclusion of the wildness suits my nature
Reclusive has been my temperament since the time's birth
Swooping, shocking, then retiring, pouncing on the prey
I do all this to keep my blood warm.

The lives of the Al-Qaeda men finding safe havens in the mountains ranges between Pakistan and Afghanistan exactly conformed with

Dr Iqbal's words. They swooped down from their Hindu Kush nests to pounce on their prey: NATO forces in Afghanistan and the Pakistan Army on its side of the Durand Line.

After 9/11, there were two categories of Al-Qaeda members: those who were associated with external operations and connected to Al-Qaeda's worldwide networks, and those who were required to make preparations for a long war against the United States and its allies in Afghanistan. Khalid Sheikh Mohammad, Ramzi bin Shib, Abu Zubaida, and others were associated with external operations, and it was therefore suitable for them to reside in Pakistan's urban centers. All of them were arrested in Pakistani cities. But more formidable Al-Qaeda military commanders such as Khalid Habib and Abu Laith al-Libi, who were associated with Al-Qaeda's military strategy in Afghanistan and who had lived in the Pakistani tribal areas from 2001, died in the mountains.

Whether in Pakistan's cities, or in its tribal areas, however, the mission of all Al-Qaeda members was not to live in hiding but to carry out missions against US interests. Al-Qaeda members in urban centers were arrested because they had been active in the field when they appeared on the intelligence radar. Similarly, Al-Qaeda commanders such as Khalid Habib and Abu Laith al-Libi were killed in the field.

To live in the Pakistani tribal areas was a strategic decision taken by Al-Qaeda. There is no better terrain in the world to fight a guerilla operation than the area between Pakistan and Afghanistan. It is a natural fortress that makes for the best defensive as well as offensive positions, and there are secret tunnels to provide safe retreats and from which deadly attacks against an enemy can be launched undetected. The selection of the right terrain had always been critical to the Al-Qaeda plan against threats while it was orchestrating a war against the Western armies. It was like a magic castle in the *One Thousand and One Nights* tales surrounded by an astounding maze that makes access by an enemy next to impossible. Al-Qaeda could never have undertaken such maneuvers anywhere else in the world, whether in the mountains of Yemen, the deserts and cities of Iraq, or Somalian jungles, as they were able to against NATO and the Pakistan Army in the Hindu Kush, and the adjoining mountain ranges which lean southwards to the western Pakistani province of Balochistan and westwards into areas of Iran down to the Arabian Sea. This is territory where no conventional army or special forces brigade can operate, even with the most sophisticated of weapons in world history. Only a rag-tag militia which roams as free as the mountain eagle can survive and fight.

HOW THE TALIBAN MANEUVERED

A long journey undertaken from dusk till dawn through the Hindu Kush, in Kunar (Afghanistan) and Mohmand and Bajaur in Pakistan, gives a glimpse of what a war in the Hindu Kush is like, albeit between the world's richest, largest, and best-equipped army and the poorest of the world's rag-tag militias.

I was almost done with my journalistic work in the Kunar Valley when my Taliban host Zubair informed me of a possible raid on his village situated in the Sarkano district. Zubair, I, and two other Taliban members left Zubair's house in a hurry at dusk after saying evening prayers. It was May 15, 2008, and we were walking up the track of the village to the mountains to cross into Mohmand.

Because of me, a native of an urban center who was totally unfamiliar with mountain treks, the Taliban moved slowly. Our walk began when the shadows of the darkness descended over a lush green valley. We took cover under trees on hearing noises of blasts followed by gunshots and helicopter gunships hovering in the skies above us to impede our passage. We were pretty sure that some Taliban groups had attacked a NATO position in a nearby village, but we were not sure which one. Before we moved on, we wanted to be certain we knew where the battle was going on.

Soon the noise of helicopters compounded by the sound of drones flying over our heads forced us to move faster. Often after the Taliban attacks, NATO forces would fan out over the area and round up suspects. We did not want to face such a situation so we moved towards a sanctuary from where we could proceed to our destination in Pakistan unhindered.

My guides reassured me that soon we would reach a safe house, but in the dark I could not see any sign of human life. Over narrow ridges, through water streams flowing through the mountains, stumbling over stony rocks, we came to an area surrounded by trees. When we entered the hollow we saw a small mud hut. That was the safe house of the Taliban.

My Taliban guide Zubair talked over the wireless and in a short while informed me that the Taliban had attacked the Korangal area from several directions, as well as the Nawa Pass near the Mohmand border – the route we had used to enter Afghanistan. Zubair said that because of the new situation we would have to take the long route home and return to Pakistan through Bajaur. We simply changed direction from east to west, exactly the same way as the Taliban changed their positions when they were chased. If they were to engage in battle on the Mohmand side in Pakistan, they would enter through Bajaur. After traveling a small distance I could see why no conventional army could gain advantage in such a vast area, especially when the militants had all the routes covered. From where the militants were positioned they could spot any foreign army easily, and target it with minimum damage to themselves. Against this, for any invading forces chasing the militants on foot through the narrow mountain passes, fast-flowing streams, and thick jungle, the place was a death trap.

Zubair decided on a route through a thick mountain forest. The destination was now Bajaur, and this further showed me how the terrain itself would fight against an invader. We worked our way through the forest which provided good cover, but the going was tough, with thorny bushes ripping our clothes to the skin. Zubair told me that if the United States were to airdrop personnel into this forest, the militants had dozens of caves to hide in and would not be found. At dawn, we entered Pakistan along with many villagers from nearby villages who were also going to Bajaur to buy flour and other food items. Early morning prayers with the Taliban on the mountain tops unveiled the whole region: we could see Kunar, Nuristan, Mohmand, and Bajaur through the mountain haze. The Taliban choice of this inhospitable terrain was apparent: huge deserted spaces where hardly anyone passes in months, yet a region replete with life-sustaining sources such as spring water, fruit trees, vegetables, and some game.

The wild terrain was perfect for Al-Qaeda to recruit people, organize militias, and provide them with training. High-profile Al-Qaeda leaders such as Osama bin Laden and Dr Ayman al-Zawahiri lived in those areas for a long time. Zawahiri was spotted twice around Bajaur and attacked by CIA drones, but this only happened only when he chose to attend a dinner in a populated center in Bajaur. Although the United States was aware of the Al-Qaeda leaders' presence in the area, it was unable to orchestrate any cohesive action against them. The United States did launch several operations in the Hindu Kush in pursuit of bin Laden "dead or alive," but its forces were nearly always surrounded by Taliban guerrillas and sustained heavy casualties.

AN INSURGENT WORLD IN THE HINDU KUSH

The Hindu Kush connects with several smaller ranges (the Spin Ghar, Tora Bora mountains, Suleman Range, and Toba Kakar) and forms a corridor which passes through Pakistan's tribal areas and the Afghan border provinces all the way down to the Pakistani coastal area of Balochistan. This approximately 1,500 kilometer corridor spreads across Pakistan, Afghanistan, and Iran, down to the Arabian Sea, a region of the Indian Ocean. It is an amazing labyrinth which can hide an entire world inside it, and it provides a large area for renegades and outlaws to travel safely from Afghanistan to Iran without being accosted by security forces.

This terrain had earlier facilitated the 11-year-long war against the Soviets by successive *mujahideen* and Taliban governments in Afghanistan, and was now the strategic backyard of the Islamic resistance as a natural safe haven for Al-Qaeda. The major irritant was the influence of the government of Pakistan. Pakistan governed the region under old British colonial laws, and even before 9/11, when it came under US influence, it aimed to increase its authority by urbanizing the remote and tribal areas which had been a safe haven for all kinds of outlaws for centuries.

Pakistan's seven tribal areas (see page xix) were from the time of British colonial rule a buffer between Afghanistan and British India. They were run by bureaucrats known as "political agents," who represented the governor of the North West Frontier Province (now Khyber Patyoonkhwa). After the partition of British India and the emergence of Pakistan as an independent state, more or less the same arrangement continued. The political agent reported to the governor of the former NWFP and completely different laws were applied in this tribal belt. The tribal chiefs were the most important units of governance.

Subsequent to the Taliban's defeat in 2001, Al-Qaeda invested all its money and energy in capturing and influencing this area, and effectively used this historical and natural buffer between Afghanistan and Pakistan as a strategic hedge to fight the United States and its allies. Al-Qaeda was certain that even the world's most advanced weaponry would fail to defeat the militant movement in this type of terrain. Before 9/11, there was no need for Pakistan to deploy troops on its western borders – that is, the tribal region. However, after 9/11 Pakistan came under US pressure and was forced to deploy 80,000 troops there. This number rose with the passage of time. Al-Qaeda anticipated that the circumstances after

9/11 would change the dynamics in the region, and that the Pakistan Army would play a hostile role against it. Therefore from 2001 onwards Al-Qaeda focused on complete control of the territory. That is the reason why there was not much fighting in Afghanistan against NATO troops from 2002 to 2004.

Only after Al-Qaeda had gained effective control of the area did it focus its attention on fighting in earnest against NATO in Afghanistan. Al-Qaeda then spent two years on capacity building for coherent guerrilla warfare in Afghanistan. At the same time it established strong bases from where the militants could fight – if necessary, against both US and Pakistani forces.

Initially Al-Qaeda's influence was limited to South Waziristan, North Waziristan, and parts of Bajaur. But over the passage of time it cunningly crafted circumstances to change the old colonial model of the political agent's office and replace it with militant local militias running the show. Al-Qaeda then promoted and spread this arrangement to the rest of Pakistan's tribal areas, and by 2008 all seven of Pakistan's tribal agencies were seen to be under the influence of Al-Qaeda-inspired militants.

From 2002 to 2008 it was a continuous struggle. Pakistan might have prevented Al-Qaeda strengthening its strongholds in the tribal areas, and indeed did make some efforts to outmaneuver the organization. However, Pakistani officials failed to grasp that Al-Qaeda's real advantage lay in it being an ideologically motivated movement which could not be confronted by military operations without judicious political actions. Pakistan launched several operations from 2004 to 2007 in South and North Waziristan following the pattern of regular military missions. The operations lacked macro perspective and coherent strategy. For instance Musharraf's government did not carry out military operations against the militants supported by a "national" message defining a political process. Against this, the militants used the Islamic ideology as their main weapon. Thus, even after their initial defeats or retreats, they were able to make comebacks and aggressively expand their sway over the Bajaur, Orakzai, Kurram, Mohmand, and Khyber Agencies. In short, the militants always had a broader macro strategy in their minds whereas the Pakistan Army carried out operations within a much narrower prism. There was, at the same time, another factor which eventually went in favor of Al-Qaeda.

Following the 9/11 attack, Pakistan's military establishment expected a US defeat within five years. In anticipation of this Musharraf held a series of meetings with several top Jihadi and religious leaders including Maulana Fazlur Rahman, Maulana Samiul Haq, Hafiz Muhammad Saeed, Qazi Hussain Ahmed, and Fazlur Rahman Khalil. He asked them to lie low for five years with the view that the situation would change after this period. Musharraf was convinced that the United States would eventually have to leave this theater of war and Pakistan would be able to revert to its previous policies of supporting the Islamists in Afghanistan, while fueling the separatist movement in Indian Kashmir. Commitment to this military doctrine thus prevented Pakistan from launching an all-out war against the militants in the tribal areas. With this in mind Pakistan's armed forces kept hostilities at minimum levels, convinced that once the United States left, Pakistan would be able to reconnect with the tribes.

However, this was a misreading of an evolving situation. The United States could never have left the theater of war within five years. In fact, the war flared up further after five years, with hostilities reaching levels where it became impossible for the United States to even consider an early exit. Gradually all the states of the region became embroiled in fighting the Islamic insurgents. Pakistan, especially, became so deeply enmeshed that its army was left with no option but to conduct an all-out war against the insurgents. But it was too late. The boat had been missed. The militants had expanded their capacity to retaliate to a level where they were able to manipulate and maneuver the war to their advantage. Their first choice was to limit operations only to particular belts of Khyber Patyoonkhwa and south-west Balochistan, both of which areas touched the Durand Line. However, when Pakistan's military operations expanded, the militants broadened their range of operations to include cities.

This strategy stunned Pakistan's military establishment. The militants unleashed attacks and established strong insurgent pockets in all the major cities of Khyber Patyoonkhwa including Dera Ismail Khan, Bannu, Lakki Marwat, and Kohat. People even feared the fall of Peshawar to the militants in 2008–09.

Earlier, Al-Qaeda had jarred establishment nerves by opening a new war front in the middle of Pakistan's capital, Islamabad, with the Lal Masjid affair in July 2007. After that, Al-Qaeda spread its war throughout Pakistan to open an enlarged long-term theater of war. From the tourist resorts of the Swat Valley they took the war to Buner in 2009. Buner is only 65 miles away from Islamabad as the crow flies. All of this was planned to rattle Western forces in their Pakistani and Afghan border bases and enable Al-Qaeda to entrench its positions for future battles. A befuddled Pakistan Army danced to the tune of the militants. They were dragged in the direction the militants wanted them to take.

Decision makers in Washington made qualified estimates of the militants' strength as guerrillas poured through Pakistan's tribal areas into Afghanistan to play havoc with the Western coalition forces from 2006 onwards. Washington immediately moved towards implementing a new strategy. Devised in late 2007, this strategy focused on training the Pakistani armed forces on counter-guerrilla operations, primarily by building up their capacity to corner and capture militants inside Pakistan. The United States sent hundreds of private defense contractors to train Pakistan's armed forces for this task. These contractors bought land inside Pakistan to train the armed forces in counter-insurgency tactics, and simultaneously planted electronic surveillance equipment to trace the movements of the militants. As a consequence, both countries were able to develop mechanisms for far better intelligence sharing. By August 2008 this translated into well-coordinated joint micromanagement of the theater of war. With that and the information Pakistan had collected earlier on militant hideouts, the United States was able to pinpoint and shoot specific targets employing CIA Predator drones.

US forces and the Pakistan Army continued coordinated operations on their respective sides of the Durand Line, but this accomplished little more than drain their energies and resources. By 2008 Al-Qaeda's ideology was too deeply entrenched in the minds of the mountain men, their strategy so clearly marked on every mountain, rock, and stone in the tribal areas, that the militant leaders felt little worry facing the world's best armies. They had the advantage of the free mountain eagle which flies at will from one high pass to another, while the thick forests and soaring mountains helped their scattered rank and file to regroup and live to fight another day.

From 2008–10, the Pakistan Army and NATO launched three powerful and determined military operations around the Hindu Kush on both sides of the Durand Line. Each time the Pakistan Army made claims of success, but each time after the curtain had lifted Al-Qaeda was seen to be in control of affairs in the theater of war.

TRIBAL INSURGENCY: A BATTLE BEFORE THE REAL BATTLE

The US decision-making corps had lumped Pakistan and Afghanistan into one theater of war in 2008–09. This was a late realization of the situation. The Afghanistan-specific war till 2007 had allowed Al-Qaeda to reinforce its position and by the time reality dawned, the United States had missed its cue. Al-Qaeda had already designated Pakistan and Afghanistan as a single theater of war in planning the 9/11 attack on the US mainland, anticipating that without planning battlegrounds in both Pakistan and Afghanistan, its war on the West would be a non-starter.

Had Al-Qaeda not migrated to Pakistan's tribal areas and not envisaged a battle plan against two hostile armies (NATO in Afghanistan and the Pakistan Army in Pakistan), its guerrilla operations in Afghanistan would have died down by the end of 2002 and its retreating forces would have been rounded up and decimated by early 2003. But Al-Qaeda had already identified Pakistan and Afghanistan as a single theater of war, and it based its entire strategy on this. Its initial focus was to reinforce its positions and bases in Pakistan's tribal areas to fight the Pakistan Army, but the war against the NATO forces in Afghanistan was always its actual goal, and it knew that goal could not be realized without preserving its mountain strongholds in the Hindu Kush and other mountain ranges in Pakistan and Afghanistan. A geographical study of the region explains why.

At the crossroads of south-east Afghanistan and Pakistan's north-western borders, the Afghan province of Nangarhar borders Pakistan's Khyber Agency, Orakzai Agency (connected through some passes), and part of Kurram Agency. The Afghan province of Paktia borders Kurram Agency. The Afghan provinces of Kunar and Nuristan border Pakistan's Mohmand and Bajaur agencies, as well as the Chitral region. The Afghan provinces of Khost and Paktika border Pakistan's tribal North and South Waziristan. From South Waziristan a route passes through Pakistan's non-tribal areas through extremely rugged territory all the way to south-west Balochistan, across the border from which are situated the Afghan provinces of Helmand and Kandahar.

The Afghan provinces have always been the Taliban's spiritual heartlands, while Pakistan's tribal regions in the north-west and non-tribal regions in its south-west were their strategic backyard – the home of Taliban support. The battle that the United States and its allies faced was to secure the control of the Taliban heartlands in Afghanistan. Therefore all of NATO's combat forces and combat operations focused on south-east and south-west Afghanistan. Had any confrontation been possible against NATO forces in south-east or south-west Afghanistan, the Taliban would not have retreated in 2001. The reason is that south-east Afghanistan, apart from the provinces of Kunar and Nuristan, comprises flat plains. No province of south-east Afghanistan offers the type of environment that facilitates a sustainable guerrilla war. The exceptions are the defiant Hindu Kush and its adjoining mountain ranges, which have natural cover and passes that allow fighters to retreat into Pakistan's tribal areas to regroup again for fresh attacks inside Afghanistan.

The Islamic spirit is traditional and inbuilt among the tribes living in the Hindu Kush. This virtually guarantees support for Al-Qaeda and Taliban during their retreats and offensives, while a network of Islamic seminaries runs across the face of the land, acting a natural breeding ground to boost the numbers of Al-Qaeda and Taliban diehards. In this near-perfect arrangement for Islamic militancy, the one irritant was the Pakistan-government-backed tribal system in all seven of its tribal agencies. Al-Qaeda was well aware that all of its geographical, ideological, and resource advantages could wash away if the Pakistan government intervened at the behest of the United States. But Pakistan's tribal areas are also the weak link of the state of Pakistan. These areas have an estimated population of 3.3 million, and are the most impoverished part of the nation. Despite being home to 3 percent of Pakistan's population, they contribute only 1.5 percent to gross domestic product. The literacy rate here is a low 17.42 percent, which is well below the 43.92 percent national average.

The tribal areas had become part of Pakistan under a special dispensation. No Pakistani laws were to apply there. Governance was to follow the pattern of British colonial rule, with the old colonial laws applied. The tribal areas are said to enjoy an autonomous status, but in fact they are in the firm grip of Pakistan's military establishment, which governs the region as would any foreign army managing a colony. Under the old tribal system, the authority of the political agent appointed by the central government to oversee affairs was limited to "protected areas": that is, roads and government buildings – nothing beyond this. The tribal areas themselves were governed by *riwaj* (customary laws). The political agent was bound to follow *riwaj* when operating in these areas. That is why the agent was called a political agent rather than an administrative officer. The agent had to deal with the tribes politically. Even today, there is no *thana* (police station), no *katchari* (lower court) and no police force. Tribal laws see to all disputes on the basis of *riwaj* overseen by the *jirga* (tribal council). There are major concessions in taxation. But all of this does not come free.

In return for these concessions (and these are collective concessions from which the tribes all benefit), there is collective responsibility, – a trade-off with every tribe responsible for the security of its own areas, called *apni mitti ki zamdari* (responsibility for one's own land). This entails that roads in these areas remain open for the political administration to carry out its historical responsibilities without hindrance, which loosely translates into free access for traditional law-enforcing agencies, like the Frontier Corps (a paramilitary force comprising of Pashtuns only) and *khasadars* (tribal police) to oversee affairs.

The arrangement is that the tribes are reminded that in exchange for the concessions granted, it is their collective responsibility not to allow their territory to be used as a sanctuary for anti-state elements and criminals. If there is a violation of the agreement, the Frontier Crime Regulations (FCR) can be brought into play. Thus, if there is a violation by a tribe or an individual, the first step is to call a *jirga* of the tribal elders and give them a reasonable period of time to rectify the problem. If the matter is not rectified, pressure is exerted on the offending tribe through penalties and stoppage of its allowances. If that does not work, punishment is meted out, starting with the close family of the offending individuals. They can be arrested under the FCR. But as collective responsibility is central to the equation, if that still does not work, the FCR (or in other words, the state) is entitled to impose an economic blockade on the tribe by sealing its shops and freezing its accounts. If nothing works, punitive military action is taken.

Al-Qaeda looked to understand the weaknesses of the tribal system to bend tribes to its will. It had to spread the feeling that the tribes were living under foreign occupation, and to lay the grounds for launching a rebellion against the state of Pakistan. Al-Qaeda went two steps beyond this. It did not merely address the grievances of the tribes against the state, it declared the Pakistani establishment "heretical" as an ally of the foreign occupation forces in Afghanistan. It then insisted the tribes break their ties with Pakistan to establish Islamic Emirates in all seven of the tribal agencies, and next pressed for the appointment of local *ameers* (chiefs) for each tribal area, and a "Grand *ameer*" for the entire tribal belt. This arrangement began in late 2007, by which time thousands of youths had joined with the militants. By 2009–10, the militants' strength had risen close to 100,000 armed men. For the local tribes that was the end of colonial rule and the beginning of self-governance, for which they were thankful to Al-Qaeda.

REVOLUTION IN THE MOUNTAINS

By 2005–06 Pakistan's tribal areas were a new world. Hundreds of tribal chiefs and local clerics in South Waziristan, North Waziristan, and Bajaur had been denounced as spies for the Pakistan Army and the United States. They were either killed or forced out. These tribal chiefs and the clerics had been henchmen of Pakistan's remote-controlled tribal system. Their elimination caused a complete collapse of the tribal system. Al-Qaeda filled the vacuum.

Each tribal area produced a few especially powerful pro-Al-Qaeda militants. They took de facto charge of the system. Some incidents established their complete control. Of these, the most significant occurred in December 2005. A group of Taliban fighters were heading to Khost to launch an operation in Afghanistan when they were stopped by some criminals demanding money for safe passage. The Taliban refused, and were allowed to pass. However, a few kilometers down the road the criminals fired a rocket and blew up their vehicle. Four Taliban belonging to the Wazir tribe were killed. The incident outraged local supporters of the Taliban, who converged near Miranshah and warned people to leave their homes if these were located near safe-havens for criminals. A raid was then conducted on one criminal sanctuary. In the fierce 15-minute gun battle that followed, several gangsters were killed, others were seized, and many fled.

Over the next three days, according to a video, the Taliban smoked out numerous criminals from their hideouts all over North Waziristan. Many were executed at mass rallies in the Miranshah Bazaar ("The Taliban's bloody foothold in Pakistan", *Asia Times Online*, February 8, 2006).

Al-Qaeda put its foot down after that powerful show of Taliban force, and advised the Taliban to continue with their program to eliminate vices and promote virtues in society. The local militants then set up checkpoints, and by January 2006 started dislodging the checkpoints of Pakistan's security forces. The local *jirga* system was next replaced by Islamic courts.

The Islamic state of North Wazirsitan came into being at the start of 2006, as did almost simultaneously the Islamic state of South Waziristan. The message traveled to Bajaur, Mohmand, and Orakzai, and by the end of 2007, Al-Qaeda had brought the whole movement under the umbrella of the Tehrik-e-Taliban Pakistan, a conglomerate of different militant groups from Pakistan's tribal areas. There was one commander in each tribal area, and all these commanders came under one *ameer*. This political dispensation conclusively replaced Pakistan's old tribal system.

The tribal areas had already become Al-Qaeda's main base for global operations. Under the new dispensation, Al-Qaeda now had complete ownership of Pakistan's tribal belt. North Waziristan was Al- Qaeda's focal point, with the town of Mir Ali and villages on its outskirts turned into Al-Qaeda colonies. Locals shared their homes with the Al-Qaeda militants. Later, this arrangement spread to the other tribal areas such as South Waziristan, Khyber Agency, Orakzai Agency, Mohmand, and Bajaur. Al-Qaeda's media wing, Al-Sahab and Ummat, was established in these areas with state-of-the-art studios in Bajaur, South Waziristan, and North Waziristan. The studios produced propaganda videos which were later distributed throughout Afghanistan, Pakistan, and Iraq.

By late 2005, the Taliban and Al-Qaeda, who were widely believed to have been completely routed from Afghanistan, had not only successfully regrouped and entrenched themselves in Pakistan's tribal areas, but had created a strong natural fortress where their armies were fully protected. Nobody could disconnect them from their supplies, and they launched frequent attacks on their enemies – the Pakistan armed forces and NATO.

Even before the old tribal dispensation had been displaced in late 2007 by the Tehrik-e-Taliban Pakistan, the Taliban spring offensive in 2006 had stunned the world. According to the West, the Taliban strength in Afghanistan was no more than 2,500, but in 2006, uninterrupted streams of Taliban fighters emerged from Pakistani tribal areas and played havoc with NATO forces. Although the Taliban suffered massive casualties, they still managed to establish a reign of terror in Afghanistan.

In a knee-jerk reaction, the United States started building military bases on Durand Line crossings near Pakistan's tribal areas, but these bases turned out to be sitting ducks for the militants. The militants carried out so many attacks on them that by October 2009 NATO announced the abandonment of all its military bases on the Afghan–Pakistan border.

The new environment called for a change of all previous strategies and equations in the region. Washington arrived at the conclusion that without declaring the whole region a single theater of war, the war in Afghanistan could not be won. That was how the term

Af–Pak was coined. As a result, within a period of 18 months the United States carried out 86 drone missile strikes inside Pakistani territories and launched several military operations. But everything, including the geography and the tribal order, continued to go the way of the militants. Even when the Pakistan Army carried out attacks from the Pakistani side and NATO forces launched assaults from the Afghan side, with drones firing missiles from the skies and the Pakistan air force bombing Taliban and Al-Qaeda positions, the Hindu Kush and adjoining mountain ranges served to protect them.

The militants did sustain some losses, and 18 of their top commanders were killed by drone strikes including Abu Laith Al-Libi, Khalid Habib, Baitullah Mehsud, and Tahir Yaldochiv, but Al-Qaeda's five-year-long plan in the tribal areas to use geography as a fortress was so well-placed that the numerous drone strikes and the military operations were unable to dent their long-term purpose.

Meanwhile Western capitals and Pakistan were working together for the conclusive defeat of the militants in the tribal areas by banking on secular parties like the Awami National Party (ANP) making ground inside the tribal areas and propping up certain tribes against Al-Qaeda and the Taliban. On the other side, a military campaign was launched to crack down hard on the militants, but Al-Qaeda was satisfied it had enough war resources to hold its fortresses in the tribal areas for another few years. In the meantime it was working on its other project – to reestablish geographical connections with the Arab world, Turkey, and the Central Asian republics in order to build more fortresses for new theaters of war. All roads went through Iran.

AL-QAEDA TAKES STEPS FOR BROADENING TIES WITH IRAN

In 2009, Al-Qaeda forged an alliance with the Iranian Jundullah organization led by Abdul Malik Rigi (executed by the Iranian authorities in 2010). The agreement was that Rigi would facilitate the militants' movements on Iranian smuggling routes to Turkey, the Central Asian Republics, and to Iraq and back. In return Al-Qaeda would help Rigi with money and training to carry out terror missions in Iran.

Al-Qaeda was cognizant of the fact that Jundullah's enabling access to the terrain would be limited, but it anticipated a huge turnout of human and material resources to connect Central Asia, the Middle East and Turkey, and Pakistan's tribal areas in the coming years. It was aiming at a long-term plan that came to a head suddenly because of an incident involving a diplomat.

Tehrik-e-Taliban Pakistan led by Hakeemullah Mehsud abducts an Iranian diplomat, November 13, 2008

At about 7.30 on the morning of November 13, 2008, Iranian diplomat Heshmatollah Attarzadeh was in the Hayatabad neighborhood on his way to the Iranian consulate in Peshawar, where he had worked for the previous three years. Peshawar is the capital of North West Frontier Province, recently renamed Khyber Pakhtoonkhwa to reflect its dominant ethnic Pashtun population.

Attarzadeh's car was intercepted by two other cars and, in a hail of bullets, forced to stop. Attarzadeh was seized by two armed men, bundled into one of the vehicles and taken to South Waziristan. This was the home of the TTP. Attarzadeh's bodyguard, a Pakistani police officer, was shot dead in the first exchange of gunfire.

The incident made international headlines and Iran's Foreign Ministry called it an "act of terrorism." A day before Attarzadeh's abduction, a US aid worker had been shot and killed outside the Iranian consulate in Peshawar. Typically in such abductions, a ransom demand quickly follows. In this case there was only silence. There followed long negotiation between Iranians and Al-Qaeda, during which time some rapport between the two had developed. Al-Qaeda had once had good relations with Iran, but these had soured because of a couple of incidents during the Taliban regime's ascendancy. The first was when eight Iranian diplomats were killed (where, how, and by whom was moot). Since Al-Qaeda had been the Taliban's ally at the time, Iran had taken umbrage. In addition, Abu Musab al-Zarqawi, a Jordanian militant allied with Al-Qaeda, had carried out some telling operations against the United States in Iraq. In some of his operations he had targeted Iraqi Shiites as well as the revered shrines of the descendants of the Holy Prophet Muhammad. As a consequence, Al-Qaeda and Iran had drifted apart. However, in the changing international circumstances it was inevitable that Iran and Al-Qaeda would draw closer. The negotiations between

Al-Qaeda and Iran over the release of the Iranian diplomat helped build a rapport.

As a result of that rapport, Iran released Iman bin Laden, the daughter of Osama bin Laden, and then released several other Al-Qaeda members it had detained after 9/11 when several of them had tried to get out of Afghanistan through Iran (read "An ATOL Exclusive: How Iran and al-Qaeda made a deal," *Asia Times Online*, April 30, 2010). In return Al-Qaeda released the captured Iranian diplomat in March 2010. Although Iran and Al-Qaeda developed ties which might be useful for the movement of pro-Al-Qaeda militants in the region, Al-Qaeda's ties with Iran's Jundullah remained stronger – a backup arrangement in case its relations with Iran soured again.

The stage was set for Al-Qaeda by 2010 to open up new theaters of war in Central Asia as well as in the Middle East, but its central headquarters remained South Asia, and in particular the Pakistani tribal belt. Hundreds of drone attacks rained down from the skies. Dozens of land-based military operations were conducted and dozens more lay in store, but Al-Qaeda's tribal belt fortress stood up to the battering – a trap sprung for the world's top armies to come and exhaust their energies and resources.

AN AMAZING MAZE

The Hindu Kush and other mountain ranges along the Durand Line are natural fortresses for Al-Qaeda but at the same time a strategic corridor which takes their fight from eastern Afghanistan to western Afghanistan, and from southern Afghanistan to northern Afghanistan. This is the magical terrain which criss-crosses through the rugged mountains of southern Afghanistan to Iran, and from there on to the Indian Ocean and back all the way up to China and Central Asia. This intricate maze is linked with the Pamirs, which are aptly called the *Bam-e-Duniya* (the roof of the world).

This is the terrain where the entire political and cultural dynamics are controlled by Al-Qaeda, taking the Taliban's battle from the southern Pashtu-speaking regions of Pakistan and Afghanistan through to Northern Afghanistan's predominately Dari-speaking anti-Taliban region. This is Al-Qaeda's "iron curtain" which repels the powerful armies of NATO and Pakistan and helps the Taliban and Al-Qaeda to continue their forward march to Kabul. There are at least three safe points through the Pakistani Mohmand, Bajaur, and Chitral areas along the Hindu Kush at which Al-Qaeda and the Taliban find easy access through Afghanistan's Kunar and Nuristan provinces to the north-eastern Taghab Valley in the Afghan province of Kapisa. This takes them to the gates of Kabul to carry out their attacks. Kapisa is predominately a Tajik province, but Taghab is majority Pashtun.

Every year, at least 2,000–5,000 fighters are launched through this corridor into Afghanistan. These fighters live in the Hindu Kush, regroup and train there, and then launch their attacks on a rotational basis. They leave Nuristan and Kunar ungovernable and through the same corridor, they take control over the Taghab Valley, from where they strike Kabul time and again.

NATO has conducted several military operations, including its longest operation ever, Operation Lion Heart, in Kunar and Nuristan, while its allies the Pakistani armed forces embarked on their sister operation *Sher Dil* in Mohmand and Bajaur. The latter operation started in late 2008 and ended in early January 2009, but the porous border failed to eliminate the militants. They simply dispersed and regrouped. NATO and the Pakistan army carried out several more missions later in 2009 and 2010, but the militants continue to dominate the terrain. From the self-same sanctuaries, Al-Qaeda emerges and carries out attacks on Islamabad and other parts of Pakistan.

The story of their success unfolds when you examine the frequent points of cross-border infiltration between Pakistan and Afghanistan. There are names for the passes but in fact these do not represent any one particular route. They merely signify that in an area there may be a dozen passes through which people from both countries travel, be they traders, smugglers, or militants.

To explore this region – which calls for a good map and a powerful four-wheel drive vehicle – is to be astonished by the acumen of Al-Qaeda, and how intelligently it has spent time on harnessing its resources over the past several years before beginning battle. At the same time it is to be shocked by the naivety of the United States and its allies, the richest and the most resourceful nations of the world, in being lured into Al-Qaeda's Afghan trap and not realizing the real battle strategy rotates around the geography of the Pamir region. NATO gathers its resources in Nuristan and Kunar and urges Pakistan to collect its army to block the militants in Bajaur and Mohmand. Their combined air powers bomb the militants and lob artillery shells at them as if they are running down from the mountains to attack them. Both forces are apparently oblivious to the fact that over the past several years the militants have adopted an evasive routine after initiating skirmishes, not going down to Kunar or Nuristan to be arrested and killed by NATO, and not venturing in the direction of Mohmand and Bajaur to be killed or arrested by Pakistan. Instead they hit and run through the forests and the mountain passes to the Pakistani regions of Chitral and Dir, with the armies not pursuing them through the mountains for fear of becoming sitting ducks.

In the last two years Pakistan has relocated a significant portion of its army to its western border and opened fronts all along the tribal belt on the insistence of Washington to block the militants' channels. While this may have slowed down the militants' movements, it has not led to their killing or capture.

The following are frequently traveled routes in the region:

- Arandu Chitral (Pakistan – P) to Nuristan (Afghanistan – A).
- Dir (P) to Kunar (A).
- Bajaur (P) to Kunar (A) (two routes).
- Mohmand (P) to Kunar (A).
- Khyber (P) to Nagarhar (A). Two routes: one is the legal route through the Torkham border crossing, and the other is an illegal route through the Terah Valley (P) to the Tora Bora mountains (A) and Kurram (P).
- Teri Mengal (P) to Nagarhar (A), four routes.
- Kurram Agency (P) to Paktia (A), two routes.
- Kurram (P) to Khost (A).
- From North Waziristan (P) there are four frequent routes from Lowara Mandi (P) to Khost and Paktika (A). There are three frequent routes from North Waziristan (P) to Paktika (A) and two routes from South Waziristan (P) to Angor Ada (both A-P), the most prominent.
- There are a total of 16 frequent routes in Khyber Patyoonkhwa and FATA.
- There is one legal route through Balochistan, which is through Chaman to Kandahar. All other frequently traveled routes are used illegally. Nushki in Chagi (P) to Ghaznali in Kandahar (A) and Dalbandin (P) to Barabecha (A) are illegal routes.

Militants criss-cross these passes, sometimes entering Afghanistan and sometimes Pakistan. For instance, militants enter from Nuristan (A) into Pakistan through Arandu Chitral when NATO conducts an operation. Chitral is a peaceful Pakistani hill station where militants stop and go to the Pakistani area of Dir. From there they once again enter Kunar. This roundabout goes on and on making it impossible to guard this huge stretch of porous border between the two countries.

Under a plan for cleansing the militancy from the Pakistani tribal areas, the local population was asked to leave their homes. According to the UN Office for the Coordination of Humanitarian Affairs, approximately 450,000 people were displaced from South Waziristan. Almost 100,000 were displaced from the tribal areas of Mohmand and Bajaur, and several thousands were displaced from the Khyber and Orakzai agencies. There was consensus between the Pakistan army and the US military that once civilians had left the areas, the militant sanctuaries could easily be bombed, and if the militants tried to flee to Afghanistan, US forces would spot and eliminate them. The Pakistan Army would then try to prop up the tribal leaders under the old tribal system, and with US financial support Pakistan's tribal areas would be put under firm control, with Pakistani policing and the court systems overseeing affairs. However, that plan remains a distant dream, with the militants playing their games of "hide and seek" with the international forces and the Pakistan Army through the dozens of passes in the Hindu Kush. In Dr Iqbal's words, it is "swooping, shocking, then retiring, pouncing on the prey."

During military operations in Bajaur and Mohmand in Pakistan, and Kunar and Nuristan in Afghanistan by the US forces, the militants carried out relentless attacks. According to ABC News the Taliban attacked a US base in Kamdesh in Nuristan and killed eight US and eight Afghan National Army soldiers. The Taliban claimed the killing of nine US soldiers and over 100 Afghan National Army soldiers besides taking prisoner 30 men from the Afghan National Army. The attack was one of its fiercest, and forced US General Stanley McChrystal to abandon all US border posts. As a result, a major portion of the Afghan province of Nuristan fell to Al-Qaeda-led militants. The militants then invited international channels in November 2009 to show their occupation of all the abandoned US bases.

A series of military operations were launched in different tribal regions beginning in 2002–03 and running through 2010, but they were unable to lessen the influence of the militants. After each operation the militancy simply changed shape. For instance the period 2009–10 was supposed to be the toughest time for the militants as the Pakistan Army had opened up fronts against them in South Waziristan, Orakzai, Khyber Agency, Mohmand, and Bajaur. Simultaneously CIA drones carried out attacks on a daily basis. In response, the militants simply splintered and came up with a standard guerilla strategy. From South Waziristan, they melted into parts of North Waziristan and let the military occupy the area abandoned. After the military's ground deployment was completed the militants used the mountain passes through Shawal and made their way back over the rugged mountains to fight and recapture the military bases in South Wazirsitan.

An identical strategy was applied in Mohmand and Bajaur. Militants traveled through the mountains into Nuristan (Afghanistan) and Chitral (Pakistan) and as soon as the military had been deployed on the ground, they ransacked their positions. In the coming months this game was not repeated here, but expanded from the South Asian to the Central Asian region demarcating the boundaries of the Islamic Emirates of Khurasan (see page xiii). The magical terrain was again to determine Al-Qaeda strategy.

The terrain has already taken the Taliban-led insurgency from south-west Afghanistan to the northern Afghan regions of Baghlan and Kunduz, and subsequently into Central Asia, where Islamist sleeper cells in Uzbekistan, Tajikistan, Turkmenistan, Kyrgyzstan, Chechnya, and the Chinese province of Xingjian were prompted to rise and revive the Islamic Emirates of Khurasan through the Pamirs. This took in the Gorno-Badakhshan province inTajikistan and the Badakshan province of Afghanistan, which connects with the Tian Shan mountains along the Alay Valley of Kyrgyzstan in the north. To the south it joins the Hindu Kush along the Wakhan Corridor in Afghanistan and Pakistan. To the east it ends on the Chinese border or extends to the range that includes Kongur Tagh in the Kunlun Mountains. These were the natural tracks connecting Al-Qaeda's South Asian theater to its Central Asia future theater of war.

This terrain of Hindu Kush and Pamir is thousands of years old, but the *One Thousand and One Nights* tales of Al-Qaeda moved on from 9/11 to years of struggle stained with blood to change the structure of the terrain. The rocks and the mountains had provided some measure of defense for tribal insurgencies in the past, but the Al-Qaeda-inspired revolution turned each rock and stone in the rugged mountains into an unassailable fortress.

8

THE THEATER OF WAR

The defense of Muslim lands is recognized by Muslim academics as the first obligation of the Islamic faith. But the way that the Soviet invasion of Afghanistan in 1979 sparked the imagination of Muslims for Jihad in the true sense of the word had not been witnessed for least 500 years. Muslim academics across the globe unanimously recognized the need for Jihad and declared it the responsibility of every Muslim to fight against the Soviets. And, as a result, thousands of young Muslim youths from all over the world poured into Afghanistan to fight alongside their Afghan brethren.

Their determination to participate in the Jihad in Afghanistan was greater even than the earlier Muslim battles to reclaim the holy land of Palestine, although Afghanistan was neither a sacred place for Muslims, nor the heartland of Islam, and by no means a rich country. In fact, Afghanistan was one of the poorest Muslim countries in the world and had played little, if any, role in international or Muslim world politics.

In 2001, when the United States announced it would attack Afghanistan, the resolve of Muslim youths to resist this occupation of a Muslim land was fortified. Jihad then became a household call. The Muslim youths who poured in did not require any religious decree or formal command to fight against the United States. They understood Afghanistan was to be the future bastion of Islamic and Jihadi activity, above and beyond the deserts and urban centers of Iraq, the mountains of Yemen, and chaotic Somalia.

US support for Afghan resistance against the Soviet Union in the 1980s was an act of vengeance for the US defeat in Vietnam. But this needed the mobilization of all possible Soviet enemies, including the international Islamic movements, to support the Afghan Jihad. If the United States had managed to lay the foundation of a Jihadi headquarters to drain the resources of the mighty Soviet empire, this might have allowed it entry into the Central Asian region. The

United States could then have turned that territory into a flashpoint which could bring about the disintegration of the rival Soviet bloc and its ideology, all the way up to the Berlin Wall. With that in mind the United States offered support for the Jihadi operation in Afghanistan, which sought to bleed the Soviets dry and force their retreat at least from this area. However the United States simply did not have the wherewithal to complete this strategy.

What really rallied the thousands of Muslim fighters worldwide was the resources that poured in as a consequence. This enabled them to strategize the Afghan Jihad against the Soviets, but from the perspective of their own thinking, which remains even to this day the Prophet Muhammad's (Peace Be Upon Him) 1,400-year-old saying. It is memorized by every Muslim:

> We [I and my family] are members of a household that Allah [SWT] has chosen for a the life in the Hereafter over the life of this world; and the members of my household [Ahlul-Bayt] shall suffer a great affliction and they shall be forcefully expelled from their homes after my death. Then there will come people from the East carrying black flags and they will ask for some goods [essential survival items] to be given to them. But they shall be refused such service. As such, they will wage war and emerge victorious, and will be offered that which they desired in the first place. But they will refuse to accept it till a man from my family [Ahlul-Bayt] appears to fill the Earth with justice, as it has been filled with corruption. So whoever reaches that [time] should come to them, even crawling on ice/snow, since among them is the vice-regent of Allah [Khalifatullah] al-Mahdi.
> (Sunan Ibn Majah, v2, Tradition #4082, The History of Tabari al-Sawa'iq al-Muhriqah, by Ibn Hajar, Ch. 11, section 1, pp. 250–1)

This saying of the Prophet Muhammad heralded the emergence of a Muslim army from the region of ancient Khurasan, which in the Middle East is referred to as the East, and comprises parts of modern Afghanistan, Pakistan, Iran, and Central Asia. (The black flag is the flag of the Muslim army and the white flag represents the Muslim state. The black flag also represents war.) This saying of the Prophet Muhammad is read along with the following saying which actually draws the boundaries of the theater of war:

Na'im bin. Hammad in al-Fitan reports that Abu Hurayrah, said that the Messenger of Allah said "A group of you will conquer India, Allah will open for them [India] until they come with its kings chained – Allah having forgiven their sins. When they return back [from India], they will find Ibn Maryam [Jesus] in Syria."

(from *Kanzul-Ummal*, a collection of the Prophet Muhammad's sayings)

A religious decree for defense of Muslim lands has been issued several times over by religious scholars with reference to occupied Muslim-majority territories. These include Indian Kashmir, the Araakan province of Myanmar, the Muslim regions of the Philippines and Thailand, and, most of all Palestine, the second most sacred site for Muslims. When this religious decree was extended to include Afghanistan as well, a flurry of Muslim youths went to this country. Pakistan then became the transit point for thousands of youths, who went into Pakistani colleges and universities where they spent eight months on education and four months waging Jihad in Afghanistan. Muslim liberation movements in locations all over the world, such as Kashmir and Palestine, which had been considered relics of the past, found new hope in the Afghan Jihad. Their members and supporters left their home regions and made Afghanistan their focus. In Afghanistan they were oriented for years in militant camps, and when they went back to their regions, they restarted their insurgencies with new zeal, perspective, and ideological spin. Two of the best examples of this are Palestinian Hamas and the Kashmiri Hezbul Mujahadeen in the mid and late 1980s respectively.

This movement towards Afghanistan rotated around the Prophet Muhammad's saying which referred to the basic theater of war of the "End of Time" battles as Khurasan. From there it was to move on to the neighboring region of India, from where all the Muslim forces would be mobilized towards the Balad-al-Sham (Syria, Lebanon, and Palestine) to fight the final battle for liberation of Palestine, and then revive the Caliphate.

While the international Jihadi brigade was regrouping in Afghanistan and Pakistan, ISI was staffed by Islamists who were the direct handlers of the Afghan Jihad and no different in their thinking from the international Jihadis. When they launched the forward strategy in the Central Asian regions of the Soviet Union to orchestrate the defeat of the Red Army in Afghanistan, the centrifugal force was again this saying of the Prophet Muhammad, with the strategy underscored that Afghanistan was to be the main battlefield and Pakistan's tribal areas the strategic backyard of the Muslim resistance. From there the theater of war was to branch out into Central Asia, India, and Bangladesh. The ISI molded the whole theater of war and oriented volunteer groups accordingly.

The organization known as Harkat-ul Jihad-i-Islami came into existence with the help of the Pakistani military apparatus. Harkat-ul Jihad-i-Islami was the first Pakistani Jihadi organization, and was formed in 1984. It hailed from the Deobandi school of thought. It used to recruit youths for the Jihad against the Soviets. The premier Islamic party of the country, Jamaat-e-Islami, was already very active in the recruitment of Pakistani volunteers and sending them for the Jihad. Actually, the raising of human resources was not an issue for the Jihad against the Soviets, as there was already a very powerful indigenous Afghan resistance movement which did not really require any external fighters to assist it.

The real motivation behind the formation of Harkat-ul Jihad-i-Islami was to draw out the boundaries of the theaters of war – beyond Afghanistan – in the Central Asian Republics and in India. It was pure coincidence that after 9/11, first the Pakistan's military establishment's "strategic depth" pattern in Afghanistan and then the whole Jihadi network which the Pakistani intelligence apparatus had set up through the Harkat-ul Jihad-i-Islami slipped from the ISI's hands and fell into the lap of Al-Qaeda. From then on Al-Qaeda used both the Afghan theater and the Jihadi network to define the boundaries of the theaters of war according to its own perspective and strategic direction.

The network of Harkat-ul Jihad-i-Islami had emerged from Deobandi Islamic seminaries. Its commanders were educated in different Deobandi schools, which were also their main recruitment grounds. The Deobandi school of thought has always been the most influential political, religious, and Sufi school of South and the Central Asia. Although the Darul Uloom Deoband (an Islamic school) was founded in 1879 by Maulana Qasim Nanoonthvi in the district of Saharanpur Uttar Pradesh (India), it was actually a deep-rooted religious, Sufi, and political legacy of Central Asian Naqhsbandi Sufi order adopted by various South Asian Muslim reformists. These included Mujadid Alf Sani (1564–1624), Shah Waliullah 1703–1762), and Shah Waliullah's grandson, Shah Ismail (1779–1831). Sheikh Ahmed Sarhendi, better known as Mujadid Alf Sani – which means a reformist for next ten centuries – inspired strict monotheist Islamic values against the Mughal emperor Akbar's secular order of Din-e-Ilahi, to force the Mughal dynasty to revert back to the Islamic system. The hardline Sunni orthodox Mughal ruler, Aurangzeb Alamgir, is said to be the byproduct of Sarhendi's teachings.

Similarly, with the rise of the Hindu Marhattas and the decline of the Mughal Empire, Shah Waliullah appeared on the horizon. Shah Waliullah, a Naqshbandi Sufi like Sarhendi, continued the legacy of Sheikh Ahmad and through his writings, pointed out the faultlines in the social, political, educational, economic, and spiritual orders which had caused of the decline of Muslim rule in India. Shah Waliullah's influence ran through the whole region from Central Asia to South Asia, and that is why when he wrote a very detailed letter to Ahmad Shah Abdali (a warlord from Kandahar) asking him to give up his life of ease and fight against the Marhatta dynasty, Abdali invaded India and ransacked the Marhatta dynasty.

Shah Waliullah's teachings were carried forward by his son Shah Abdul Aziz and grandson, Shah Ismail, the ideologue of the pioneering Jihadi movement in South Asia in the beginning of the nineteenth century. This influence of the Shah Wali Ullahi family thus laid the foundation of the Darul Uloom Deoband.

The Darul Uloom Deoband was a trustee of Shah Waliullah and his family's legacy and promoted *madrassas* (schools of Islamic learning) across the whole of South Asia. It also promoted the different Sufi orders of Qadri, Chushti, Suharwardi, and Naqshabandi. The majority of Sufi Khaneka in the extended South and Central Asian region are affiliated with the Deoband School of thought. Last but not the least, this school of thought was the flag bearer of all the Jihadi movements from the nineteenth century onwards, such as the Syed Ahmed Brelvi, the Faraizi movement, and the Reshmi Romal movement (the twentieth-century silk hand-kerchief movement), leading into the twenty-first-century Taliban movement.

The Darul Uloom Deoband launched the movement of religious education through a trained faculty, and promotes a network of Islamic seminaries from the Northern Caucasus and Central Asia to Bengal and Myanmar. The political map of the whole region changed in the twentieth century as the Caucasus and Central Asian areas were occupied by the former Soviet Union, while some areas were captured by communist China, both of which banned religious education. However, the migrant Central Asian Muslims in northern Afghanistan, including Badakshah, Balkh, Mazar Shareef, and Takhar, retained their old religious linkages.

The Darul Uloom Deoband school of thought was the major

academic influence under which scattered Central Asian religious and Sufi orders were united. It also trained Muslim academics in India and sent Muslim scholars back to Afghanistan, where they built large and small *madrassas* to revive old religious values, Sufism, and politics.

After the partition of British India, several leading religious scholars of the Darul Uloom Deoband came to Pakistan and established Islamic seminaries there, such as the Jamiatul-Uloomul Islamia in Binori Town, the Darul Uloom in Karachi, and the Jamia Ashrafia in Lahore. The International Islamic University founded in the late 1970s in Islamabad was also influenced by the Deobandi school of thought. These religious schools became centers of learning for the whole region, and Muslims of Uzbek, Tajik, and Turkoman origin who had fled the Soviet Union because of its religious restrictions, as well as Muslims from the Chinese province of Xingjian, and from Myanmar and Bangladesh, migrated to the Islamic republic of Pakistan.

Some of them sent their children to the Islamic seminaries of the Deobandi schools where they were provided with free board and lodging, food, clothing, and education. Pakistan's intelligence apparatus tapped this network to extend its reach from Central Asia to Bangladesh through the formation of the Harkat-ul Jihad-i-Islami of Pakistan. They then tapped these schools as the major source of recruiting Central Asians to pitch them into proxy wars against the Soviet Union in the Central Asian Republics and the Caucasus. The Harkat-ul Jihad-i-Islami simultaneously recruited Pakistanis, Kashmiris, and Bengalis (Bangladeshis) trained in Afghanistan for "bleed India" operations after the Soviets had been defeated. However, they soon became too big to be controlled by Pakistan's intelligence apparatus. Meanwhile, a network of Muslim students from Central Asia was being trained for guerrilla operations around the world. These students were first sent to training camps of organizations which had Tajik and Uzbek roots, then transferred to Afghanistan for further training in the camps of Hizb-i-Islami Afghanistan led by Gulbaddin Hikmatyar, and Jamaat-e-Islami led by Afghanistan's Professor Burhanuddin Rabbani and Ahmad Shah Masoud. These two major *mujahideen* organizations had a sizeable number of commanders in northern Afghanistan, where a number of students from Pakistani seminaries were also being prepared by them to mount an insurgency against the Soviets in Central Asia.

Both the Hizb and the Jamaat were ideologically close to Egypt's Muslim Brotherhood. They had not only read the revolutionary teachings of Syed Qutb and Hasan Al-Banna but were also under the influence of ultra-radical Arab fighters, as most of these Arabs had fought against the Soviets under the banner of the two Afghan organizations. Muslim Central Asian fighters were earlier orientated to Deobandi Sufi religious values. Their subsequent inclusion in Jamaat-e-Islami and Hizb-e-Islami's training camps, and their inter-action with Arab militant camps, familiarized them with Muslim Brotherhood literature. Those connections actually laid down Al-Qaeda's roots in Central Asia.

The ISI's initial target was to tap into the underground Naqshbandi Sufi movements in then Soviet Muslim territories, and these students infiltrated Central Asia through Hizb-e-Islami Afghanistan, Jamaat-e-Islami Afghanistan, and Harkat-ul Jihad-i-Islami, with the dual tasks of cultivating the Sufi orders, as well as ordinary Muslims who had continued practicing Islam despite the repressive Soviet political system.

Trained in the Afghan Jihadi camps, the Central Asian youths connected with the underground Sufis and prompted them to revolt against the Soviet system for the restoration of Muslim values. Thousands of Holy Qurans were smuggled into the Central Asian Republics, together with the literature of the Muslim Brotherhood. These efforts bore fruit in Central Asia's political arena when the foundations of the Islamic Renaissance Party were laid in Tajikistan in 1990, and then later in Uzbekistan and other parts of Central Asia.

The establishment of the Islamic Renaissance Party was a proxy operation against the Soviet Union, backed by the CIA and perpetu-ated on the ground by the Saudi and Pakistani intelligence agencies with the help of Afghan *mujahideen* and the Pakistani Jihadi orga-nizations. But with the seeds of radical Islam planted, matters began to spin out of the control of these agencies.

The Soviet Union collapsed in 1991 and this further emboldened the Islamic Jihadi movements in Central Asia. The Uzbeks, Tajiks, Turks, and Chechens who had participated in the Afghan Jihad went home after the liberation of their territories in September 1991. There was then a US campaign to promote democracy in the Central Asia Republics, but the Jihadis rejected the idea of democracy and established underground Islamic cells aiming to promote Islamic revolution throughout Central Asia. These Islamic cells were ideo-logically motivated by Muslim Brotherhood teachings and initially supported the ideology of Hizbut Tahrir, a non-militant Islamic revolutionary group which stood for the establishment of a caliphate but through a demonstration of street power rather than armed militancy. But they later turned to Akramia, a breakaway faction of Hizbut Tahrir, which believed in militancy. A sizeable number of Islamic Renaissance Party members also joined the underground Islamic militant movements.

During the Tajikistan civil war in the early 1990s, underground cells played a significant role. At the height of hostilities in 1992 most of the people owning allegiance to the Islamic Renaissance Party and other underground Islamic cells fled to Afghanistan. Jamaat-e-Islami Afghanistan's commander Ahmad Shah Masoud brought these Islamic groups into his fold and organized them under the banner of the United Tajik Opposition, which had regrouped in northern Afghanistan. The husband of the chief of Hizb-e-Islami Afghanistan, Gulbaddin Hikmatyar's niece, Humanyun Jarir, played a major role in sending these volunteers from northern Afghanistan into the Central Asian Republics to fuel the unrest.

Meanwhile, Central Asian Islamic militants needed financial backing, which nobody offered except the Arab camps in Afghanistan. The ideological connection was the persuasion that Osama bin Laden used, and this was strengthened by the financial support he provided to the Uzbek, Chechen, Chinese (eastern Turkestani), and Tajikistani fighters. As a result, all these factions moved from northern Afghanistan to Kabul and Kandahar under the Pashtun-dominated Taliban government in Afghanistan.

After the US invasion of Afghanistan, this Central Asian diaspora moved to the Pakistani tribal areas, mostly to North and South Waziristan. Interestingly, except during the initial fight after the US invasion of Afghanistan, Chechen, Uzbek, and Chinese fighters were mostly not used in the Afghan battle. Al-Qaeda deliberately held them in reserve. The ultimate purpose was to eventually send them back to the Farghana Valley (the boundaries of which touch almost all of the Muslim republics of Central Asia, as well as Chechnya and the Chinese province of Xingjian), and from there expand the war to encompass the whole region.

GHAZWA-E-HIND

By the early 1980s Jamaat-e-Islami's Al-Badr camp came under the command of Bakht Zameen Khan, who organized a network of thousands of Pakistani volunteers to fight against Soviet forces in Afghanistan. Their main training camps were established in the Afghan province of Paktia near the Pakistani regions of Parachanar,

Khost, and Nangarhar. Initially the ISI used Al-Badr's camps to train Kashmiri separatists, and the largest indigenous Kashmiri organization, Hezbul Mujahadeen, was raised in Al-Badr's Afghanistan camps.

However, ISI's strategists felt that for the Ghazwa-e-Hind (the promised "Battle for India") there was need for a structure which stood on more solid foundations. Al-Badr camps were run by the Jamaat-e-Islami, whose men came from a middle-class urban background. They had been educated in secular schools. They were committed to the cause of Jihad, but their commitments were unlikely to be lifelong (no more than five years at best) because of their background, which was part of their being.

ISI's Ghazwa-e-Hind project required networking not only in Kashmir but in the whole of India – and in India's neighboring countries like Nepal and Bangladesh. There was a need for people who came from simple rural backgrounds with no leanings towards a middle-class "upward mobility" structure. The Harkat-ul Mujahadeen, whose network was governed by the Deobandi school of thought – from Central Asia to Bangladesh – was therefore thought more suitable for the Ghazwa-e-Hind operations.

Pakistani ISI almost simultaneously opened theaters of war in Central Asian regions and in Indian-held Kashmir in the late 1980s, when various newly organized Kashmiri Islamic militant organizations including Harkat-ul Jihad-i-Islami and Hezbul Mujahadeen confronted Indian security forces in Indian Kashmir.

Harkat-ul Jihad-i-Islami applied the same strategy in India as it had earlier applied in Central Asia. India was a far easier place to lay down networks. Initially the Qadri Sufi order was used as a cover for ISI activities. One of the top Sufi clerics in Pakistan, Mubarak Ali Shah Gilani, cooperated with the ISI on that front, and soon an underground network was laid in India with the help of Sufis, especially in Hyderabad Deccan.

While Kashmiri militants escalated hostilities the Indian underground network was asked to keep a very low profile. The network was to enhance its activities on the recruitment front only. Soon the Ghazwa-e-Hind project had reached Uttar Pradesh, where its target was youths being educated in secular schools. By the late 1990s, Aligarh University became a hotbed of underground Islamic militant intrigues, but there was not as yet any plan for the launch of real Jihadi activities in India.

Meanwhile, Harkat-ul Jihad-i-Islami had firmly established itself in Bangladesh through networks of Deobandi Islamic seminaries.

The purpose, however, was not to disturb the social and political structure of the country, but to facilitate the future Ghazwa-e-Hind project for a steady supply line of Muslim fighters from Bangladesh once Jihadi activities had begun in India. The timeframe was closely linked with the hype on the Kashmiri separatist movement.

After the death in a plane crash of General Zia-ul-Haq and the formation of a new government led by the Pakistan Peoples Party, the era of Islamist generals such as General Hamid Gul in Pakistani military headquarters came towards an end, and strategies such as Ghazwa-e-Hind transformed into "bleed India" projects became more of a purely functional proxy operation rather than a deep-rooted Jihadi perception.

Harkat-ul Jihad-i-Islami was still the favored network, but in the late 1990s the Pakistani establishment suddenly stopped pushing Ghazwa-e-Hind. Instead it dreamed of the creation of a greater Pakistan stretching from Afghanistan (from a strategic depth angle) to Bangladesh. The Central Asian module of the military establishment was shelved in the late 1990s.

This was the time when the Jihadi elements started looking in another direction, although still cooperating with the Pakistani military establishment. A hardline Deobandi Taliban rule in Afghanistan was the great morale booster for Jihadis reared by Pakistan's military establishment. But the Jihadis were also closely monitoring newly emerging equations. The events of 9/11 changed the world, as well as the Jihadi mindset.

THE HARVEST IS READY BUT …

Pakistan's ISI's forward strategy in the 1980s against the Soviet Union (and against India) was ready to deliver desired national goals on the regional strategic front when 9/11 happened in 2001. But, by that time so many events had taken place that it was Al-Qaeda which benefited from the harvest.

Earlier, thousands of Farghana Valley fighters of ethnic Uzbek, Tajik, and Turkish origin, along with fighters from the Chinese province of Xingjian and the Republic of Chechnya, gathered in an Afghanistan under Taliban rule. The diaspora from Central Asia and North Caucasus badly needed money, arms, and training to fuel insurgencies in their home regions. The Taliban provided them with sanctuaries, but it did not have enough money to keep its own movement afloat, leave alone fund insurgencies elsewhere.

As a result, dozens of Chechens, Uzbeks, and the Chinese left Afghanistan and settled in Turkey. Turkey provided them with housing and money, and encouraged their struggle, although under the strict vigilance of the state's intelligence apparatus. That situation was unacceptable to commanders such as Juma Namangani and Tahir Yaldochiv of the Islamic Movement of Uzbekistan and Hassan Mahsum of the Eastern Turkestan Islamic Party (China), who had progressively lost control over their men living in Turkey. But they did not have alternative sources of funding. Al-Qaeda took advantage of this and developed close contact with these groups. It provided them with money and training. Although there is no proof of the organizational attachments of these groups with Al-Qaeda, there is no denying Al Qaeda's ideological and financial influence over them in the late 1990s.

That was the time when the Pakistani Jihadi organizations reared by ISI became a serious threat to India. According to one estimate, between 1980 and 2000 approximately 600,000 Pakistanis and Kashmiris had been trained in different Afghan militant camps, and at the time of 9/11, at least 100,000 Jihadis were active in Indian Kashmir (they used to be launched from Pakistan on a rotational basis). These insurgents not only troubled the 400,000–800,000 Indian security services (including Indian Army, police, and paramilitary forces) but emboldened the Pakistan Army to orchestrate military adventures like the Kargil Operation in 1999. Militants also dared to hijack an Indian aircraft, took it to Kandahar, and then exchanged the passengers with their prisoners who were languishing in Indian jails.

The Jihadis also carried out an attack on the Red Fort in Delhi in December 2000 and even planned an attack on the Indian parliament in December 2001. Simultaneously, the Harkat-ul Jihad-i-Islami was gaining a firm foothold in Bangladesh at the instigation of the ISI to pave the way for the rout of the pro-India elements there. Harkat carried out an assassination attempt on Sheikh Hasina Wajid and many of her supporters in 2000. This brought India under so much pressure that an alliance that supported a coalition with Pakistan won the Bangladeshi elections in 2001.

By the year 2001, strategically speaking, Pakistan had become the most influential country from Central Asia to Bangladesh. It was about to translate that for a better bargain with India as well as Iran and the United States when 9/11 occurred. The entire world changed, and so did Pakistan's strategic objectives.

AL-QAEDA SPLITS THE SPOILS OF WAR

Pakistan's Afghan policy made a U-turn after 9/11, and the country provided logistic support and airfields to the United States to facilitate its air and ground assaults on Afghanistan by the end of 2001. The Taliban were routed in Afghanistan and, under immense US pressure, the Pakistan-based Jihadi outfits which had trained in Afghan camps and stood opposed to the US invasion of Afghanistan were banned. However, Pakistan's President General Pervez Musharraf held meetings with senior Jihadi leaders and assured them that a US presence in Afghanistan would last no more than five years, so they needed to be patient and bear with Pakistan's about-turn of freezing Jihadi activities. The barely veiled deal was that as soon as the United States withdrew from Afghanistan, Pakistan would revert to its Jihadi policies again. But those who planned the 9/11 incident were acutely conscious of the events that would follow the devastating attacks on the US mainland. They were well aware that the distance between Pakistan's military apparatus and the Jihadi dispensations was bound to widen to the point where Pakistan did not have much choice but to support the US war.

The thousands of Jihadis assembled in Afghanistan were equally aware that they faced persecution, jail, and oppression, and so they made their way to the Pakistani tribal areas to join up with Al-Qaeda. With that the entire Jihadi assets of the ISI (raised over two decades) fell into the lap of Al-Qaeda. And with this, Al-Qaeda was able to expand the boundaries of the theater of war from Central Asia to Afghanistan and across to Bangladesh.

HARKAT-UL JIHAD-I-ISLAMI: FROM ISI TO AL-QAEDA

In 2005, the formidable operational commander of Harkat-ul Jihad-i-Islami, Muhammad Ilyas Kashmiri, became convinced after his second release from ISI detention that US pressure had permanently disabled the Pakistan Army's capacity to revert to its pre-9/11 role as the supreme strategic force in the region. He therefore decided to abandon his struggle in Kashmir, and moved to fight in Afghanistan.

Kashmiri was familiar with Afghanistan as he had first trained and fought there back in the 1980s, before he went to Kashmir. He took his family along with him this time and migrated to North Waziristan. His initial aim was to fight alongside the Afghan Taliban against the NATO forces. However, as he spent an increasing amount of time with the international Jihadi network, his views changed. He no longer saw things through the narrower prism of Kashmir's liberation. His struggle against India for Kashmir's freedom remained a driving force, but it widened to encompass a global Islamic war view.

Razmak, a small town in North Waziristan, became Kashmiri's new home, and he set up his training center there. Kashmiri was a charismatic commander who had accomplished wonders against the Indian forces throughout India. He had a great rapport with the Jihadi community. As a result, his presence in North Waziristan brought forward hundreds of militants from the Kashmiri battle-field to Afghanistan. These fighters abandoned their struggle in Kashmir and moved to North Waziristan ready to be launched into Afghanistan against the NATO forces.

By mid-2006, Kashmiri's camp had impressed everybody. He had retired officers from Pakistan's military services, former commanders of elite Jihadi organizations such as Laskhar-e-Taiba, and his own 313 Brigade of blooded fighters trained by the ISI's India cells. Al-Qaeda's leader Mustafa Abu al-Yazid and ideologues like Abu Waleed Ansari and Sheikh Essa drew close to Kashmiri and influenced his thinking, ideology, and strategy. These Al-Qaeda leaders had earlier interacted with many Jihadi commanders including Fazlur Rahman Khalil (of Harkat-ul Mujahadeen), Masood Azhar (of Jaish-e-Mohammad), and Abdullah Shah Mazhar, and feared that the Pakistani Jihadi commanders could not emerge from the steel frame constructed for them by the ISI. Their assessment was that the Pakistani Jihadi commanders could never think beyond the strategic boundaries drawn in their minds by the ISI. They knew too that the local tribal commanders were prey to a thought process constrained by tribal and Pashtun traditions. They were incapable of thinking beyond Afghan or Pashtun boundaries.

Kashmiri, however, was different. He had a mind which was intuitively inventive. He had maintained discipline in coordinating with the Pakistan Army against the Indian forces in Kashmir, and strictly adhered to Pakistani strategies in that context. However, he had developed his own operational procedures while providing valuable assistance for the Pakistan Army to strategize its future strategic options.

Kashmiri was an original thinker. He was not prone to knee jerk-reactions and his decisions were a result of considered thought. His interaction with Al-Qaeda in Razmak had fired his imagina-tion, and Al-Qaeda found that he and they were exactly on same wavelength. There is no other example of a non-Arab coming as close to Al-Qaeda as he had done. Within months his ideas so impressed Al-Qaeda that it had no hesitation in pulling him into its inner circle. By 2007 he had become a full-fledged member of Al-Qaeda's *Shura*.

Towards the end of 2007 Kashmiri came up with a comprehensive battle plan which surprised even Al-Qaeda. It envisioned the promised "End of Times" theater of war in the East, which Al-Qaeda's best military brains had visualized, but saw no way of implementing. Kashmiri presented his thesis on this. There was bound to be a strategic alliance between NATO, the Pakistan Army, and the Indian forces for the defeat of Al-Qaeda and Taliban in South Asia. Kashmiri came up with a military plan to counter their joint efforts.

India was the central element in this plan, and Kashmiri aimed to revitalize the Jihadi network in that country and orient it to harmonize with Al-Qaeda's strategy and ideology. The ISI-built network still held firm in India, but as a result of the multiple pressures over Pakistan owing allegiance to the US invasion of Afghanistan, the network had been marginalized. Kashmiri looked to direct this Jihadi network to matters such as the destruction of India's nuclear arsenal. He calculated that this would create so much friction between the two countries that India would turn against Pakistan. Kashmiri targeted three plausible results from this strategy:

- The dissolution of the strategic alliance between India, NATO, and Pakistan against the militants.
- Trapping Pakistan and India in a conflict which would immediately force Pakistan to relocate its forces from the western borders (in the tribal areas) to the eastern borders (near India) and thus give free rein to militants to fight against NATO troops.
- In the case of a war, India would put a naval blockade on Pakistan which would create problems for the land-locked Afghanistan-bound NATO supply line from the Arabian Sea.

Kashmiri wanted to create a permanent theater of war in India, as Pakistan had done in the 1990s in Kashmir. His aim was to destabilize India with a planned pattern of terror plots. He then spent several months revitalizing the old ISI networks in India, employing a twofold approach to accomplish this mission.

Kashmiri had connections with the old Harkat-ul Jihad-i-Islami assets in India and Bangladesh. The connections were already there, but Al-Qaeda's aid was needed to strengthen and broaden them. Previously Harkat-ul Jihad's network had operated mostly in southern India. Kashmiri used his connections in the Pakistani Jihadi networks and made contact with its underground cells. The most useful contact in this regard was with SIMI (the Students Islamic Movement of India). Previously SIMI had been a student arm of Jamaat-e-Islami, India, but it had since severed its ties with the parent organization. SIMI had subsequently hailed Osama bin Laden a true *mujahid*. Kashmiri was aware of this turn of events so he quickly tapped into his connections to expand his outreach in Uttar Pradesh and Delhi.

The Mumbai attack on November 26, 2008 came from a meticulous Kashmiri plan which entrusted the task to team members comprising retired Pakistani army officers who cunningly manipulated an ISI forward section and the Laskhar-e-Taiba. The plan was perfect for a confrontation between India and Pakistan. But sanity prevailed in Washington, and the timely intervention of the United States prevented open hostilities between the two countries.

After the Mumbai carnage failed to start a war, an almost identical but much bigger plot to simultaneously attack the National Defense College in Delhi and some of the Indian nuclear installations was unveiled. But war was again prevented with the arrests of David Headley in Chicago and Kashmiri's Indian cells in Pakistan.

The *Ghazwa-e-Hind* for which Kashmiri had prepared the ground all over India lay pending, and since a war drum is often beaten before a war, for the first time Kashmiri emailed a letter to me, which was tantamount to a declaration of war. The email documented the talks between the Indian and Pakistani foreign ministries in the shape of dossiers.

Kashmiri wrote:

> We warned the international community to play their role in getting the Kashmiris their right of self-determination and preventing India from committing brutalities in Kashmir, especially in Bandipur, raping women, and behaving inhumanly with Muslim prisoners.
>
> We warn the international community not to send their people to the 2010 Hockey World Cup, IPL [the Indian Premier League – a cricket competition involving international players] and Commonwealth Games [to be held in Delhi later that year]. Nor should their people visit India – if they do, they will be responsible for the consequences.

We, the *mujahideen* of 313 Brigade, vow to continue attacks all across India until the Indian Army leaves Kashmir and gives the Kashmiris their right of self-determination.

We assure the Muslims of the subcontinent that we will never forget the massacre of the Muslims in Gujarat and the demolition of Babri Masjid [a Muslim mosque destroyed by Hindu militants in 1992]. The entire Muslim community is one body and we will take revenge for all injustices and tyranny.

We again warn the Indian government to compensate for all its injustices otherwise they will see our next action. From 313 Brigade.

(quoted in *Asia Times Online*, February 13, 2010)

Kashmiri had no history of interacting with the media. The first time he interacted was with me on October 9, 2009, to announce in an interview that he was alive and had not been killed in a CIA Predator drone strike as had been reported. The email he sent on February 13, 2010 was perhaps his first statement to the media. It was written when Kashmiri had actually finalized his Ghazwa-e-Hind project.

The second part of Kashmiri's battle plan was to instigate rebellion in the Central Asian Republics, the alternative US supply route for Afghanistan, through which 15 percent of NATO's supplies came to northern Afghanistan. This was an easier task. All Central Asians are natural born fighters, more so even than Afghans and Pakistani tribesmen. But they lack knowledge of modern warfare techniques, one of the basics of which is the ability to read the mind of the enemy. Kashmiri was the one who trained the Central Asians and Chechens (as he had previously trained Afghan guerrillas) on how to penetrate enemy lines by using their security uniforms and by various other networking tools. In addition, the sophisticated attacks in Moscow and Dagestan by the Chechen guerrillas in March 2010 were spin-offs of Kashmiri's training.

Kashmiri took up the necessary training programs for the Chechen, Uzbek, Uighur, Tajik, and Turkish fighters, first orienting them with mobilization patterns, response, and the strategic doctrines of modern armies. The second part of their learning program dealt with modern guerrilla warfare. The techniques were the same as Kashmiri had employed in Kashmir, then in Afghanistan.

Kashmiri is an acknowledged expert in the art of reading the enemy's mind and guiding guerrillas through gaps left by the enemy, but he always used trial terror tactics first (like serial cracker blasts) to measure the response time and mobilization pattern of the security forces. He then he made plans to fit that pattern. After they had been fully trained, Kashmiri encouraged the return of the Central Asian and the Chechen fighters to their homes via Turkey.

In Kashmiri's battle plan the central theater of war remains Afghanistan and the Pakistani tribal region until the Indian and Central Asian insurgencies set their respective territories ablaze. Kashmiri believes that once insurgencies pick up pace in these areas, the Hindu Kush passes will allow a natural channel to flow to Central Asia. Infiltration through the Arabian Sea, and actions across the Pakistan and Bangladeshi land borders would follow to expand the war theater into India.

Al-Zawahiri was thrilled when he heard Kashmiri's plan and its details. Al-Qaeda had tried to work out the zones of war for the "End of Times" battle, but failed to connect the pieces of the puzzle. It was left to Kashmiri to strategize the ideological paradigm, and Kashmiri had the resources in India to make that job much easier. So Al-Qaeda installed Kashmiri as the head of its military committee to first finalize the Ghazwa-e-Hind project, and next coordinate the Central Asian insurgencies.

The Pune bomb blast in 2010 was carried out by Al-Qaeda's 313 Brigade, led by Kashmiri. Al-Zawahiri was supposed to make an announcement taking responsibility for the attack in a video speech, but at the eleventh hour it was decided that since the Pune attack was not noteworthy enough even to serve as the curtain raiser for Al-Qaeda's entry into the Indian war theater, Al-Qaeda should remain silent. This permitted a hitherto unknown organization, the Laskhar-e-Taiba Al-Alami, to claim responsibility for the attack through an email. It was thereupon decided that all future attacks would be claimed by Al-Qaeda to begin the mobilization of Jihadi groups in India following the pattern of attacks in Indian Kashmir, Pakistan, and Afghanistan.

This was the ISI plan drawn up 30 years ago with Harkat-ul Jihad-iIslami, Jamaat-e-Islami, Muslim Brotherhood connections, Islamic seminaries, and Sufi networks of constructing a theater of war from Central Asia to Bangladesh to defeat the Soviet Union in Afghanistan, and simultaneously to acquire the right of self-determination for Kashmiris in India. Thirty years later, Al-Qaeda simply refurbished the plan after sketching out its ideological boundaries, to prepare the greater theaters of war of Khurasan and Ghazwa-e-Hind for victory, before its armies, holding the black flag aloft, entered in the Middle East for the final battle against the Western world.

EPILOGUE

David Coleman Headley (48) and Tahawwur Hussain Rana (48) were accused by US federal authorities in Chicago on October 27, 2009, of plotting against the employees of a newspaper in Copenhagen. Headley was accused of traveling to Denmark to scout out the *Jyllands-Posten* newspaper offices and a nearby synagogue, for an attack by terrorists. On December 8, 2009, the FBI additionally accused Headley of conspiring to bomb targets in Mumbai, and providing material support to LeT, a militant Pakistani Islamist group; and aiding and abetting the murder of US citizens in the 2008 Mumbai attacks.

Headley pleaded guilty to all charges on March 18, 2010. He faces life in prison and a US$3 million dollar fine when he is sentenced.

Headley's and Rana's arrests complicated the story of the 2008 Mumbai attack. US intelligence believes that the action was carried out by LeT – allegedly a proxy arm of the Pakistan Army – in connivance with Al-Qaeda. In fact, Headley was Al-Qaeda's mole in LeT, through which Al-Qaeda hijacked the ISI's blueprints and used them to broaden its regional agenda. However, the more Headley's statements were made public, the more complicated the situation became. Headley told his interrogators that the ISI paid out PKR2.5 million and provided logistical support to carry out the Mumbai operation. Meanwhile Ajmal Kasab, the only surviving Mumbai attacker, had already confessed to being trained and equipped by the ISI.

I documented these facts in my December 2, 2008, reportage in *Asia Times Online* of how meticulously Al-Qaeda had hijacked the ISI and LeT plans for fuelling the Kashmiri insurgency. I had documented that an ISI forward section was behind the attack, but that they had planned a very low profile proxy operation, of a type both India and Pakistan regularly undertake against each other. But Al-Qaeda, with the help of its network, turned the event into an international act of terror which brought Pakistan and India to the verge of war – a war that was only narrowly avoided by timely US intervention.

This is typical of the type of Al-Qaeda operation which the world has witnessed in Afghanistan, Iraq, and Pakistan, but for which most people had failed to understand the motives. Despite both Headley and Rana identifying figures such as Kashmiri, retired Major Haroon and retired Major Abdul Rahman as responsible for the India operations, the Indian establishment and US counterterrorism experts continue to suspect the Pakistan Army and its proxy LeT of being behind the Mumbai carnage. At one point they even thought that the Pakistan Army and Al-Qaeda had developed relations to operate against India together!

In 2010, when I look at the events that transpired, I am fully convinced that the author of 9/11 must have been an avid reader of the Arabic classic *Alf Laila Wa Laila* (*One Thousand and One Nights*), anticipating as he did a comprehensive dialectic beyond 9/11, and the following US invasion of Afghanistan which devastated the Al-Qaeda network. As a result, there was a mass migration of Al-Qaeda members into the Pakistani tribal areas. From there began a new series of events which originate from 9/11 and give birth to a new range of immortal tales which go all the way from Central Asia to India and Bangladesh, as might be seen by somebody flipping through the pages of *Alf Laila Wa Laila*.

Al-Qaeda's *Alf Laila Wa Laila* is a collection of tales with each new tale throwing up a stream of new characters in the theater of war in South Asia after 9/11. It is presented at a juncture when a new phase of Al-Qaeda's war on the West has only just begun. As in 2002, when the United States was absolutely convinced of Al-Qaeda's obliteration, it tells of the birth of a new generation of fighters – such as Kashmiri's 313 Brigade – committed to an Al-Qaeda agenda which stretches all the way up from North Africa.

Al-Qaeda achieved its aims through the 9/11 attack. It succeeded in creating a Muslim backlash against the West and Westernized Muslim rulers. By attacking the US icons of supremacy, the Twin Towers in New York and the Pentagon in Washington, Al-Qaeda challenged the "cowboy" mentality of the United States and succeeded in instigating anger against the arrogance of power that brought the United States to the swamp of Afghanistan.

The United States had a free pass into Afghanistan. It thought it had already annihilated Al-Qaeda and was not wrong when it announced its destruction. Dozens of top Taliban leaders fled to Pakistan. The middle cadre of its leadership was either killed or arrested. Taliban footsoldiers melted into the tribal weave of Afghan society. The entire resistance had died down by 2002. The

United States announced victory and a road map through the Bonn
Agreement (2001) to acknowledge the need for a US and NATO
presence in Afghanistan until democratic institutions in Afghanistan
were restored.

For the United States that was the endgame in Afghanistan, but
for Al-Qaeda it was only the beginning of a new story. A long-term
stay for the United States and its allies meant they would be trapped
in Afghanistan and Al-Qaeda would be able to set up a battle dispensation to bleed them to death in the trap it had set. Al-Zawahiri
was the person who structured the next phase of operations. This
included reviving Al-Qaeda cadres, devising new strategies, and
building new bases in Pakistan.

Al-Zawahiri was not an ordinary person. He was the last Emir
of the Egyptian Islamic Jihad. He was the planner of a long recruitment process from amongst Egypt's civil and military officials aimed
at launching a coup in the country against the rule of then President
Anwar Sadat. Egyptian officials got wind of the plot and carried out
a successful counter-coup in which dozens of people were rounded
up. But al-Zawahiri had equipped the organization with contingency
plans directed through various cells, to ensure Islamic Jihad would
survive the blow. Thus, while the Egyptian government's crackdown
on the organization had successfully countered the coup, Islamic
Jihad had Sadat assassinated at the hands of Egyptian army officer
Khalid Islamboli.

The astute al-Zawahiri drew a precise picture of the US invasion
of Afghanistan and its effect on Al-Qaeda. In the post 9/11 era we see
al-Zawahiri applying the same strategy in Afghanistan that he had
earlier applied in Egypt. This included penetrating Pakistan's armed
forces, and creating different cells with horizontal command structures so that if one cell was penetrated by security agencies, another
cell would immediately become operative. Al-Qaeda followed this
design of "planned replacement" with the tribesmen who joined the
organization when they arrived in Pakistan from Afghanistan.

However, al-Zawahiri did not see any direct role for the few
hundred Al-Qaeda operatives who had migrated from Afghanistan
into Pakistan, except to inspire a new generation of "Sons of the
Soil" (*Ibnul Balad*) fighters fortified by the Al-Qaeda vision and
its ideology. That was the nucleus of the whole strategy on which
irregular resistance would turn into popular global resistance against
the West. And this is Al-Qaeda's battle hymn.

How Al-Qaeda was structured for fighting this war was crucial.
Had it been structured with a centralized control and command

system like any regular army and used standard weaponry, it would have lost the war by mid-2002, as appeared to be the case during the developments which had left Al-Qaeda in the lurch after the US invasion in Afghanistan. At the time, the United States was convinced that it had broken Al-Qaeda's back. However, the organization had strong enough foundations to structure a new strategy stemming from the unshakeable commitment of its founding members.

Al-Qaeda leaders such as al-Zawahiri had spent decades working with the Muslim Brotherhood in Egypt and helped found several underground organizations. Such men were familiar with the dialectical process of state clashes with underground organizations – and the consequences. Al-Zawahiri knew exactly how to react in trying circumstances and how to generate resources to wage a new war. Al-Qaeda devised its strategy in such a way that the team, characters, and leadership at the time of the US invasion of Afghanistan in 2001 quietly receded into the background and a new team of players subscribing to the Al-Qaeda ideology emerged. This continued until 2003, but there were new strategic dimensions.

Other Al-Qaeda leaders of al-Zawahiri's experience enabled them to anticipate the enemy and prepare multi-layered counter-moves. The approach Al-Qaeda employed for a recovery in its war against the United States was to prepare layers of leaders and adherents, focused first on first understanding the enemy's mind; second on knowledge of the enemy resources; and third, expanding the war into the wider South Asian region to drain the enemies' resources, with the obvious intent of reducing the status of the United States to that of a more easily assailable enemy.

In pursuit of this, Al-Qaeda's leadership morphed into three segments:

- Osama bin Laden featured as the symbolic and charismatic spiritual figurehead, supported by monetary contributions from around the world, and attracted young Islamists to join the anti-US war.
- The visionary al-Zawahiri defined the Al-Qaeda ideology to draw all of this cadre under a single ideological umbrella, as well as to set broad parameters of the war, with himself as the chief strategist.
- There were several (changeable) operational chiefs, who while adhering to al-Zawahiri's ideological mission of war against the West's presence in Muslim lands, formulated operational procedures according to need and circumstance.

For public consumption, Osama bin Laden was the leader, but the real direction of the whole game came from al-Zawahiri, whose ideas had been instilled into a select group of people with a sense of purity of purpose. They comprised battle-hardened teams groomed in the South Asian theater of war over decades. From each such team, one person was installed as the operational field commander, and if he was killed or captured, another was readily available to replace him. In the new situation there was no time or space for Al-Qaeda to hold regular meetings to decide on strategy and disseminate day-to-day orders. The team had to be trusted to shape events on its own, and not stray away from Al-Qaeda's broader strategy of global war.

The modus operandi to achieve this was muffled in multilayered plans. These plans set the stage of the living *Alf Laila Wa Laila* tales – in which one story appears on the pages with a line of characters and, as each story ends, its characters fade into the background, but the tales move on with another story of equally motivated characters.

The margin of failure was thus minimized with multiple layers and folds cushioning the impact of any attack, and an unending stream of actors ready to play their roles in new actions. In other words, where one plan failed, another plan with a new team would immediately replace it. This *Alf Laila Wa Laila* drama, even today, goes by the original script, whether by way of Al-Qaeda action against an enemy and the enemy's reaction to this, or an action by the enemy against Al-Qaeda and Al-Qaeda's reaction to that.

The person who fired the imagination of Osama bin Laden and al-Zawahiri for the 9/11 attack was Khalid Sheikh Mohammad, a US-educated Balochi, raised in Kuwait. He was arrested in Rawalpindi in 2003. It was he who conceived a situation where the United States would believe it had won outright victory and so work towards developing a strategy envisaging a long-term stay in Afghanistan. Khalid had reasoned that the single blow of 9/11 would drag the United States into the Afghan net, and from there the inhospitable Afghan terrain would slowly but surely drain US material resources to a point from which it would never be able to recover. There was also the conviction that although the United States might mercilessly butcher Al-Qaeda's human resources at the outset, Al-Qaeda's spiritual and ideological strength would breed a long line of poverty-stricken Muslims ready to fight the war anew. That was why Pakistani and Afghan impoverished tribal areas were chosen by Al-Qaeda as the initial theater of war. In addition to this, Pakistan was a country under an Islamist military dictator, General

Zia-ul-Haq, who had already begun to move away from the normal pattern of third-world social development.

In the 1980s and 1990s Pakistan's military establishment encouraged the formation of the Jihadi community in Pakistan's rural areas to fuel the insurgency in Indian Kashmir. That influence spread all the way from Central Asia to Bangladesh, and raised another generation of militants. The Taliban rule in Afghanistan had inspired them, and the Jihadi *madrassas* network in Pakistan had increased their numbers many times over in a few short years. Al-Qaeda was certain that it would successfully use these assets to fight the United States and then capture the larger network to expand the theater of war from Central Asia to Bangladesh.

Put another way, there was faith that while the United States might be able to inflict repeated defeats on Al-Qaeda and kill one generation of militants, another generation of militants would surface in a short space of time and the US war machine would ultimately run out steam. Al-Qaeda, meanwhile, would move from strength to strength until victory was assured in Afghanistan to hail the promised Mahdi's arrival for the final battle. Muslim armies would then join hands and march from South Asia to the Middle East, and inflict a conclusive defeat on Israel to usher in a Global Caliphate. This particular perspective helped Al-Qaeda expand the boundaries of its operations, weaponry, human resources, and ideology for a type of war not witnessed in the region before.

In the next few years a new generation of fighters were raised, which though local and owning first allegiance to the Taliban, were ultimately led by Al-Qaeda. They are sons of the soil and generally understood as Taliban, but as they are not part of Al-Qaeda's organizational set-up, so I call these recruits the Neo-Taliban or Al-Qaeda's "blood brothers." Unlike the traditional Afghan Taliban, who mostly live in south-west Afghanistan and south-west Pakistan and adhere to Pashtun tribal traditions, these Neo-Taliban live in the Federally Administered Tribal Areas (FATA), and stand against state-supported tribal dispensations. These Neo-Taliban are today to be found in many parts of South Asia. They have massacred local tribal chiefs, or forced them to leave. They have assassinated dozens of traditional clerics. They live on both sides of the Afghan–Pakistani border, believe in a global Muslim brotherhood, and subscribe strictly to radical Islam. Both the traditional Taliban and the Neo-Taliban fight against NATO forces in Afghanistan. But while for the traditional Taliban the war begins and ends in

Afghanistan , the Neo-Taliban's war starts from Central and South Asia and ends with the emergence of the Global Caliphate.

The Neo-Taliban, who evolved through the testing circumstances of the US invasion of Afghanistan, the US bombings, and state oppression of Jihadi organizations by the Pakistani government, extend from south-east Afghanistan to Karachi. They were the ones who set the stage for Al-Qaeda to develop its huge bases in Pakistani tribal areas to fuel the theater of war in Afghanistan. They enabled the Afghan Taliban to capture 74 percent of Afghanistan by 2009, and helped expand the war from Pakistan into India, while Al-Qaeda opened new war fronts in Yemen and Somalia.

In the post-9/11 scenario the game plan was going exactly as Al-Qaeda wanted. The US supposed victory in Afghanistan had encouraged it to invade Iraq in 2003. However, the US invasion of Iraq came as something of a surprise – and bonus – to Al-Qaeda. It had planned a single trap for the United States in Afghanistan, but the United States had fallen into two different traps.

Abu Musab al-Zarqawi, formerly a non-Al-Qaeda leader of an anti-Shiite group, was already in Iraq. Al-Zawahiri awarded him the Al-Qaeda franchise for Iraq to stir up sectarian strife so that Iraq's theater of war would be more complicit. The violence that resulted made Iraq ungovernable. However, this was a diversion. The real war was still to be fought in Afghanistan, as Al-Qaeda's control of the Iraqi resistance movement was still tenuous.

Al-Qaeda had tried to influence local resistance groups in Iraq with the idea of an "Islamic Emirates of Iraq," but the experiment failed. The reason was that there are over two dozen organizations involved in the Iraqi resistance, and the majority of them are associated with the Muslim Brotherhood. They take their guidance from the Muslim Brotherhood councils in the Middle East as well as in Europe. The local franchise of the Muslim Brotherhood in Iraq, Hezbul Islami Al-Iraqi, is already in Iraq's parliament, with its leaders holding important positions including the office of vice-president of Iraq. These groups openly negotiate with the United States. The United States also holds dialogue with the Iraqi resistance in Turkey. The United States has no problem dealing with either, but provide no quarter to Al-Qaeda's foreign fighters in Iraq.

The Iraqi indigenous resistance groups have huge differences with Al-Qaeda, especially regarding its strategy to create crises through sectarian violence. Al-Qaeda focuses on trapping the United States in the Afghan quagmire. The Iraqi resistance aims at liberating

Iraq with the withdrawal of the US forces from its territories. This divergence in approach left Al-Qaeda isolated in Iraq, and so in 2007–08 Al-Qaeda turned to Afghanistan, leaving the war against the West to the local Iraqi resistance.

In Pakistan and Afghanistan, Al-Qaeda acquired the ability to shuffle the pack. From 2002–05 it kept its eyes on Pakistan's tribal areas to provide franchises as part of its regrouping program. The game-plan in 2006 was to win the war against US and NATO troops in the Taliban heartland of south-west Afghanistan. I went to Helmand in November 2006 and visited all the important districts. The Taliban were in complete control there, with NATO's presence barely visible only in the capital, Laskhar Gah, and a few other places, where NATO's British troops were mainly restricted to their bases. The Taliban's comeback compelled Washington to look for a radical shift in its political and war strategy.

Washington then began to use Pakistan for negotiations with the Taliban, on the one hand, and for the elimination of Al-Qaeda's structures on the other. The fallout of this was that in 2007 Al-Qaeda moved into Pakistan's capital Islamabad and into the scenic Swat Valley in Khyber Paktoonkhwa. The expansion of the war from the tribal areas to Pakistan's urban centers aimed at puncturing Pakistan's peace process efforts with the Taliban. In Iraq, Al-Qaeda was never permitted this kind of leverage. Thus, despite Iraq's Arab origin, Al-Qaeda was left with little choice but to pursue its war on the West in Afghanistan. However, setting up a theater of war in South Asia was no less of a challenge. It was an attempt to pass on to indigenous tribes the revolutionary ideas of a few hundred Arabs not even remotely connected with local culture or traditions.

Although some leading ideological thinkers such as Mustafa Abu al-Yazid and Abu Waleed Ansari were killed in US Predator drone attacks, there were still some seasoned Arab ideologues such as al-Zawahiri present. Each had been a long-time affiliate of Egypt's Muslim Brotherhood and spent several years in the Afghan Jihad. They knew exactly how to network their future actions in these areas. They did not interfere in local affairs, but had on constant call tribesmen who had either trained in Al-Qaeda camps, or interacted with them in Afghanistan. The dilemma of Western analysts was that they never tried to understand Al-Qaeda and its dialectic. Most of the time they viewed the Al-Qaeda-inspired events either in isolation or from the wrong perspective – as was the case with the Mumbai attack of 2008.

The US war in Iraq and Afghanistan continues to drain billions of dollars of taxpayers' money, and the war is getting increasingly untenable. Each year US think tanks discover new Al-Qaeda strategies against the United States, and by the time the United States comes up with counter strategies, Al-Qaeda has moved in a different direction in its war against the Western coalition.

US intelligence did its homework thoroughly before launching the war against Al-Qaeda. It researched Islamic resistance movements down the decades and minutely studied the French occupation of Algeria in 1830 and the resistance there led by the famed Abd al-Qadir. Algerian resistance never permitted smooth sailing for the French in Algeria, and at one time controlled one-third of Algeria, even to the point of knocking on the door of the country's capital. The British occupation in Egypt ran much the same course, as did the Russian occupation of the Caucasus, and the British occupation of India. Each of these occupations resulted in fierce Muslim resistance inspired by liberation movements and reformist movements undertaken on the fundamental precepts of revolution.

The US invasion of Afghanistan and later of Iraq was launched on the understanding of these earlier models of Muslim resistance movements and therefore, subsequent to the swift defeats of the Taliban and Saddam Hussain respectively in Afghanistan and Iraq, power was as quickly as possible transferred to local politicians with US forces standing in support. In Afghanistan, Provincial Reconstruction Teams (PRTs) of roughly 60 to 100 military combat personnel were put in place as a show of force in outlying urban areas, but they only managed to provide limited security to local projects. In Iraq, on the other hand, US forces in Baghdad and other troubled cities withdrew from the urban areas, sequestering themselves in armed camps and limiting their presence in the cities.

The United States sought to convey the impression to the local population that they were not living under foreign occupation forces but under an independent sovereign government. It took three and a half years in the case of Afghanistan and in Iraq only a year before this US strategy fell apart and armed resistance against the foreign occupation forces began in both countries.

The international community, including the United States, the United Kingdom, Pakistan, Turkey, Iran, Russia, Saudi Arabia, and India saw the war on Al-Qaeda as a unique conflict where for the first time in history the militant networks were engaged in a power struggle against nation-states. They failed to realize that it was not simply an alliance of various international groups whose foundation had been laid in Afghanistan, but in fact the rediscovery of a dialectical process understood by a group of battle-hardened people after a 20-year-long underground struggle in the Middle East against the Soviet Union.

Afghanistan is the catalyst of many international dramas including 9/11. The main drama, however, remains the exploration of the dialectic through which Al-Qaeda elevated its status from a simple insurgency to a global resistance movement aiming to organize a backlash of the Muslim population to set up a mechanism under which the resources and the arsenal of the Muslim majority states can be used after bringing the state machinery to the point of collapse.

In early 2009, Pakistani militants seized huge parts of Khyber Paktoonkhwa. The entire police force of the civil administration defected, and defections also became common among army personnel. This was a time when Al-Qaeda looked to seize some batteries of the Pakistan Army, convinced the war could conclusively be decided in favor of militants in Pakistan as well as in Afghanistan. However, Pakistan's newly installed chief of army staff, General Ashfaq Parvez Kayani, realized the danger and employed maximum force against the militants, compelling them to disperse. This was, of course, only to be a temporary arrangement as Pakistan, the United States, and Saudi Arabia each saw Al-Qaeda as no more than a minor irritant. In keeping with the US war strategy, they fought a low-intensity anti-insurgency war with all steps taken, whether political, economic, or military, to keep that particular perspective in mind. However, the fact of the matter is that Al-Qaeda can only be understood by going through its *One Thousand and One Nights* tales and the cast of characters, charisma, ideology, and the myths and realities that appear in them.

Today, Osama bin Laden is in the background. Dr Ayman al-Zawahiri is invisible. A large number of Al-Qaeda legends such as Mustafa Abu al-Yazid and Abu Waleed Ansari have been killed in drone attacks. Khalid Sheikh Mohammad and Abu Zubaida, along with dozens of other key operators, are under arrest. However, the saga of Al-Qaeda's *One Thousand and One Nights* tales continues with new strategies and new characters. For Al-Qaeda these are just measures to keep the West running from pillar to post until it exhausts itself and Al-Qaeda can announce victory in Afghanistan. Al-Qaeda next aims to occupy the promised land of ancient Khurasan, with its boundaries stretching from all the way from Central Asia to Khyber Paktoonkhwa through Afghanistan, and then expand the theater of war to India.

The promised messiah, the Mahdi, will then rise in the Middle East and Al-Qaeda will mobilize its forces from Ancient Khurasan for the liberation of Palestine, where a final victory will guarantee the revival of a Global Muslim Caliphate.

NOTES

1 Commander Muhammad Ilyas Kashmiri is a former Kashmiri militant who commands his own 313 Brigade group and is also a member of Al-Qaeda's *Shura* (council).
2 Sirajuddin Haqqani has been called the most dangerous commander in Afghanistan. He is the son of a legendary Afghan commander during the Soviet invasion, Jalaluddin Haqqani.
3 Qari Ziaur Rahman is the most dangerous Afghan commander in the eastern Afghan provinces of Nuristan and Kunar. He is allied with Al-Qaeda.
4 The Tora Bora are the mountains situated in the Afghan province of Nangarhar.

PROLOGUE

1 David Coleman Headley, formerly known as Daood Sayed Gilani, born June 30, 1960, is a Chicago-based Pakistani American, who conspired with militants and ex-military officers to launch the 2008 Mumbai attacks and other terrorist activity. He changed his Muslim name to an Anglo name to hide his Muslim identity to make travel to India easier.
2 Abdullah Yusuf Azzam was born in Palestine in 1941 and assassinated by a bomb blast on November 24, 1989, in Peshawar, Pakistan. He preached in favor of defensive jihad by Muslims to help the Afghan *mujahideen* against the Soviet invaders. He raised funds, recruited, and organized the international Islamic volunteer effort of Afghan Arabs through the 1980s, and emphasized the political ascension of Islamism.
3 The United Islamic Front for the Salvation of Afghanistan, more commonly known as the Afghan Northern Alliance, was a military-political umbrella organization created by the Islamic State of Afghanistan in 1996. The organization united various ethnic groups of Afghans to fight the ethnically Pashtun Taliban.
4 The Bamiyan Buddhas were two sixth- century monumental statues of standing Buddhas carved into the side of a cliff in the Bamiyan valley,

227

in the Hazarajat region of central Afghanistan. They were dynamited in 2001 on the orders of Mullah Omar.

CHAPTER 1

1 Laskhar-e-Taiba means Army of Pure. It is a Pakistan-based organization which is fighting in Indian Kashmir to support the Kashmiri separatist movement. The organization was banned in 2002. It operates under the name of Jamaatut Dawa.

2 Hafiz Muhammad Saeed is the chief of Jamaatut Dawa, a charity organization that is widely considered to be a cover organization for the LeT militants. India considers him one of its most wanted terrorists because of his alleged ties with LeT and its involvement in attacks against India. The United Nations declared Jama'at-ud-Da'wah a terrorist organization in December 2008, and Hafiz Saeed a terrorist as its leader.

3 Salafi is a Muslim school of thought followed particularly in Saudi Arabia.

4 Jamaat-e-Islami (JI) (or Islamic Party) is a Muslim religious and political party in Pakistan. It was founded on August 26, 1941 in Lahore by Muslim scholar Syed Abul Ala Maududi, and is the oldest religious party in Pakistan.

CHAPTER 2

1 The Frontier Crime Regulations (FCR) comprise a set of laws enforced by the British Raj in the Pashtun-inhabited tribal areas of north-west British India. The same laws are still enforced in Pakistani tribal areas.

2 The Durand Line theoretically marks the boundary between Pakistan and Afghanistan.

3 Gulbaddin Hikmatyar was the chief of his own faction of HIA, a former interim prime minister of Afghanistan, and is now a Taliban ally against the western coalition in Afghanistan.

4 Moulvi Younus Khalis, who was born in 1919 and died in 2006, was the leader of his own faction of HIA. Khalis was resistance leader against the Soviet invasion in Afghanistan in the 1980s, and a Taliban supporter after the US invasion of Afghanistan.

5 Jamiat-e-Ulema-e-Islam (JUI) (the society of Islamic scholars) is a political party in Pakistan. The party has split into two separate groupings. One is led by Maulana Fazal-ur-Rehman and is known as Jamiat Ulema-e-Islam (Fazlur Rehman) (JUI-F), while the other is led by Maulana Sami ul Haq and is known as Jamiat Ulema-e-Islam (Sami ul Haq) (JUI-S).

6 The PPP is a center-left political party in Pakistan affiliated with the Socialist International. It is the largest political party in Pakistan,

and leads the ruling coalition in the country. To date, its leader has always been a member (directly or through marriage) of the Bhutto family.

7 The ANP's main electoral influence is in the Pashtun-dominated areas of the Khyber-Pakhtoonkhwa, Baluchistan, and Sindh provinces of Pakistan. Historically it clams to be a continuation of the National Awami Party.

8 The MQM is the fourth largest political party overall, and the largest liberal political party, in Pakistan. It is generally reckoned to hold immense mobilizing potential in the province of Sindh.

9 The PML(Q) is a centrist, conservative political party. This present form of the Pakistan Muslim League was formed prior to 2002 general elections by ex-President Pervez Musharraf.

CHAPTER 3

1 The Kargil War was an armed conflict between India and Pakistan that took place between May and July 1999 in the Kargil district of Kashmir and elsewhere along the Line of Control (LOC) that defines the boundary between disputed Indian Kashmir and Pakistani Kashmir.

MAPS

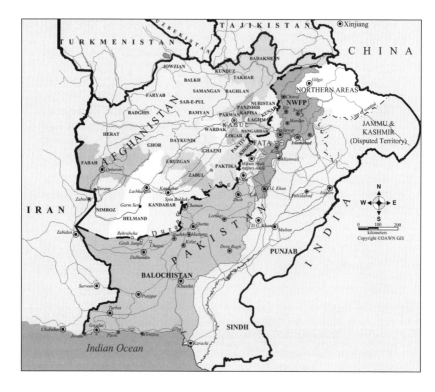

Map 1 Pakistan and Afghanistan, administrative areas

Map 2 The Mohmand and Bajaur agencies of Pakistan
and adjoining areas

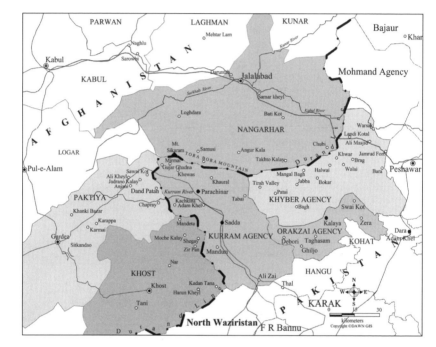

Map 3 The Khyber and Kurram agencies of Pakistan and adjoining areas

Map 4 North and South Waziristan, Pakistan and adjoining areas

Map 5 The Afghan/Pakistani border around Kandahar and
Balochistan

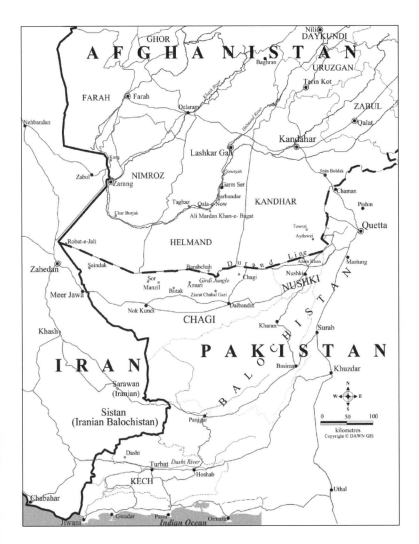

Map 6 Border regions between Iran, Pakistan, and Afghanistan

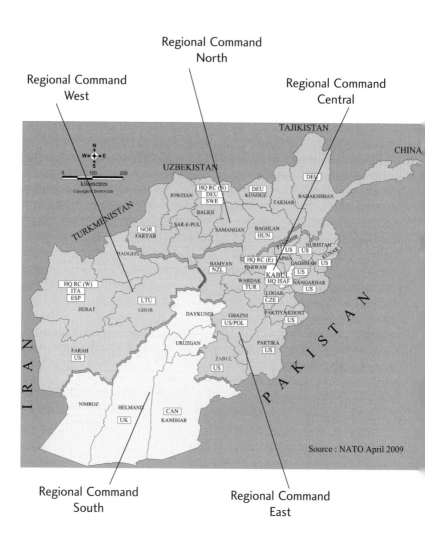

Regional Command
North

Regional Command
West

Regional Command
Central

Regional Command
South

Regional Command
East

Map 7 NATO Regional Command areas in Afghanistan

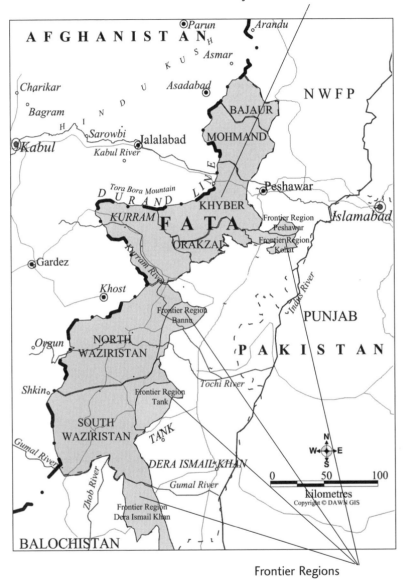

Map 8 Pakistan's Federally Administered Tribal Areas (FATA)

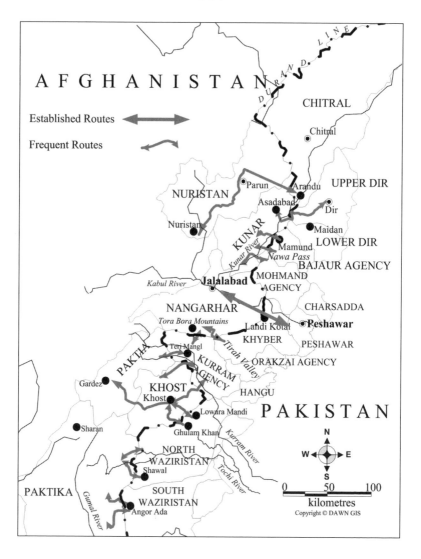

Map 9 Established and frequently used routes across the Afghan/
Pakistani border

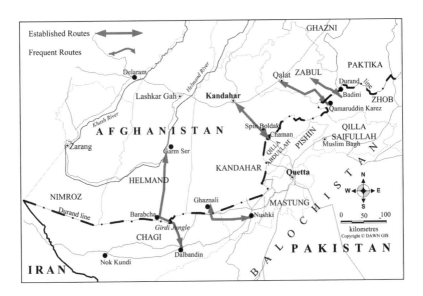

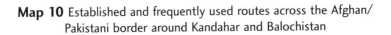

Map 10 Established and frequently used routes across the Afghan/
Pakistani border around Kandahar and Balochistan

INDEX